LAUGHING HISTORIES

Laughing Histories breaks new ground by exploring moments of laughter in early modern Europe, showing how laughter was inflected by gender and social power.

"I dearly love a laugh," declared Jane Austen's heroine Elizabeth Bennet, and her wit won the heart of the aristocratic Mr. Darcy. Yet the widely read Earl of Chesterfield asserted that only "the mob" would laugh out loud; the gentleman should merely smile. This literary contrast raises important historical questions: how did social rules constrain laughter? Did the highest elites really laugh less than others? How did laughter play out in relations between the sexes? Through fascinating case studies of individuals such as the Renaissance artist Benvenuto Cellini, the French aristocrat Madame de Sévigné, and the rising civil servant and diarist Samuel Pepys, *Laughing Histories* reveals the multiple meanings of laughter, from the court to the tavern and street, in a complex history that paved the way for modern laughter.

With its study of laughter in relation to power, aggression, gender, sex, class, and social bonding, *Laughing Histories* is perfect for readers interested in the history of emotions, cultural history, gender history, and literature.

Joy Wiltenburg, Professor Emerita of History at Rowan University, studies the cultural history of early modern Europe. Her publications include *Disorderly Women and Female Power in the Street Literature of Early Modern England and Germany* (1992) and *Crime and Culture in Early Modern Germany* (2012).

FIGURE 0.1 Jan Massys, *A Merry Company*

Source: © Album/Alamy Stock Photo

LAUGHING HISTORIES

From the Renaissance Man to the Woman of Wit

Joy Wiltenburg

Routledge
Taylor & Francis Group

LONDON AND NEW YORK

Cover image: Jan Massys, *A Merry Company* © Album/Alamy Stock Photo

First published 2022
by Routledge
4 Park Square, Milton Park, Abingdon, Oxon OX14 4RN

and by Routledge
605 Third Avenue, New York, NY 10158

Routledge is an imprint of the Taylor & Francis Group, an informa business

© 2022 Joy Wiltenburg

The right of Joy Wiltenburg to be identified as author of this work has been asserted in accordance with sections 77 and 78 of the Copyright, Designs and Patents Act 1988.

British Library Cataloguing-in-Publication Data
A catalogue record for this book is available from the British Library

Library of Congress Cataloging-in-Publication Data
Names: Wiltenburg, Joy, author.
Title: Laughing histories : from the renaissance man to the woman of wit / Joy Wiltenburg.
Description: Abingdon, Oxon ; New York, NY : Routledge, 2022. | Includes bibliographical references and index.
Identifiers: LCCN 2021059439 | ISBN 9781032162065 (hardback) | ISBN 9781032162072 (paperback) | ISBN 9781003247517 (ebook)
Subjects: LCSH: Laughter—Social aspects—Europe—History. | Sex role—Europe—History.
Classification: LCC BF575.L3 W57 2022 | DDC 152.4/3—dc23/ eng/20220308
LC record available at https://lccn.loc.gov/2021059439

ISBN: 978-1-032-16206-5 (hbk)
ISBN: 978-1-032-16207-2 (pbk)
ISBN: 978-1-003-24751-7 (ebk)

DOI: 10.4324/9781003247517

Typeset in Bembo
by Apex CoVantage, LLC

CONTENTS

FIGURES

PREFACE

This book is a departure from some academic comfort zones: the narrow field of specialty where one can be confident of one's knowledge, and the established topic with widely recognized importance. I'm very aware of its unorthodoxy, as its portraits of laughter range across time and space in ways that may make some historians nervous. All I can say is, I did this on purpose.

In pursuing memories and experiences of laughter in its social habitat, I've been informed by some theories about laughter, especially those that examine how laughter exercises social power. Readers in search of extended dissection of theories will need to look elsewhere, however. Those looking for a lot of laughs themselves might be a little disappointed too, but there are some amusing nuggets.

It was from Erik Midelfort that I first learned about the historical importance of folly. He has inspired many of his students into adventurous studies—seemingly foolhardy, but original and rewarding. We wished we could get the "ship of fools" into the title of a festschrift for him a few years ago (*Ideas and Cultural Margins in Early Modern Germany*, edited by Marjorie Elizabeth Plummer and Robin B. Barnes). At least now I can give laughter some of its due, and also thank him again for his remarkable mentorship.

Many generous colleagues have aided me in this possibly daft project. I'm especially grateful to those who have read and commented on portions of the manuscript, including Sara Beam, Tom Cohen, Fara Dabhoiwala, Ute Lotz-Heumann, Erik Midelfort, and Ann Tlusty. Many thanks to the members of the Rowan History Department works-in-progress seminar, who have read work from this research at multiple stages: Keith Aksell, Cory Blake, Emily Blanck, Bill Carrigan, Mikkel Dack, Kelly Duke-Bryant, Josh Gedacht, Stephen Hague, Jim Heinzen, Melissa Klapper, Janet Lindman, Jody Manning, Scott Morschauser, Chanelle Rose, Debbie Sharnak, Katie Turner, and Edward Wang. I've benefited greatly from the advice and support of Joel Harrington, Mary Lindemann, Fran Dolan, and many others who may not even remember the help they gave me, including Martin Ingram, Tom Robisheaux, Lyndal Roper, Carla Roth, and Jeff Watt. My literary agent, Amaryah Orenstein, has been a marvelous reader and supporter of my work (and special thanks to Melissa Klapper for referring me to her!). Thanks also to the editors and readers for Routledge, to Rowan University and the College of Humanities and Social Sciences for research support, and to Gurkirat Dhillon for his research assistance one summer.

As always, my husband, Rick Womer, has supported me in every way possible, from helping me photograph sources to reading drafts to enduring my bouts of angst. I know how incredibly lucky I am.

A note to lovers of language: I have taken the liberty of modernizing some English spellings and punctuation for readability. I thought it only fair, when passages from other languages have been translated into standard English.

INTRODUCTION

Laughter and Early Modern Europe

"I dearly love a laugh," declared Jane Austen's heroine Elizabeth Bennet, boldly asserting her right to joke. In a scene full of haughty and serious social superiors, it was a declaration of independence. And it was her wit and laughter, among other charms, that won her the love of the somber Mr. Darcy, despite his loftier social place. Yet, some fifty years earlier, the Earl of Chesterfield's influential letters had put forward the most repressive of anti-laughter advice—all based on maintaining a deportment that showed social superiority. It was "the mob" that would laugh out loud. The gentleman, and presumably also the lady, should merely smile to show their appreciation of clever wit. Not everyone agreed with Chesterfield, even among his social equals, and Austen was writing fiction, but the contrast raises historical questions: how did social rules constrain laughter? Did the highest elites really laugh less than others? How did laughter play out in relations between the sexes? Is there change over time in how and when people laugh? If we take delight in the laughter of Elizabeth Bennet, are we responding to a "modern" type of laughter? And what about our own laughter, which we perceive as natural and spontaneous? Has it too been historically conditioned, and if so how?

Questions like these form the starting point for this book. The pursuit of them has led back into the centuries before Austen's novel and into many permutations of laughter. For all its seeming frivolity, laughter is powerful. It disrupts the ground of social encounters, creating shifts of meaning that cannot be accomplished with serious modes of speech and behavior. This power makes it a significant mode of social negotiation. In early modern Europe, we find a huge array of functions for laughter and its close partner humor: men using it to assert masculine prestige, women using it to disarm gender hierarchy, aristocrats using it to distinguish themselves from social inferiors, social climbers using it to form new relationships, and all sorts using it in sexual play. We find, on the other hand, the fear of others'

DOI: 10.4324/9781003247517-1

laughter constraining people's choices and enforcing conformity. The case studies in this book dive into a range of laughter scenarios and laughter types, each in a different historical context. The result is purposely a patchwork, not a grand narrative with claims of continuous development; still, the broad transformations that marked the transition from medieval to modern society left their mark on laughter. Each study opens up different insights into the power of laughter, as well as its complexity. Laughing is easy to do—not always so easy to understand. Early modern laughter shows us much that is familiar, with practices and assumptions that continue into modern Western society. We will also find some puzzles that remind us of the strangeness of the past, and of laughter itself.

The clash between Austen and Chesterfield points to the contested status of laughter. Many societies have imposed conventions and rules on laughter to tame its ambiguity and unpredictability, but its past in Western culture has been especially checkered. Nearly everyone nowadays approves of laughter. Not only is it fun, but it is widely thought to be good for you. This has not always been so. Laughter in Europe encountered suspicion from multiple sources, over many centuries. Already in the classical writings of Greece and Rome that grounded Western learning, one finds traces of the Chesterfield attitude of class-based laughter control. The dominance of Christianity brought attacks on laughter from a very different direction, tainting it as worldly, ungodly, or immoral. Not all Christian thought was hostile to merriment, of course, and it's doubtful how far the austerity of some moralists impinged on the enjoyment of everyday Christians. There was plenty of laughter in the Middle Ages, whatever the most humorless theologians thought; there was even some in monasteries. Still, there was a long strain of negativity. In the early modern period, controversy over laughter came to a head, as it was both weaponized and celebrated. In the course of these centuries from 1500 to 1800, it was the positive view of laughter that won out. But if the early modern period may have finally put the main anti-laughter forces to rest, it also birthed some peculiarly modern notions. To understand the roots of modern attitudes toward laughter—from the demand for a sense of humor in prospective mates to the (modern and stubborn) idea that men are better at humor—we need to look to the past.

Laughter and Early Modern Europe

The early modern era is an important one in the history of laughter. The centuries between 1500 and 1800 saw a host of changes that shifted European society decisively away from medieval patterns. The connections between large-scale early modern changes and laughter may not be obvious, but they emerge on closer inspection. Capitalism, for example, seems hardly a laughing matter, but the market growth of the early modern era turned comedy into a commodity. The rise of literacy and the invention of printing intersected with the growing market economy to advance the sale of new, reproducible products designed to elicit laughter. Jestbooks, songs, satires, stage comedies—all could now be sold to a much wider audience. These laughter products affected the shifting reputation and practice of laughter among literate circles, as did the intellectual movements associated with the Renaissance and later the Enlightenment. Did the growing market value of laughter contribute to a more positive cultural valuation of it?

Another major early modern trend, the development of powerful national states, may seem even further afield from laughter than economic change. Yet, in scholarship inspired by Norbert Elias's concept of the "civilizing process," state-building has been linked with much broader changes in manners and customs, including attempts to curb raucous outbursts of laughter.[1] In examining the history of manners in European society, Elias traced how the rules of polite society applied increasing restraints and reticences to bodily functions from spitting to sex. These changes, in turn, he associated with the courtly world where political power was increasingly consolidated. The theory has inspired fruitful scholarship examining themes from violence to laughter, although it is vulnerable to some criticism. Elias's concept of the "before" picture of the Middle Ages has nettled medievalists with his assumption of an unbridled expression of natural drives before the early modern "civilizing process."[2] Further, he implied that manners and ideas trickled down in one direction, from elites to the masses—another idea that tends to dissolve on closer inspection. If the fork was first introduced among the rich, one can find counter-examples of trends that spread upward to elites from humbler levels of European society during these centuries, such as the freedom of youth to choose their own spouses. In any case, ideas of civility may have quieted some of the loudest laughter, at least among elites, but they also promoted the cultivation of their own forms of wit and pleasantry.

A seminal work more closely focused on laughter, from Mikhail Bakhtin, will be explored more fully in the next chapter. He too had a theory of change, in this case drawn from Marxist analysis of class conflict and the early modern growth of bourgeois society. In his view, the popular laughter of the masses, typified by the rowdy belly laugh of carnival celebration, increasingly gave way after the Renaissance to the sterile snicker of the bourgeoisie. The parallel with Elias's observations is evident, in the association of polite restraint and decorum with higher social status. One can also relate these ideas to the findings of social historians who have traced growing social discipline in the sixteenth and seventeenth centuries. Even as those with pretensions to gentility policed their own manners, authorities in both church and state sought to curb disorders in society more broadly. The push for more control was made possible by the growth of more effective judicial systems, increasingly staffed by men with a legal education—yet another development of early modern statebuilding. Along with a crackdown on crime, measurable in growing caseloads, there was increasing suppression of popular festivities like carnival, which were seen as seedbeds of immoral and disruptive behavior.[3]

Not directly focused on the early modern period, but taking a broad sweep from ancient to modern, is Barry Sanders's overview of laughter's history, *Sudden Glory*. Drawing mainly on literary sources, and partly inspired by Bakhtin, Sanders views laughter as a tool of the oppressed, empowering women and peasants in face of attempts at suppression from above. His subtitle, *Laughter as Subversive History*, expresses this appealing idea, and I almost wish I were convinced.[4] As we shall see, however, laughter in historical practice has been too slippery for such a label, just as it has stymied the many attempts to form a comprehensive laughter theory.

European society in the Middle Ages was by no means as simple as its popular image often suggests. As far back as one cares to look, there were people who did not fit easily into the traditional tripartite scheme of clergy, nobility, and peasants. Nevertheless, the early modern centuries saw a massive expansion and differentiation of "middle" statuses that departed from that scheme. Social mobility increased in dual senses: first, in literal movement from place to place, and second, in transition across levels of status. Geographical mobility can be traced in the high levels of anxiety about vagrants, in the population movements caused by religious conflict and warfare, and in migration from countryside to cities. None of these were completely new, but they bulked larger in early modern concerns about social stability and change. While movement from one social status to another could go in any direction (not always upward), growing literacy and education offered a notable path of social ascent. Many of the laughter testimonies in this book emerge from the growing ranks of professionals who owed their enhanced rank, prestige, and prosperity to their education and abilities. Such social transitions involved the forging of new identities, helping spark the new urge toward autobiography while demanding new calibration of one's behavior, including one's laughter.

Like the social history of the early modern period, intellectual history points to this era as one of ferment over the status of laughter. Renaissance humanists argued about it far more than their medieval predecessors. With their revival of classical practices of rhetoric that sought to move the emotions of an audience, humanists saw humor and ridicule as powerful weapons in debate. As Quentin Skinner has argued, this focus on demolishing the arguments of one's opponent strongly highlighted the aggressive potential of laughter.[5] Many Renaissance commentators insisted that the essence of laughter was scorn and mockery, the feeling of superiority that was famously defined as the passion behind laughter by Thomas Hobbes in the mid-seventeenth century. There were dissenters from such views, but it was only in the eighteenth century that laughter began to receive more vigorous defense from thinkers like Francis Hutcheson—even at the time when the anti-laughter strain in manners represented by Lord Chesterfield was reaching its height.

Moving the story of laughter into the modern era, Daniel Wickberg has examined growing cultural approval in the nineteenth century for a quality that came to be called the "sense of humor." Now taken for granted as a desirable quality—and a frequent criterion for dating and mating—the sense of humor is a modern concept. Looking at American culture, Wickberg argued that the growing valuation of a sense of humor arose from modern, post-Enlightenment ideas of a distinctive, individualist personality. Appropriate responsiveness to the laughable came to be appreciated as a positive and even necessary human trait. This was an important change. And yet, in studying mainly theories of laughter rather than practice, Wickberg identified some novelties that were actually much older, such as the ability to laugh at oneself.[6] This quality gained new prestige in the modern age, but we will find people laughing at themselves much earlier, including Felix Platter in the sixteenth century and even some French aristocrats in the age of the Sun King. If the gap between Hutcheson and Chesterfield reminds us of the differences among contemporaries, the longer history of self-directed laughter shows us the distance between discourses of laughter—what people think and say about it—and what they actually do.

So, one can point to a range of developments over the early modern period, from the marketing of laughter to new expectations of laughter decorum, shifting perceptions of the moral implications of laughter, and developing ideas about humor and laughter as positive components of the individual personality. Of course, our evidence about these changes comes overwhelmingly from either prescriptive writings—telling people what they ought to do or think—or what I've called laughter products—writings intended to make people laugh. What about laughter in practice, in the lived experience of everyday social interactions where most laughter takes place? About this we know much less, and this book is an attempt to fill some of the gaps in our knowledge about actual occasions of laughter in the early modern past.

Pursuing Laughter

Some readers may wonder whether laughter has a history at all. It is often assumed to be a universal that is essentially constant over time. Certainly, one can find laughter in all human societies, in all times and places. It seems that even some animals laugh, in contrast to the view of ancient authorities like Aristotle. Yet there are obvious cultural differences in laughter. Anything that varies by social setting is subject to time and change, and therefore has a history. Historians in recent decades have uncovered histories of many things that once were viewed as unhistorical: the human body, emotions, sex, and gender, to name a few.[7] Similarly, things that were once considered beneath serious notice—such as food, sleep, noise, or clothing—turn out to reveal a great deal about both change and continuity in human experiences over time.[8] All societies have laughter, but expressed in different ways and aroused by different things. Given the near-infinite variety of human societies and subgroups, there cannot be a single thread to this story. Laughter has not a history, but histories.

Even within a given society, of course, laughter differs according to social class and subculture. One may think in clichéd fashion of the guffaws of the peasant versus the smirk of the aristocrat in pre-Revolutionary France. A word like guffaw, with its echoes of animallike sound, captures a discomfort with uncontrolled laughter that has led to extensive social regulation according to status and situation. Laughter is different in public settings than in private—in mixed-gender sociability than in single-sex groups. It is different when evoked by social superiors from the reverse: what does it mean to laugh at the boss's joke, as opposed to trying to get him (or her) to laugh—or laughing *at* the boss? And, of course, laughing at superiors, inferiors, or anyone else classified as "other" is a practice with a very long history indeed. In fact, one feature of what some theorists describe as "otherness" is a boundary of laughter: the other is laughed at, whereas the social bond of laughing together creates a space of shared community, if only momentary.[9]

The multiple forms and meanings of laughter make it notoriously difficult to pin down and analyze. As Mary Beard has remarked in tracing the history of laughter in ancient Rome, many have come to grief in their attempts to form a unified theory of laughter, from ancient times to modern.[10] Among the many theories about laughter, three standards have come to the fore in the modern era. The "superiority" theory, most famously expressed by Thomas Hobbes in the seventeenth century, sees laughter as delight in a sudden perception of inferiority or defect. The "incongruity" theory, associated with the more benign outlook on laughter of thinkers like Francis Hutcheson and Immanuel Kant in the eighteenth century, is more morally neutral: it says we laugh at the sudden reversal of our expectations. The "relief" theory sees laughter as offering a relaxation of tension, whether release of psychic energy in the thinking of Sigmund Freud or the restorative recreation of earlier commentators.[11] Notably, these laughter theories all concentrate on humor and the causes of laughter. They also focus on the individual laughing and the reasons for that behavior. In Hobbes, there is an element of social relationship, in order for the laugher to feel superior to someone—but still, we are largely in the realm of individual psychology, asking what is going on in the mind, heart, or body of the one who is laughing. As Lucy Rayfield has observed in a recent article, these theories pay scant attention to laughter's effects, in contrast to the thinking of the Renaissance.[12]

What about the functions of laughter in the largely social contexts where laughter takes place? It's quite unusual for people to laugh alone, except in response to comic media, another social product. (This finding not only appears in modern studies but also was observed in earlier centuries.)[13] In this book I am less interested in what people were laughing *at* than in what they were laughing *for*. What were they doing with laughter, and how did it affect their relationships with the people around them? And, since we learn about this laughter from recorded memories of it, why was the laughter important to them? Rather than seek a unifying theory, I look for laughter where it lived. Laughter has been an important element of social interaction in a wide range of historical contexts. In linkage with its close confederate humor, laughter appears throughout this book as a mediator of social power—whether in personal self-assertion, the formation of social bonds, the undermining of hierarchies, or the enforcement of customary rules.

Laughter is both a physical action of the body and a social response. It expresses a feeling of the laughing individual and communicates a signal to others. Commentators have differed on whether laughter is a passion or emotion in itself, or merely the sign of one.[14] Unlike the standard range of emotions, however, laughter can be linked to a bewildering array of feelings: amusement, embarrassment, contempt, defiance, delight, friendliness—and the list could go on. In the messages it sends to others, laughter is equally varied. A remarkable feature of laughter is the fact that even though it always communicates, it has no explicit content. (Everyone knows how explaining a joke will kill it.) This ambiguous quality allows laughter to work in ways that reasoned argument could not. Laughter can take us beyond officially prescribed norms and assumptions, into a realm where we find many surprises. People did not necessarily have to defy the rules; sometimes, they could just laugh at them. So, for example, with all the constraints and disapproval female rulers had to deal with, it is striking to find Margaret of Austria laughing her way through a highly successful career as imperial governor of the Netherlands in the early sixteenth century. At humbler social levels, one can find both women and men joking in ways that subtly undermined gender stereotypes. Skills in negotiating the tricky terrain of laughter could make a real difference in the degree of freedom—sometimes called "agency"—that individuals could exercise. Conversely, laughter could be used to enforce conformity without rules or proclamations, when aberrant behavior became the object of ridicule.

This study focuses on the laughter of social interaction. Laughter in response to humorous entertainment, the form that may come most easily to mind for many, is less complicated. The comedian, or in one of the common early modern forms, the seller of printed jestbooks, is aiming to be funny, and audience laughter is the sign of success. This laughter is the stuff of comedy and the subject of a huge body of literary scholarship. But laughter that is raised by comic performances, or even by purposeful joking, is hardly its most prevalent form. It was in the early modern period, with its expansion of media and the market, that laughter-producing entertainment became a major product for sale, from print to theater performance. But everyday laughter is not very much like comedy. Studies of laughter in modern society find that in everyday interactions it is rarely a response to something funny. Instead, laughter appears as a social signal. As Robert Provine has observed, "laughter has more to do with relationships than with jokes."[15] As in the range of feelings associated with laughter, its social messages cover a wide spectrum. It can be used to dominate and intimidate, to express social inclusion or enforce exclusion, to placate and soothe, to invite intimacy, to express scorn—here again, the list is long. It is only in its particular occasions and contexts that its meaning can be read.

Attention to social context can help us tease out the distinction between humor—an intentional spur to laughter—and laughter itself. Successful humor does often elicit laughter, of course, but laughter is far from a passive response to amusing stimuli. Laughter takes an active role in defining a communication or situation as nonserious. The sociologist Anton Zijderveld has offered a helpful formulation of this role of laughter: it signals a shift into the mode of playing with accepted meanings.[16] Putting this idea together with the fact that its triggers may not even be "funny" in themselves, we can see laughter as even more powerful. The shift of social meaning that occurs in joking can be accomplished by laughter, even when there is no joke.[17]

Although there are studies of laughter from the perspectives of various disciplines including biology, psychology, sociology, and linguistics, there are few cross-cultural investigations to shed light on its variations according to culture, place, and time. Studies that place laughter within particular social and cultural contexts have tended to focus on humor rather than laughter itself, partly because humor is easier to study. Humor can be embodied in texts and images—jokes, comedies, satires, caricatures, cartoons—that can be extracted, collected, and analyzed. Also, studying humor can be fun because you get to retell amusing jokes and anecdotes. (Studying laughter is fun too, but there are fewer jokes.) In recent years, in addition to Beard's study of laughter in ancient Rome, historians have begun pursuing its ramifications across centuries and continents from medieval England to twentieth-century China.[18] This book aims to contribute to this growing body of knowledge about laughter and its histories.

Memorable Laughter

How many times did you laugh today? Yesterday? You've probably forgotten, even if you are one of the few people who keep a daily journal. One modern study of laughter frequency found an adult average of some 18 laughs per day, a good enough number to go on with, although of course there is no way to quantify the laughter of the past.[19] People laugh a lot, but the vast bulk of that laughter goes unrecorded. There are good reasons why most of what we know about early modern laughter comes from theory and entertainment rather than daily practice. The search for sources to tell us about everyday laughter is a search for records of remembered laughter. Most laughter disappears from memory, but some makes such an impression that it is written down, either by the one who laughed or by someone who witnessed it. The laughter in this book is laughter that mattered to people in the past. In fact, sometimes it mattered so much that they may have invented it to fit the occasion! Like any historical sources, accounts of laughter are not pure reflections of reality. They are filtered through the perceptions and purposes of those who have left them for us.

The central sources for this book are texts that historians sometimes call "ego documents," a term that includes various kinds of personal accounts—diaries, memoirs, autobiographies—as well as some oral testimonies, such as those recorded in court cases. Another commonly used term for many of these sources is "self-writings." I have incorporated evidence from a range of genres, looking for accounts of laughter in social interaction, with some attention as well to related uses of humor. Of course, the different types of sources require an eye to their particular purposes, audiences, contexts, and conventions. Letters, for example, may not be "ego documents" or "self-writings," depending on their purpose. The business letter and diplomatic correspondence differ markedly from intimate letters that may share many features with the journal or diary, which again differ from public letters intended for a wider audience. Laughter can find its way into any of these types, but its functions and messages differ, both for the authors and for historians.

Europeans of the early modern period produced masses of written texts. Literacy was already rising among the more prosperous and urban social strata in the late medieval period. It was the increasing demand for reading matter that sparked the invention of printing in the fifteenth century, to speed up book production for the growing market. At the same time as more people began reading, more began writing. People wrote to each other across distances; they also wrote about their own lives. Already in the sixteenth century we find increasing numbers of autobiographies, a genre that had largely languished during the Middle Ages. Correspondence too was burgeoning, both with the revival of letter-writing as a literary form among learned elites, and with an increased exchange of informal letters among families and friends. The explosion of written verbiage was a feature of public life as well, with expanding bureaucracies and an increasing demand for written records. Judicial proceedings, for example, increasingly needed to be written according to formal standards in order for judgments to be legal.

Where in all these texts do we find laughter? In all this early modern recording of experiences, laughter appears in many different corners. Still, uncovering it is a challenge. Courts may have turned to meticulous recording, but no one keeps an archive of laughter cases! Digital searching is a great help, but the ever-growing digital corpus does not extend very far into manuscript sources, except for some that later made their way into print. There are many areas the search box cannot reach. I have mined a number of these obscurer veins of laughter, but there are undoubtedly more to be found, especially in areas beyond my language limits (English, German, French, and a bit of Italian and Latin). Of course, given the many varieties of laughter as well as geographic and chronological spread, it is impossible to be comprehensive.

My strategy instead has been to look for tips of the icebergs—personal accounts that are especially rich in laughter, to explore the different types of laughter practice that they illuminate. The case studies in each chapter offer laughter stories that are distinctive to an individual, but also relate to larger contexts of laughter in their time. Clearly, these individual laughers should not be taken as typical inhabitants of their time and place, or even as the most important or most representative in their laughter. The very fact that they wrote or had their stories recorded marks them as exceptional, and some of them were undoubtedly jollier than the norm. Also, for all the early modern growth in literacy, it remained largely the mark of a privileged minority. Readers will readily perceive the prevalence of sources from elites, although some voices do emerge from below. My purpose is not to claim that I can paint a thorough picture of laughter practices in early modern society. Rather, I want to explore laughter's different modes in social negotiation, as well as the shifts we can observe according to place, time, and social milieu.

The laughers in this book are not invented characters. They were all real people with real experiences. Yet our access to their stories comes only through surviving texts, created from their memories and, as I have suggested earlier, designed to serve the purposes of their own time and not ours. I have selected them for the richness of their testimonies and also for the ways in which they offer distinctive entry points into the social action of laughter. No doubt it would be possible, and equally valid, to approach the history of early modern laughter through a completely different set of people and places. (In fact, I would be quite eager to read that history!) While it would be different from mine, it would surely encounter many of the same uses and variations of laughter that I have found in studying these eventful centuries.

★★★

The following chapters move both thematically and chronologically—not tracing a single line of development but offering a shifting kaleidoscope of the guises of laughter. We open with a consideration of laughter's power in the broad scale of social politics. Did body-based humor raise a leveling laughter that brought elites down to the level of the masses, as Mikhail Bakhtin suggested? By examining uses of laughter from low and high, peasant to king, one finds complex dynamics of laughter and power. We meet a range of laughers, from the printers made famous by Robert Darnton to the diplomats and royals, including female rulers, who used laughter for political aims.

The case studies of individual testimonies open with two sharply contrasting versions of Renaissance laughter, the hostile and the friendly. Looking at these laughers in context offers us avenues into the broadly competing positive and negative views of laughter in European society. The Renaissance artist Benvenuto Cellini serves as an exemplar of aggressive laughter. His self-promoting autobiography creates a towering persona, chronicling his many triumphs, especially those over rivals and enemies. Laughter appears here mostly as a sign of defiance and scorn, though he also enjoyed depicting congenial laughter with his highborn patrons— another signal of his success. His story takes us into the negative side of laughter and the long anti-laughter tradition. His near-contemporary and opposite in laughter, the Swiss physician Felix Platter, wrote a very different story of his life. Here the laughter of social bonding brought people together, from courting couples to school chums. We find laughter across differences of religion and status, along with many fans of laughter's benefits, notably doctors who valued its contributions to physical and emotional health.

The issue of gender in the social history of laughter deserves a whole book of its own, but the case of Dorothy Osborne offers a distinctive entry point into women's laughter and the role of laughter in gender relations. We find Osborne making fun of male pretensions and gender stereotypes, yet petrified at the prospect of becoming the object of ridicule. Was laughter a tool of female agency or a means of keeping women under control? Well, yes to both. At the same time, with its role in courtship and sexual play, laughter itself could become tinged with sexual suspicion, especially for women.

While each chapter takes a central individual as its focus, the shifting themes of laughter do not follow a strict chronology. The courtly tradition of laughter takes us to Madame de Sévigné and the seventeenth-century court of Louis XIV, but for context we take a flashback to the sixteenth century and Baldassare Castiglione's influential handbook *The Courtier*. Elites had long been cultivating their own brand of laughter, and while courtly deportment may have stifled the belly laugh, it did not curb ridicule. Sévigné became famed for her witty letters, written to her daughter but also circulated among their friends. She championed a laughter that was largely good-humored, but the exclusionary laughter of the court could humiliate those who missed the fine points of behavior and hierarchy.

If laughter could put people down, it could also help raise them up. Samuel Pepys was a close contemporary of Sévigné and even wrote his famous diary before she began her famous correspondence. Unlike her letters, which she once described as being passed around "like the Holland Gazette," Pepys's was a private record, intended for himself alone. A rising English civil servant under the restored monarchy of Charles II, Pepys depended on his relations with people of higher rank in carving out his social success. Laughter was important to him, both for personal enjoyment and in negotiating his place across differences of status. In an age that combined sharp consciousness of rank with rising social mobility, skills in managing laughter could be a powerful tool.

Hester Lynch Thrale takes us into the eighteenth century to follow the impact of the growing market for laughter products. Best known for her friendship with the formidable Samuel Johnson, Thrale was also an author in her own right. Her extended project in self-writing, the *Thraliana*, began as a collection of anecdotes and finished as a diary. She archly referred to it as a "jestbook"; laughter provided the frame and impetus for preserving her life's memories. She rated her friends and acquaintances for their wit, among other aspects of their character. The stories of others in her circle, such as Arthur Murphy and James Boswell, show us the valuation of laughter as social currency. Laughter-related qualities served as one measure of social performance. Did the spread of a less personal, marketable laughter, detached from its social context, contribute to the positive view of laughter that increasingly prevailed?

Laughter Approaches the Modern Era

Laughter has had a markedly checkered history in Western society—with suspicion coming both from elite squeamishness about bodily contortions and from Christian critiques of ungodly mockery. When Renaissance humanists sought to revive the powerful rhetoric of classical times—inspired by the oratory of Cicero and the biting satire of Juvenal—they brought new attention to the potential of laughter as a weapon. Well-placed ridicule could undermine the position of an opponent far more effectively than simple argument. The humanist cuts and thrusts of wit were largely literary, embodied in the texts that proliferated with the new technology of printing. At the same time, cultures of honor and reputation emphasized the damage that mockery could inflict. In the exclusive circles of the royal court, ridicule was an intimidating force. Law courts often treated the laughing insult as actionable harm. Themes of public laughter like cuckoldry were the stuff of litigation when applied to actual people, especially those of higher status.

It was in the early modern period that these negative views of laughter reached their height. It was also in this period that they were overtaken and passed by the positive valuation of laughter that has come to prevail from the eighteenth century onward. We can see a range of factors contributing to the evolving status of laughter, from the growth of the laughter market to the spread of "civilizing" manners and changing ideas about women and their relationship to laughter. Some might argue that the laughter so valued by modern society since the eighteenth century is a tamed version, stripped of some of its earlier bite. The many uses and guises of early modern laughter form a complex picture that should caution modern readers against taking laughter for granted. The laughter of modern society is a natural human enjoyment, but also the product of a long evolution.

Notes

1 See, for example, Chris Holcomb, *Mirth Making: The Rhetorical Discourse on Jesting in Early Modern England* (Columbia, SC: University of South Carolina Press, 2001); Norbert Elias, *The Civilizing Process: The History of Manners*, trans. Edmund Jephcott (New York: Urizen Books, 1978).

2 For example, see Barbara H. Rosenwein, *Generations of Feeling: A History of Emotions, 600–1700* (Cambridge, UK: Cambridge University Press, 2016).

3 See Mikhail Bakhtin, *Rabelais and His World*, trans. Hélène Iswolsky (Cambridge, MA: MIT Press, 1968); Peter Burke, *Popular Culture in Early Modern Europe*, 3rd ed. (Farnham, England, and Burlington, VT: Ashgate, 2009), 289–332; Ronald Hutton, *The Rise and Fall of Merry England: The Ritual Year 1400–1700* (Oxford: Oxford University Press, 1994).

4 Barry Sanders, *Sudden Glory: Laughter as Subversive History* (Boston: Beacon Press, 1995).

5 Quentin Skinner, "Hobbes and the Classical Theory of Laughter," in *Visions of Politics: Volume 3, Hobbes and Civil Science* (Cambridge: Cambridge University Press, 2002), 142–76, ProQuest Ebook Central.

6 Daniel Wickberg, *The Senses of Humor: Self and Laughter in Modern America* (Ithaca: Cornell University Press, 1998), esp. 8.

7 Studies are legion, but for example: Thomas Laqueur, *Making Sex: Body and Gender from the Greeks to Freud* (Cambridge, MA: Harvard University Press, 1990); Jonathan Sawday, *The Body Emblazoned: Dissection and the Human Body in Renaissance Culture* (London and New York: Routledge, 1995); Rosenwein, *Generations of Feeling*; Jan Plamper, *The History of Emotions: An Introduction* (Oxford: Oxford University Press, 2015); Faramerz Dabhoiwala, *The Origins of Sex: A History of the First Sexual Revolution* (London and New York: Allen Lane, 2012).

8 Again, just a few examples: Ulinka Rublack, *Dressing Up: Cultural Identity in Renaissance Europe* (Oxford and New York: Oxford University Press, 2010); A. Roger Ekirch, *At Day's Close: Night in Times Past* (New York: Norton, 2005); Emily Cockayne, *Hubbub: Filth, Noise, and Stench in England, 1600–1770* (New Haven: Yale University Press,

2021); C. M. Woolgar, *The Culture of Food in England, 1200–1500* (New Haven: Yale University Press, 2016).

9   See, for example, the recent work examining "laughter communities" in Werner Röcke and Hans Rudolf Velten, eds., *Lachgemeinschaften: Kulturelle Inszenierungen und Soziale Wirkungen von Gelächter im Mittelalter und in der Frühen Neuzeit* (Berlin and New York: de Gruyter, 2005).

10 Mary Beard, *Laughter in Ancient Rome: On Joking, Tickling, and Cracking Up* (Berkeley: University of California Press, 2014); similarly, Robert Favre, *Le rire dans tous ses éclats* (Lyon: Presses Universitaires de Lyon, 1995), 7.

11 For a useful summary, see John Morreall, "Philosophy of Humor," in *The Stanford Encyclopedia of Philosophy* (Winter 2016 Edition), ed. Edward N. Zalta, https://plato.stanford.edu/archives/win2016/entries/humor; for more extended discussion, John Morreall, *Comic Relief: A Comprehensive Philosophy of Humor* (Malden, MA: Wiley-Blackwell, 2009).

12 Lucy Rayfield, "Rewriting Laughter in Early Modern Europe," in *The Palgrave Handbook of Humour, History, and Methodology*, ed. D. Derrin and H. Burrows (Springer Nature, Switzerland AG, 2020), 71–91, https://doi.org/10.1007/978-3-030-56646-3_4.

13 See Robert R. Provine, *Laughter: A Scientific Investigation* (New York: Viking, 2000), 45.

14 See, for example, Anca Parvulescu, *Laughter: Notes on a Passion* (Cambridge and London: MIT Press, 2010), 6–7; Rod A. Martin, *The Psychology of Humor: An Integrative Approach* (Amsterdam: Elsevier, 2007); Wallace L. Chafe, *The Importance of Not Being Earnest: The Feeling Behind Laughter and Humor* (Amsterdam: John Benjamins Publishing, 2007).

15 Provine, *Laughter*, 3; on the lack of funniness in pre-laugh comments, see 36–42.

16 Anton C. Zijderveld, "Humor, Laughter, and Sociological Theory," *Sociological Forum* 10, no. 2 (1995): 341–45, https://www.jstor.org/stable/684995; see also Chafe, *The Importance of Not Being Earnest*.

17 For a classic treatment of shifts of meaning in joking, see Mary Douglas, "Social Control of Cognition: Some Factors in Joke Perception," *Man: The Journal of the Royal Anthropological Institute* 3 (1968): 361–76.

18 For example, see Beard, *Laughter in Ancient Rome*; Peter J. A. Jones, *Laughter and Power in the Twelfth Century* (Oxford: Oxford University Press, 2019); Colin Jones, *The Smile Revolution: In Eighteenth Century Paris* (Oxford: Oxford University Press, 2014); Christopher Rea, *The Age of Irreverence: A New History of Laughter in China* (Berkeley, CA: University of California Press, 2015).

19 Rod A. Martin and Nicholas A. Kuiper, "Daily Occurrence of Laughter: Relationships with Age, Gender, and Type A Personality," *Humor: International Journal of Humor Research* 12, no. 4 (1999): 355–84; this is likely an underestimate because it is based on self-reporting.

FIGURE 1.1   Margaret of Austria as a widow, portrait by unknown artist

Source: KHM–Museumsverband

1

LAUGHTER AND POWER

The Politics of Laughter

One day in 1576, Agrippa d'Aubigné shared a laugh with the future King Henry IV of France, in a scene packed with themes of high and low, power and subordination. Aubigné was on the road with Henry, then King of Navarre, when they stopped to eat at a village. The king felt the urge to relieve himself and took the opportunity to defecate into a hamper. But the hamper's owner, an old peasant woman, was incensed. While he was in the very act, she rushed at him with a billhook (a sharp-edged agricultural tool) "and would have split his skull" if not prevented by Aubigné himself. For Aubigné, the incident was comic, even though he claimed, half-seriously, that he had saved the king's life. To make Henry laugh, he composed a mock epitaph, suited to the occasion if the king had died "such an honorable death": "Here lies a king, o wondrous end,/Who died, as God permitted,/Of a billhook thrown by an aged crone,/As in her hutch he shitted."[1]

This incident raises a host of questions about the role of laughter in relations of power. The scene gives us extremes of status from top to bottom, and of humor from the lower bodily function to linguistic wit. The appropriation of the hamper—clearly a valued item of the peasant's property—for such a defiling use underlined the extreme assumption of superiority by the king and his retinue. Clearly, Henry was in open view, the old woman's presence troubling only because she wielded a weapon. Here, in the sixteenth century, we are in the "before" stage of Elias's civilizing process, when such bodily functions were not rigorously hidden. But covering someone or their goods with shit was still offensive, as the woman's reaction shows. In practical terms, of course, it created a disgusting mess. The hamper was a storage vessel for food, adding the implication that she and her family should eat shit. The action effectively placed the woman and her possessions below the level of the king's excrement.

The anecdote offers food for thought in relation to Mikhail Bakhtin's seminal work on the power of popular laughter. In his view, laughter that lampooned the

DOI: 10.4324/9781003247517-2

messy workings of the body was a strong force in symbolically disrupting the hier-archy and dignity of the established order. But Aubigné shows a side of scatological humor that is very different from the equalizer celebrated by Bakhtin. Here the excrement intensifies hierarchy; the king's messy body offers just one more mode of degrading his inferiors. Of course, the comedy is enhanced by other elements of the social contrasts as well. The peasant is not only lowly but female; not only female but old; not only old and female, but violently angry. The rage of women, presumed to be impotent, is a long-lived comic stereotype. It appeared in medi-eval drama, such as in the character of Noah's shrewish wife, and has survived into modern times in the cartoon image of the wife chasing her husband with a fry-ing pan or rolling pin. In this incident, we may well doubt whether the woman was really as violent as Aubigné claims; in fact, readers are probably not meant to take her very seriously as a threat. The incident was "not worthy" of inclusion in Aubigné's larger historical work on the period, but only figured as an anecdote in the personal account of his own life that he wrote for his children. We do not know either whether she was what we would call old—what would that have meant to the youthful king and his entourage? Henry and Aubigné were both in their twenties at the time. But her age, her sex, and her improvised weapon made her extra funny.

These themes provide the jumping-off point for exploring laughter and power. Is laughter subversive, overturning the status quo? Or does it serve the masters, reaffirming their authority? We can find laughter operating in both these modes, a slippery tool indeed. We look first at laughter from below, which has inspired pathbreaking work from cultural historians. Looking at a range of evidence, we consider some perennial questions: is the laughter an effective weapon, or is it a "safety valve" that disperses potential rebellion into frivolity? How can we tell when laughter is truly "popular"? Turning to laughter at the heights of official power, we consider the laughter of rulers and diplomats. Of course, on one level they laughed as everyone does; but they also mobilized laughter in distinctive ways for political purposes—leading to its appearance in political records. The theme of laughter's power continues throughout this book, but the issues raised by laughter in the traditional realm of public power—of rule, subordination, class, and political rivalry—invite us to consider a central question: how powerful was laughter really?

Laughter from Below

The first work to draw wide attention to the historical power of laughter was written not by a historian but by the Russian literary critic Mikhail Bakhtin. In *Rabelais and His World*, Bakhtin argued that *Gargantua and Pantagruel*, masterwork of the Renaissance icon François Rabelais, was not just a literary classic but a win-dow into the elusive world of popular culture and especially popular laughter. Two features of Bakhtin's argument have broader importance for historical views of the power of laughter. The first has to do with the particular type of laughter. Bakhtin celebrated the laughter of popular festivity, especially carnival, the mad season of license that preceded the sobriety of Lent. The second has to do with who was laughing and at whose expense. For Bakhtin, the belly laugh of Rabelais was the laugh of the masses of ordinary people, and it symbolically dethroned the proud elites above them.[2]

The "carnivalesque" laughter of popular celebration, in turn, had two main ways of subverting the orderly world of social hierarchy. One was the playful theme of inversion, turning the world upside down so that nothing is as it ought to be. The comic possibilities were vast—fish swimming in the air, husband and wife reversing their roles, a boy officiating as a mock bishop, a peasant honored as king. The masking and revelry of carnival offered many opportunities for changing identities and reversing high and low. Inversion appeared in many guises in public entertainment as well, from stage to song to popular print. Inversion was funny, overturning expectations with its absurd reversals of the norm. It also played fast and loose with the serious and the sacred.

A related and overlapping ground of popular laughter was what Bakhtin called the grotesque body. Rabelaisian laughter is full of untamed bodies and their orifices: gorging, swilling, vomiting, farting, pissing, shitting, coupling, even giving birth, all became part of the raucous comedy. The characters' monstrous excess, in gigantic size and in the scale of their disorderly behaviors, marked them as grotesque. Bakhtin saw a liberating symbolism in the shared bodily experience of humanity—birth, death, digestion, excretion, sex—all in their way disgusting, all unavoidably human, all matter for carnivalesque laughter. The laughs at excrement and other fleshly functions, in Bakhtin's analysis, marked the "uncrowning" of social superiors by the reminder of their shared and absurd physicality. For Bakhtin, such popular humor marked a space of freedom—if only in the imagination—that he saw as suppressed and stunted in modern bourgeois society.

But was popular laughter really subversive, or was it merely a diversion that helped reconcile the lowly to their position in the status quo? The imagined inversions were fun, but their humor depended on recognition of the normal state of things: kings and nobles ruling over peasants, husbands ruling their wives, bishops processing with suitable pomp, fish swimming in the sea and not the sky. Carnival was temporary. On the other hand, the daring license of festivity was not always kept within bounds. When real rebellion did erupt, the laughter and irreverence could undermine the everyday awe that elites hoped to maintain. Another question: were the unruly laughers really the downtrodden masses? Rabelais had an elite university education, after all, and the wealthy claimed their own part in carnival festivities. It was they who could afford the best costumes for masquerades and fund the best revels. Carnival was imprinted with Christian meanings and could be orchestrated by authorities (though they could not always control it). Even when carnival play shifted into real unrest, it was not necessarily the lower classes who got out of control. Carnival laughter does not yield its meaning easily.[3]

Laughter and Subversion

Possibly the most famous subversive laughter in history was uncovered by the brilliant Robert Darnton in his book *The Great Cat Massacre*. It was late in the 1730s, in the Parisian print shop of a lazy bourgeois master and his cat-loving wife. Creeping capitalism had blocked advancement in the printing industry to a few fortunate owners. Employees still had the old guild titles of apprentice and journeyman, but in fact were largely treated as casual labor, without any prospect of eventually becoming master printers and opening their own workshops. They thought the master printer ought to be a coworker, but he had become part of a separate, leisured class that slept late, ate fancy dinners, and kept pampered pets. When told to get rid of the howling alley cats that kept the master and mistress awake at night (skipping a couple of steps in the story here), the workers staged a carnivalesque massacre. Starting with the mistress's favorite, they slaughtered cats in an atmosphere of high revelry. According to the worker who retold the event in his life story, it roused irresistible laughter among the workers, not only at the time but in reminiscences. It was told and retold, raising hilarity every time.[4]

As Darnton has noted, the story may not have happened just as it was recounted. The semi-autobiographical account of the printer Nicolas Contat was full of embellishment, but it tells us a great deal about the workers' outlook. Darnton found many layers of meaning in their laughter, which celebrated a moment of vicarious attack on the master and mistress themselves. The workers drew on the resources of popular culture, in which symbolic role reversals and innuendos from the sexual to the supernatural were in constant play. With inversion and symbolism, they could call the mistress a whore and witch, the master a cuckold—all while pretending that they were merely following their instructions to get rid of those pesky cats. The workers' derisive laughter was not revolutionary; it did not change their objective situation. Yet it made them happy in the hilarious moment. No longer victims, they could celebrate their own power. As Darnton points out, their rebellious outlook shows a kinship with the real revolutionary upheaval that was to come half a century later.

The cat massacre was the most dramatic moment in Contat's account. It was far from the only laughter, though. Contat depicts a workers' culture in which laughter was a constant and even required element of belonging and group identity. The cat episode is sandwiched between other occasions of laughter—not all of it rebellious, but all positioning laughter as a source of power. It was laughter that exerted the power of the group over individual members, as well as laughter that marked the community of its participants. In the first instance, the unhappy apprentice Jerome became the butt of his coworkers when they found and read aloud a letter from his uncle that repeated the words, "I told you so, Jerome!" The workers were amused by all the old uncle's criticism and advice, but "I told you so, Jerome" caused explosions of laughter. The phrase became a catcall and nickname, loudly echoing through the shop—a hundred times a day, Contat tells us.[5] (Even the cat massacre only got 20 repetitions.)

Such hazing may seem unsurprising treatment of a young and vulnerable new apprentice. But everyone was fair game. When the print workers gathered for sociability and solidarity, ridicule was de rigeur. In speeches of mock formality, they made fun of one of their number—taking care not to attack honor or reputation, but telling funny stories, with the greatest applause for the most successful satire. As in the modern "roast," etiquette required that the object of ridicule take it all in good part. Even though he was expected to feel chagrin (*dépit*), "nevertheless, to merit the esteem of his comrades, he must never get angry and must laugh with the others; if he does otherwise, he will be seen as unworthy of the amusements and society of the printers."[6]

The massacre of cats was not the last laughter at the expense of the beleaguered bourgeois master, either. After their exploit with the cats, Jerome and his friend Léveillé decided to do something about their inadequate meals. Taking their skimpy meat ration to the grocer's, they had it weighed. The grocer's shop was a public space, and the customers there were quick to joke about the master's kind care in preserving his employees from indigestion. Now the master printer was the target of community ridicule. He had been slow to see the insults implied in the cat massacre, but this damage to his reputation made him livid. In rage he threw the youths out of his house—only later realizing that banishment would delight Jerome by freeing him from his apprenticeship. The apprentice packed as fast as he could, but only got one foot over the threshold before the master called him back to serve the rest of his time. Of course, this follow-up adventure became another source of repeated amusement for the print workers.[7] Whatever liberties Contat took in telling his stories, there is no mistaking the relish for laughter as both a test of solidarity and a weapon against the higher-ups.

Usually, times of popular celebration—such as carnival, May Day, and Three Kings Day—were temporary frolics that transitioned smoothly back into the regular rhythm of work. But they could sometimes become opportunities for mayhem. At carnival time in the southern French town of Romans in 1580, festivity turned to violence in a class conflict that led to deaths. But the upheaval was not really an outgrowth of the laughter, even though the holiday provided the occasion for the outbreak of long-building tensions. The town elite attempted to maintain a tone of hilarity, staging events early in the proceedings in which, according to the organizer, "there was talk of nothing but laughter and amusement."[8] The patricians put forward their own comic inversion of values, with the intention of reinforcing the normal order of things. The discontented workers mounted a rival celebration of carnival—each group using the symbols of carnival masking and play for their own purposes. It was the elite who seized the opportunity offered by mock disorder for a turn to violence, beating and killing members of the lower-class group. In fact, the elite faction had conspired ahead of time to plan its attack.[9]

Other studies have found festivities to be frequent moments of unrest—only partly because everyone had the day off from working. Religious riots, like the infamous St. Bartholomew's Day massacres of French Protestants in 1572, could not only seize on the festive occasion of a royal wedding, but also draw on the comic vocabulary of carnival in their violence. Rituals of inversion, parody, mockery, and defiling uses of excrement, which in other settings were so funny, here served to dehumanize victims. Natalie Davis has argued that these elements of play enabled people to distance themselves from the reality of what they were doing.[10] It's not clear how much there was actual laughter. Here too, though, we are not really seeing a liberation of the lowly, as broad classes joined in violence, including clerics and elites.

Laughter at the disorderly body, as Aubigné's example shows, did not always symbolically dethrone the powerful. Yet it was a constantly available means of undermining dignity. Even though carnivalesque laughter was hardly limited to the "popular" classes, the shaming potential of body humor did put a weapon in the hands of those without official power. Libel cases from England's Star Chamber in the seventeenth century show how seriously elites could take plebeian laughter. Proceedings at this court were expensive, mainly limited to the wealthy, who could bring their complaints to this court when libeled by their social inferiors. It was the unruly body—in particular, illicit sexual relations or rumors of them—that gave libelers their central ground for shaming laughter. (Of course, it was not only social superiors who were vulnerable to such mockery—more on that later—but it was the elite who could gain protection from this court.) The central role of hilarity in these libels emerges clearly from contemporary descriptions in the court records and elsewhere. The seventeenth-century clergyman John Swifte was said to be "a known and common libeler and contriver of false and slanderous libels and pamphlets" which he would "by way of jest and merriment, scoffingly sing, divulge and publish . . . at diverse and sundry times and in diverse places to diverse persons."[11] Even people who were not literate themselves could enjoy such humor at their superiors' expense, getting someone else to write songs for them or laughing and joking about scurrilous pictures posted on a tavern wall.[12] Libels were sung on "alebenches and other places in most scoffing, lewd and obscene manner" or trotted out for Christmas merriment. Complaints to the court stressed the "laughing and rejoicing" of the defendants and their friends in "scornful, deriding and infamous" enjoyment.[13]

Women as well as men were prosecuted for writing or distributing libels. In 1606, Joan Gomme of Norfolk was accused of "the making of libelous and lascivious ballads by and of her neighbors." Another writer of defamatory rhymes and songs was Mary Shepperd of Hertfordshire in 1652.[14] Verses and ballads were a common vehicle for popular ridicule, a pastime in which both sexes participated. One of the aims of the Star Chamber court was to silence the laughter when lower-class people targeted their social superiors. As Adam Fox found, defamation had formerly been considered merely un-Christian immorality but now was criminalized: "seditious if directed against persons in authority and breaches of the peace if touching private individuals."[15] Before this court, jest was no laughing matter. The element of comic derision became part of the legal standard on libels, which worked

> either by scoffing at the person of another in rhyme or prose, or by the personating of him, thereby to make him ridiculous; or by setting up horns at his gate, or picturing him or describing him; or by writing of some base or defamatory letter, and publishing the same to others, or some scurvy love-letter to himself, whereby it is not likely but he should break the peace; or to publish disgraceful or false speeches against any eminent man or public officer.[16]

Such ridicule was punishable as malicious even if its contents—such as charges of committing adultery or begetting a bastard—were true.

More explicitly political critiques made use of laughter too, of course. The spread of printing gave new scope to political satire, a huge subject of its own.[17] We can only consider a couple of examples here. Political critics sang comic songs and satires in sixteenth-century Augsburg, while in seventeenth-century England the radical Levellers mocked Puritan authority.[18] In France, Sara Beam has traced the fortunes of theatrical farces, finding a gradual suppression of bawdy humor along with political bite, as local elites showed increasing deference toward royal absolutism in the seventeenth century. Not only sex but also farting, defecation, and other low bodily functions marked the raw humor of early farces. Mockery of authority, by means of exposing this common bodily ground, was part of the license of comedy, as in the carnival celebrations analyzed by Bakhtin. But just as courts in England began seriously policing such jesting, urban officials in France increasingly sought to clean up the stage. The amateur players of earlier farces used sex and the body for comic license in risky political satire, but the increasingly professional stage of the seventeenth century was far more cautious. Formerly funny material came to be seen as scandalous and rude.[19]

Such "civilizing" of unruly laughter is a process that one can observe at various stages in European history. Peter Burke has posited a "Triumph of Lent" in the seventeenth century, as rowdy popular customs were increasingly suppressed in favor of a more sober and ordered society.[20] Yet even in the eighteenth century, historians have found pockets of public hilarity that evoke the Rabelaisian laughter of carnival. Underground and in private, of course, this strain never went away, even before the twentieth-century revival of humor that had formerly been labeled obscene. The English satirical prints of the decades around 1800 marked a golden age of caricature, in a study by Vic Gatrell. The ribald images of prominent and aristocratic individuals poked fun at their bodies and sexual peccadilloes. Like Bakhtin, Gatrell argues for a broadly liberating effect from all this disrespectful treatment of the powerful—a liberation that he finds suppressed in the nineteenth century by the increasing ascendancy of bourgeois respectability. The prints were not serving subversive political aims, however, for all their scurrility. As Gatrell notes, they were commercial products designed for a monied clientele; they were produced by artisans, but not for a "popular" audience. It was the elite crowd of people familiar with all the players of high life—particularly men—who enjoyed them, not the man or woman in the street.[21]

Antoine de Baecque, in his study of laughter cultures in eighteenth-century France, argues that laughter played a significant social and political role. Literary battles among types of laughter material, from satire to gaiety to farce, had associations of class and political bent. In the run-up to revolution, some radicals argued that the French reputation for gaiety and frivolity was a relic of the absolutist past, to be overcome now that Frenchmen had real political affairs to discuss. De Baecque has traced links between the published satires of royalist counter-revolutionaries and the actual eruptions of laughter in the National Assembly in the early years of the French Revolution. While the earnest and mainly bourgeois revolutionaries had sought an atmosphere of gravity—issuing rules that banned laughter in the chamber, along with other demonstrations of approval or disapproval, such as applause and insult—some aristocratic delegates refused to conform, disrupting the proceedings with satirical and unserious behavior. Once laughter was on the floor, however, the champions of revolution could also turn ridicule against their opponents. At a more popular level, humor was used to spread revolutionary messages. Laughter was a many-edged weapon.[22]

Popular Policing?

Libels and political satire could provoke laughter at the expense of authority figures, though they were not always "popular" in their origins and aims. Other forms of popular laughter could police relationships and behaviors in a quite conservative direction. Rituals of public mockery took various names and forms—charivari, "rough music," Skimmington and the like—and were widespread in early modern Europe. Here again, sexual behavior was a prime focus of attention. Typically led by groups of young males, these practices used their comic license to enforce widely accepted behavioral rules; the norms were their excuse, at any rate, for often abusive behavior. Those suspected of illicit sex, particularly women, were mocked and shamed; other targets included infertile couples or second marriages, particularly those with a large age difference.[23] Perhaps best known from recent scholarship is the ridicule directed against marital discord—in particular, couples in which the wife was thought to dominate or even beat her husband. In the Skimmington, an English variety, the henpecked husband or a surrogate was made to ride backwards in comic procession on an ass. To the participants it was fun: a crowd gathered "to make merry with Skimmington" at the expense of John Day of Somerset in 1653, calling him cuckold and threatening to throw his wife into a pond.[24] As Susan Amussen and David Underdown point out, while neighbors might see the Skimmington ride as an "old country ceremony used in merriment," the targets were not amused; some were driven out of town.[25] The laughter of such rituals exerted power, certainly; but hardly a liberating power.

These real–life occasions echoed the comedy of husband–hammering shrews in popular literature, a favorite theme of seventeenth–century songs and prints. Shakespeare's famed *Taming of the Shrew* was part of a much wider European genre. With all the festivity, the intent and effect was public shaming, the curbing of undesirable behavior—in this case, female uppitiness. By the eighteenth century in England, popular sanction shifted toward disciplining the abusive husband—a positive change from a modern feminist standpoint.[26] The shared theme in this type of public mockery, however, was the maintenance of an expected order, through play and laughter that mimicked reversals and violations. Literary images are not our main focus here, but they do give some evidence of what people laughed at. And, while satirical images like the shrew may have held women up to ridicule (along with their hen–pecked husbands), there were plenty of laughing women in literature too. Pam Brown has pointed to this strain of female laughter—including the laughter of shrews!—as a potential means of exerting power against the misogyny of the age.[27] We will meet more laughing women in the pages ahead.

Besides the laughter of unruly women, literature and folklore offer a wide range of laughing insurgents. The tradition of the trickster, a laughing antihero, was celebrated in print in many forms, from the German Till Eulenspiegel to the vogue for picaresque novels. The picaresque genre was successful all over Europe, with best sellers crossing borders; one could cite the Spanish novella *Lazarillo de Tormes* in the sixteenth century, along with the works of the German Grimmelshausen and the English Defoe in the seventeenth. The carefree and insouciant picaro was a literary image, but one that could cross over into autobiography. When the French artisan Jacques-Louis Ménétra came to write his much-fictionalized life story in the eighteenth century, he imagined it as a series of picaresque adventures, with himself as the trickster-hero.[28]

We can find more rebellious laughter of the rule-breaking underdog in real life, in the eighteenth-century accounts of the Ordinary of Newgate Prison in London. The Ordinary was the prison's official minister, tasked with providing religious instruction to condemned criminals. Several Ordinaries in succession were scandalized when they found prisoners were inclined to laugh instead of lament. These were largely young men, sentenced for property crimes and soon to hang. In 1714, the Ordinary complained of William Dyer, condemned for burglary, that when he admonished him to repent, "I observ'd him to fleer and snigger." Another Ordinary, in 1721, found that the 19-year-old John Jones, who had snatched a woman's purse, "Laugh'd frequently at the Prayers." In 1726, John Barton "laugh'd, and was thought to be one who provok'd some of the rest to such undecent Carriage [behavior]." In these cases and some others, the ministers reported eventual success in imposing greater seriousness, so that Barton, for instance, at execution "repented of all his Sins, and died in Communion of the Church of England." But there were some hard cases. James Carrick, at the site of his execution in 1722, "laughed and smiled upon all whom he there knew." Most appalling of all was Benjamin Campbel Hamilton, 17, on reaching the scene of his death in 1750: his "Behaviour was intolerably indecent there, talking and laughing almost all the while the

Executioner was tying them up, and using such Expressions as are better stifled than reported." These ultimate resisters could not save their lives, but they could refuse to accept the role of penitent assigned them by authority; they could keep their power to laugh.[29] In the Old Bailey records more broadly, laughter appears most often as attributed to accused criminals, evidently a suspicious sign.

Laughter at the Top

From the laughter of social subordinates, we shift to the highest centers of power. Laughter at the royal court was not trivial or casual. Far back into the early Middle Ages, merriment was part of a ritualized culture of gesture that was an important element in negotiating power relations. Historians once saw the Middle Ages as unrestrained and spontaneous, but recent scholarship shows that people knew exactly what they were doing. Emotional outbursts, whether laughter, tears, or anger, were not just an eruption of instinctive drives; they were calibrated to their occasions and designed to convey specific messages. It was a world of violence and insecurity, to be sure—all the more reason, as Gerd Althoff has pointed out, why one needed to be a skilled observer and practitioner of gesture and ceremony.[30] In political relationships, feasting and the accompanying merriment were part of the serious business of displaying and cementing solidarity. The seemingly routine descriptions of meetings and meals in medieval chronicles marked significant moments in the building of political networks. It mattered very much, Althoff notes, "how someone was received most honourably, was presented with great gifts, dined in a joyful atmosphere, or approached another person and kissed him."[31] Althoff cites Gregory of Tours on the extended celebration that marked a pivotal political move in the sixth-century Frankish kingdom, the designation of a new heir to the throne: "They feasted together for three days, and made merry and exchanged gifts, before departing in peace."[32] The ability to provoke laughter, too, was a valued quality in political debate.[33]

The laughter of the king had its own meaning. Jacques Le Goff has pointed to the king's laughter as becoming "practically obligatory" in the developing culture of the royal court starting in the twelfth century.[34] Royal laughter could operate as a means of dispensing differential favor, or as Le Goff suggests, "a way of structuring the society around him." The image of the laughing king projected confidence and ease in rule. Conversely, laughter at the king's jokes—another thing that was practically obligatory, no doubt—signaled the effective subordination of his courtiers. Henry II of England was especially known for his jokes and laughter, which were carefully recorded. Peter Jones has recently made an in-depth study of laughter at Henry's court. He argues that the ambiguous resonances of laughter allowed the king to circumvent his own growing bureaucracy and exert a personal, charismatic power. This king not only employed laughter in his own dealings but also presided over a court where laughter, ridicule, and satire were a constant source of both threat and influence.[35]

The most famous raiser of royal laughter was the court jester or fool, a fixture at European courts up through the seventeenth century. Louis XIV cultivated an image of seriousness but still kept a jester—though he appears to have been the last of French kings to do so. The jester was in a privileged position, licensed to rouse laughter by violating taboos that others had to observe. Jesters could even make fun of the ruler, up to a point. But their privilege was partly based on the fact that their position was completely dependent upon royal favor—unlike noble courtiers, who had independent sources of power, at least before the seventeenth-century rise of absolutism. In fact, wealthy nobles often kept their own jesters, along with other entertainers. Beatrice Otto has collected many examples of close relationships and affection between royal patrons and their jesting dependents. Some served for decades or for their whole lives, retaining their places through the rise and fall of more prestigious courtiers. But of course, the most fundamental source of their license was the fact that they did not need to be taken seriously. Their humor could be disruptive in the moment, skewering pretensions of the great, but dissolving in shared laughter that never disturbed the hierarchy of royal authority. Otto has found jesters across many cultures and in the most reputedly despotic of regimes. Jesters to the emperors of China, for example, were reported to crack daring jokes that could have put their lives at risk. If they were witty enough, as the famous ones were, they got away with it.[36]

The jester was a laughter professional, a performer who made a living from the ability to make a patron laugh. The decline of this figure in European courts coincided with the expanding development of comic theater and other forms of marketable laughter. Perhaps somewhat ironically, leading Renaissance jesters were a prime source of material for the growing print market for jests. The tie to named comedians gave jestbooks an attractive claim to authenticity; they were attributed to real jesters like the English John Scoggin, fifteenth-century jester to Edward IV, as well as to invented ones. Yet broader commercialization was likely part of what put the court jester out of business. Louis XIV's jester took his wit too far and ultimately lost favor, a fate that portended the general decline of the position.[37] At the same time, the development of professional theater had given royals other options for their amusement. Charles II of England had a witty courtier, Thomas Killigrew, whom some saw as a jester figure, but his real role was as a producer of plays. While he found Killigrew amusing, King Charles was also a prime patron of the playhouse, where Samuel Pepys, among other audience members, took note of the eruption (or not) of royal laughter. There were fools employed at eighteenth-century German courts, often the butt of cruel practical joking by rulers and noble courtiers alike, but the jester's heyday was clearly past.[38]

Even in modern times, of course, sociability and ceremony among political leaders are full of political significance. Diplomats and ministers pay attention to the moods of leaders and seek to read their uses of laughter. The early modern era was the first age of regular international diplomacy, an invention of the Renaissance Italian city-states that spread widely in the sixteenth century. The settled envoys at foreign courts sent back news to their own rulers—not only with information about events, but with attempts to gauge the intentions and purposes of their rivals. Moods and laughter were factors they observed but often found difficult to interpret. The laughs were part of a complex dance of gesture intended to convey a particular impression—often hiding the laugher's real thought. On the surface, much of the laughter might seem normal, natural, or even insignificant. Of course, people are going to laugh. On the other hand, as the reporters of laughter also knew, laughter in these contexts was almost never without purpose. And in fact, the diplomatic maneuvers were often integrated into occasions of sociability, such as hunting or banqueting. Laughter here could become an affair of state, important enough to figure in dispatches to their principals.

The diplomats who filed detailed reports of foreign politics for their own governments were intensely attuned to nuances of behavior. They noted when something was said laughingly, or when a sovereign or minister responded to them with laughter. The laughter of rulers was especially noteworthy; it was open to a range of interpretations and often called for particular finesse on the part of the ambassador, who then reported on his own handling of the moment. In 1518, for example, the Venetian envoy Sebastian Giustinian sought to assure Henry VIII of England that King Francis I of France sincerely wished to preserve peace. Henry "began to laugh as if he suspected deceit, and said if Francis were in earnest he would not so lightly injure Englishmen, or deny them justice."[39] Giustinian redoubled his assurances as the king ridiculed France's policies; but then two-year-old Princess Mary was brought in, and the envoy shifted to the ceremony of kissing the toddler's hand.

In this case, the king's laughter suggested disbelief. On the other hand, it could signal favor, an affable disposition to set the diplomat at ease, or an expression of appreciation for his efforts. Even such occasions as these might demand skillful maneuvers in reply, however, as the ambiguity of laughter could shift the ground of discourse in an undesired direction. Eustace Chapuys, representative of the Holy Roman Emperor Charles V, reported a conversation in 1532 in which Henry VIII spoke disparagingly of the emperor's relations with the Venetians and through them with the Turks: "He said this, laughing, putting his hand on my shoulder several times." But the laughter and accompanying gesture of fellowship did not disarm Chapuys, who "showed him the contrary, saying that I hoped the Emperor would send such an answer to his letters that he would know that there was no prince in the world who had greater desire for the good of Christendom."[40]

A case of benign laughter appeared to indicate that the diplomat had succeeded in gaining the laugher's appreciation—at least to the extent of recognizing the result of his efforts. The Venetian ambassador Federico Badoer reported such success in 1556 with King Philip (Philip II of Spain, King of England by his marriage to Queen Mary Tudor), during negotiations to bring a long series of wars to an end. In a friendly conversation with Badoer, the king expressed gratitude to the Venetian government, promising that they would soon have " 'proof positive of my goodwill in this matter and in all others hereafter, and I believe that by reason of our reciprocal goodwill there will always be sincere friendship between us';

adding very graciously, with a laugh, 'and you, owing to the good offices you have performed, will bear the blame of this.' "[41] Badoer, pleased and proud, responded with serious diplomatic courtesy:

> To this kind jest on the part of his Majesty I replied that he conferred great favour and honour upon me by speaking in this manner, and that nothing but the sincerity practised by me in all the negotiations could deserve such praise.

Diplomats also reported their own laughter, often deployed to hide their true feelings or make light of a threat. Diego Guzman de Silva, who represented Philip II in England from 1564 to 1568, was highly attuned to laughter, reporting ways in which he used it himself, as well as the levity of Queen Elizabeth (more on that later). When the French ambassador told him of the approach of a Turkish ambassador, he responded "laughingly, as if I did not attach much importance to it."[42] In response to an angry outburst from the queen's chief minister, William Cecil, over the treatment of England's ambassador in Spain, Guzman employed laughter to place himself above the fray:

> I waited a little for him to recover somewhat from his rage, and then went up to him laughing and embraced him, saying that I was amused to see him fly into such a passion over what I had told him, because I knew he understood differently.[43]

Another Spanish envoy, in the midst of tensions with England over Spain's treatment of the Netherlands in 1576, met anger with a (false) laugh: Queen Elizabeth's chief minister, William Cecil, Lord Burghley, said

> angrily, "You people are of such sort that wherever you set foot no grass grows, and you are hated everywhere." I affected to laugh at this, and said that this was like the Romans, who were hated all over the world in consequence of their bravery.[44]

The laughing off of threats, the laugh to hide serious interest, the laugh to feign camaraderie, and many other permutations were part of the diplomatic arsenal.

The records of diplomacy show striking uses of royal laughter among female rulers of the early modern era as well. Although their historical image is typically colored by the restrictions and negativity they faced, these women were also laughing—not just at the antics of court entertainers, but also with purposes of their own. Their sex made female rulers inappropriate wielders of authority in the eyes of many of their contemporaries. Kings went to great lengths to avoid female rule, which was seen as making a throne weak and vulnerable (often a self-fulfilling prophecy). Henry VIII's dramatic succession of marriages was about exactly this goal—with huge consequences for England's religious as well as political history, since he broke with Rome to get his first divorce. In France, female succession was outlawed, although even there it was not possible to avoid some regencies that placed power in female hands. Accidents of lineage, and the fact that noble birth and blood relationships took precedence even over the bar of gender, brought women into positions of rule. To take one date in the mid-sixteenth century, 1560, we can find female rulers in important realms across Europe: England, Elizabeth I; France, Catherine de Medici, regent; Scotland, Mary Queen of Scots; Navarre, Jeanne d'Albret; Portugal, Catherine of Austria, regent.[45] Female rulers were a minority, but a significant one.

Lady of Mourning, Lady of Laughter

A little-known but fascinating example is that of the Habsburg princess Margaret of Austria, who governed the Netherlands between 1507 and 1530 on behalf of two Holy Roman Emperors—her father, Maximilian I, and her nephew, Charles V. Her rule has been widely acclaimed for its successes. The classic 1911 *Encyclopedia Britannica* bestowed this rare praise: "She was a wise and prudent ruler, of masculine temper and intrepidity, and very capable in affairs."[46] The terms of this praise are somewhat ironic, given that in launching one of her notable diplomatic moves—the "Ladies' Peace" of Cambrai between France and the Holy Roman Empire in 1529—Margaret explicitly asserted that her sex made her a better negotiator. The male rulers' attachment to masculine codes of honor would not let them forget past wrongs, but "ladies might well come forward in a measure for submitting the gratification of private hatred and revenge to the far nobler principle of the welfare of nations."[47]

In addition to her successful diplomatic negotiations and political maneuvering, she was a noted patron of the arts, sponsoring musicians, poets, and artists. Her image has typically been a somber one, however, partly because of the sobriquet of "Lady of Mourning" bestowed by one of her court poets. The mourning referred to the early deaths of her two husbands, and her determination to remain single thereafter. The nineteenth-century editor of her correspondence with Maximilian, André Ghislain, even stated that the tragic early losses of her husbands, followed soon after by the death of her beloved brother, "cast an ineffaceable tinge of melancholy on the character of this superior woman."[48] This impression was likely reinforced by her surviving poetry, much of which does take the mode of lament.

And yet attendees at her court in the Netherlands had a very different impression. The English envoy, Robert Wingfield, found her habitually joking and laughing. Writing in 1522 to Cardinal Wolsey, he told of how she seemed to reproach him for some of his reports, but took his answer "in good part, and with laughing cheer, after her custom, fell to talk of other matters."[49] Wingfield even jested with her on a reputedly sensitive subject. Margaret had been raised at the French court as the future wife of the heir to the throne—a frequent custom in royal betrothals. But after becoming king, the young Charles VIII put her aside for a political marriage, to prevent Brittany from falling into Habsburg hands. Margaret has been said to bear lasting resentment for this slight; Ghislain took the trouble to argue against the idea that she remained bitter against France ever after. In any case, the matter was not so serious that she couldn't joke about it. In 1525, the French King Francis I had suffered a humiliating defeat and was imprisoned by the Emperor's forces. The English were allied with the Empire against France, and Wingfield was negotiating with Margaret about how to handle the fruits of this victory. Margaret showed Wingfield two letters from Francis asking her to intercede with the Emperor for him; he had signed the first "as written by her good son, and the second by her good cousin and friend." Francis's wife had died the previous year, and Wingfield made a joke that harked back to the failed French marriage of Margaret's youth—a jest that she relished and capped with one of her own. Wingfield

> told her, jesting, that he [Francis] had remembered better in his second letter than in the first, considering that the son might not well marry his mother. At this she laughed heartily, after her accustomed manner, and told a merry tale "how a young prince would needs marry his mistress, which was old, against his friends' mind, because he would be avenged on her for killing of his master with her cursedness;" and said, Francis might wish to be avenged upon her for the good will she had always borne to France.[50]

In this incident, Margaret compared her own attitude with the "cursedness"— shrewishness—of the woman in the story, in a comic vein. The joke hinted too at her own age—45—compared with the 30-year-old Francis. Certainly, she remembered the poor treatment she had suffered from an earlier French king; but in fact, her Habsburg ties would have put her on the opposing side in a long series of wars, no matter what her personal sentiments. Far from being perturbed by the reference to that early humiliation, she could laugh at it. This, at any rate, is the image of laughing strength that she presented to those in attendance at her court. The correspondence of Wingfield and other diplomats shows their respect for Margaret as a capable and trustworthy negotiator. Her ability to season her talent for affairs with laughter reinforced the aura of ease and confidence that impressed those who dealt with her.

Margaret's love of laughter also emerges from the correspondence of one of the noblewomen of her court, Marguerite de Croÿ. Her letters to her mistress express respect and often pleas for support in her husband's affairs, but also a playfulness that attests to their joking relationship. De Croÿ made fun of the terrible handwriting of Margaret's German scribes. She asked to be remembered to the King of England and threatened to ridicule him if he didn't behave. She referred to herself as "the mad Madame de Croÿ," joking about her wish to get better treatment in traveling than her mistress had. On another occasion, she was extremely eager for herself and a young pupil to accompany Margaret on a visit to see the "beau roy"—evidently the handsome young King of England, Henry VIII. Pleading with Margaret not to go without them, she facetiously threatened to set fire to Margaret's treasured

library at Malines, burning "all your books and spells [enchantements]." She even
included a little rhyme with pet names for her mistress:

> madame ma trocquette ma mye,
> nales pas sans no[us] je vo[us] en prie,
> ajointe mains et a jenouls,
> no[us] priro[n]s adieu pour vous.

Or, in approximate English translation, preserving the rhyme:

> O dear madame, my love, my sweet,
> Take us along, I you entreat,
> With pleading hands upon our knees
> We'll pray that God may grant you ease.

Margaret's reply does not survive, but she may have been moved by this playful
appeal; de Croÿ was present at a meeting with Henry in 1513.[51]

   Margaret's jesting habit complemented her astute political sense in making her
expert at both negotiation and rule. Wingfield, the representative of an ally, got
along with her particularly well and was able to match jest for jest, without losing
sight of her firmness in defense of imperial interests. Contemporary accounts of her
diplomatic maneuvers with rival powers hint at her ability to disarm others in trick-
ier negotiations. One observer certainly exaggerated her success in talks at Cambrai
at the start of her rule in 1508, asserting that she "was so successful in charming [the
Cardinal of Amboise] that he could refuse her nothing."[52] In fact, the two were often
at loggerheads; they tabled some contentious issues about competing claims in the
Netherlands, while negotiating a major international alliance, the League of Cambrai. The ambiguity of jest could both ease relationships and put others off guard.

The Laughter of Elizabeth

Elizabeth I of England used laughter to great effect. Her persistent deflection of
marriage offers is well known, along with the complaints of her advisors and others about her delays and vacillation on the subject.[53] Less recognized is the way
she used laughter and jest to keep people guessing about her intentions. Diplomacy over marriage negotiations was especially active during the first decade of
her reign—though even by the mid-1560s the idea that she would not marry was
spreading. Early in her reign, in 1559, the envoy of Spain wrote slightingly of the
wit of the Holy Roman Emperor's ambassador, "who is not the most crafty person
in the world," for thinking Elizabeth favorably inclined to a German match.[54] In the
event, she would not come to the point:

> After spending a good while on this chat she turned to the subject of the
> Emperor and his sons, and said she heard that the Emperor was a virtuous,

just and worthy prince, and that Maximilian was a noble and christian gentleman and a lover of the true religion. She heard that Ferdinand was only
fit to pray to God for his father and brothers as he was so strong a Catholic,
which she laughed at, but that she knew nothing about Charles, and then she
waited to hear what the ambassador would answer.

Guzman de Silva, the cheerful Spanish envoy, was at Elizabeth's court at the
height of negotiations over her possible marriage to the Archduke Charles. He
recorded multiple instances of her slippery uses of laughter to avoid firm com-
mitments and divert conversations away from the nub. She joked about marrying the son of the Turkish ruler, Suleiman the Magnificent; she even joked
about marrying the pope. Guzman traded jokes with her but was always left in
doubt about her meaning. In 1565, Guzman was promoting the marriage with
the Archduke, but also secretly promising Elizabeth's domestic favorite, Robert Dudley, that he would encourage his interests if the imperial marriage fell
through. In Guzman's conversation with the queen, her laughter hinted that she
suspected this double game:

> I said I hoped to God I should see her some day in the position I wished.
> She seized upon this at once and said, "You never speak out clearly to me,
> you have something in your breast that you will not tell me." I told her
> I could not speak more clearly than I had done as to your Majesty's [Philip
> II's] good will to the Archduke, and my own wishes could be only those of
> your Majesty. She said she still had some suspicion, but that I might be sure
> that neither the Emperor nor the Archduke should ever know it from her.
> I answered that I had no more to say than I had already said, and she replied
> that she knew my thoughts, although I would not declare them, and laughed
> very much. She is very strange.[55]

The following January Elizabeth was joking to Guzman about a possible marriage with Dudley, playing on a comparison with Mary Queen of Scots, who had
just married her countryman and cousin Lord Darnley:

> If she did marry him, she said laughingly, two neighbouring Queens would
> be wedded in the same way, but she ended the subject by saying that her
> inclination tended higher. She is so nimble in her dealing and threads in and
> out of this business in such a way that her most intimate favourites fail to
> understand her, and her intentions are therefore variously interpreted.[56]

Elizabeth's sally about marrying the pope came in response to hints at a rap-
prochement with Catholicism, when the diplomat spoke of the pope's good opinion of her. In some quarters on the Catholic side it was hoped that Elizabeth would
return to the fold, and that possibly she was only hindered by the pontiff's open
adherence to her enemies. Perhaps if she would favor the old religion, he would

recognize her legitimacy. The envoy did not trust Elizabeth in the least, however: he did not "believe she was a Catholic, although sometimes she shows signs of it, which come to nothing next day, and no doubt it is all trickery." Still, he began to "cautiously introduce the matter"

> by saying that they write me that the Pope held her person and virtues in high esteem, and there was nothing however difficult which he could do for her which he would refuse. . . . She seemed pleased with the conversation, and praised the good and pious character of the Pope, and then said, laughing, she thought he and she would get married.

He was doing his best to arrange a match with the Archduke, "but I have little confidence in her unless God himself does it all."[57]

Elizabeth loved the laughter of entertainment—she was an active patron of comedy. But her laughter was also a tool of policy. Both she and Margaret of Austria were able to draw on the prerogatives of royal laughter, while using the resonances of gender to inflect it to their advantage. In the often-polarized thinking of gender division, the female was not only the pole of weakness in contrast to male strength, but also the pole of dalliance and diversion, in contrast to the serious business of the state. Operating as rulers within codes of power designed as male, women like Margaret and Elizabeth could make purposeful use of both seriousness and laughter. Laughter's ambiguity and power to disarm created a distinctive space for political maneuvering. The evidence of laughter among female rulers may not justify talking about a "laughing regiment of women"—much as I might like to, countering the complaint of the Scottish divine John Knox. His *First Blast of the Trumpet Against the Monstrous Regiment of Women*, published in 1558 near the start of her reign, aroused Elizabeth's ire rather than a laugh. The timing was unfortunate for the Protestant Knox, since he had meant his attack to fall on the Catholic Queen Mary. There never was a second blast. His trumpet could not drown out the queen's laughter.

Laughter at the "Other"

Beyond the royal court, of course, there was downward-directed laughter among elites that paralleled the laughter from below that we examined earlier. Social subordinates were perennial targets of laughter, a tradition going back to the ancient association of comedy with low-class life. In classical conceptions of drama that held sway into the eighteenth century, the serious characters of tragedy should be upper class, preferably royalty; ordinary, "base" persons were fit subjects for comedy. Lack of the manners or education that came with birth and wealth was a common basis for ridicule. One can trace class-based associations of funniness in language, as in the English "clown," originally an untutored country fellow; the word only gradually came to refer to someone who was funny on purpose.

Similarly, the German "Schalk" meant a servant in the Middle Ages; in the early modern period it came to mean a joker or jester. There is far too much laughter from the social heights to explore here; we will meet more of it in future chapters. For the moment, it is worth observing that while rebellious laughter may have given subordinates a feeling of freedom, the converse for elite laughter was a strong confirmation of exclusiveness and superiority.

Laughter serves to include and exclude, defining social boundaries of belonging. Scholars are just beginning to explore its functions in colonial encounters of the early modern era. A complex picture emerges from the recent study by Marie-Christine Pioffet of laughter in the Jesuit Paul Le Jeune's attempt to convert the Montagnais tribe in seventeenth-century Canada. In contrast to the priest's European and Christian views, the Montagnais placed high value on laughter. While Le Jeune often perceived the natives' laughter (when he was attempting to preach, for example) as an ungodly affront, the locals cultivated laughter as a preserver of health, well-being, and sociability. Le Jeune made some feeble attempts to counter their laughter with his own—again with a negative view of laughter as essentially hostile mockery. His mission, overall, was not successful; arguably, the laughter barrier bulked even larger than that of language.[58]

Of course, one can find Europeans laughing at the perceived crudity of strange cultures, including those coming to be viewed as inferior races. References to race in the personal accounts studied here are few, though travel literature could be a more fruitful source for scholars. One marker of negative associations between laughter and racialized darkness appears in a 1615 publication by the prolific Puritan divine Thomas Adams, *The Blacke Devil or the Apostate*. Here the sinner, mired in the Devil's influence, "may feed his eye with vanities, his hand with extortions, his belly with junkets, his spleen with laughter, his ears with music, his heart with jollity, his flesh with lusts." Those accustomed to such laughing evil ways are on a path to doom, for "Can the Black-Moor change his skin? Or the Leopard his spots?" The hypocrite may put on a pretense of religion, but "when the white scarf is plucked off this Moor's face," "his black leprosy appears."[59] Interestingly, in the autobiography of Olaudah Equiano, one of the first personal accounts published by an African in Europe, the little laughter that appears is ridicule by whites. They joked about eating him when he was a very young captive in real fear for his life; they made fun later when he attempted to convert a young Native American to Christianity. Equiano chose not to portray laughter of his own, even on occasions of rejoicing when it surely occurred, such as when he was dancing in celebration of his freedom. This reticence maintained a tone of evangelical seriousness and victimhood, seeking to recruit white readers to the anti-slavery cause, while also avoiding associations with irreverent blackness.[60] How often, one wonders, did native audiences in varied colonial settings, like the Montagnais, simply laugh at the preaching of a foreign religion?

★★★

Laughter at social "others" connects back to our opening story of King Henry, Aubigné, and the old peasant woman. There we had the extreme of social distance, a man at the pinnacle—royalty—confronting the lowliest—a peasant—and of the inferior gender to boot. In that episode the laughter, like the excrement, expressed and underlined the contempt felt by high elites toward social inferiors. But one did not need to be a king or a poor peasant to experience the ways in which laughter was inflected by differences of social place and used to assert power.

The ambiguity of laughter makes it a versatile and powerful tool—for undermining the position of a rival, for disrupting a hierarchy, for expressing contempt, for disarming criticism, for shaming the nonconformist, for defining the outsider, or for concealing one's true intent. Its uses across the social and political spectrum underline its power and unpredictability. One thing can be said with certainty, though: laughter is not the opposite of serious matters—power, rebellion, rule, negotiation, social control, and violence. Instead, it has long been a significant element in the social relations and rituals where power lives.

Notes

1 Theodore-Agrippa d'Aubigné, *His Life, to His Children; Sa Vie à ses enfants*, trans. John Nothnagle (Lincoln and London: University of Nebraska Press, 1989), 27–28.

2 Mikhail Bakhtin, *Rabelais and His World*, trans. Hélène Iswolsky (Cambridge, MA: MIT Press, 1968).

3 For critique of Bakhtin's attempt to separate profane laughter from Christian orthodoxy, see Aaron Gurevich, "Bakhtin and His Theory of Carnival," in *A Cultural History of Humour*, ed. Jan Bremmer and Herman Roodenburg (Cambridge, UK: Polity Press, 1997), 54–60; on carnival's complexity, see also Norbert Schindler, "Karneval, Kirche und verkehrte Welt. Zur Funktion der Lachkultur im 16. Jahrhundert," *Jahrbuch für Volkskunde* 7 (1984): 9–57.

4 Robert Darnton, *The Great Cat Massacre* (New York: Basic Books, 1984), 75–104.

5 Nicolas Contat, *Anecdotes typographiques: où l'on voit la description des coutumes, moeurs et usages singuliers des Compagnons imprimeurs*, ed. Giles Barber (Oxford: Oxford Bibliographical Society, 1980), 42.

6 Contat, *Anecdotes*, 68.

7 Contat, *Anecdotes*, 53–55.

8 Emmanuel Le Roy Ladurie, *Carnival in Romans*, trans. Mary Feeney (New York: George Braziller, 1980), 192.

9 Ladurie, *Carnival in Romans*, 218–25.

10 Natalie Z. Davis, "The Rites of Violence," in *Society and Culture in Early Modern France* (Stanford: Stanford University Press, 1975), 152–87, 180–81.

11 Adam Fox, "Ballads, Libels and Popular Ridicule in Jacobean England," *Past & Present* 145 (1994): 47–83, 53.

12 Fox, "Ballads, Libels," 49–51.

13 Fox, "Ballads, Libels," 67, 70, 72.

14 Fox, "Ballads, Libels," 52.

15 Fox, 'Ballads, Libels," 55.

16 William Hudson, quoted in Fox, "Ballads, Libels and Popular Ridicule," 56.

17 For recent examples, see Mark Knights and Adam Morton, eds., *The Power of Laughter and Satire in Early Modern Britain: Political and Religious Culture, 1500–1820* (Woodbridge, Suffolk: Boydell & Brewer, 2017).

18 Christian Kuhn, "Urban Laughter as a 'Counter-Public' Sphere in Augsburg: The Case of the City Mayor, Jakob Herbrot (1490/95–1564)," *International Review of Social History* 52 (December 2007): 77–93; Sammy Basu, "'A Little Discourse Pro & Con': Levelling Laughter and Its Puritan Criticism," *International Review of Social History* 52 (December 2007): 95–113.

19 Sara Beam, *Laughing Matters: Farce and the Making of Absolutism in France* (Ithaca and London: Cornell University Press, 2007), 3, 9.

20 Peter Burke, *Popular Culture in Early Modern Europe*, 3rd ed. (Farnham, UK, and Burlington, VT: Ashgate, 2009), 289–334; see also Ronald Hutton, *The Rise and Fall of Merry England: The Ritual Year 1400–1700* (Oxford: Oxford University Press, 1994).

21 Vic Gatrell, *City of Laughter: Sex and Satire in Eighteenth-Century London* (London: Atlantic Books, 2006), 144, 154.

22 Antoine de Baecque, *Les éclats du rire: la culture des rieurs au XVIIIe siècle* (Paris: Calmann-Lévy, 2000), 203–34.

23 Classic treatments include Natalie Z. Davis, "The Reasons of Misrule," in *Society and Culture in Early Modern France*, 97–123; E. P. Thompson, "Rough Music: Le Charivari Anglais," *Annales. Histoire, Sciences Sociales* 27, no. 2 (April 1972): 285–312, 290; on abuses, see also Ladurie, *Carnival in Romans*, 223.

24 Susan Amussen and David Underdown, *Gender, Culture and Politics in England, 1560–1640: Turning the World Upside Down* (London: Bloomsbury Academic, 2017), 70.

25 Amussen and Underdown, *Gender, Culture and Politics*, 30; see also Martin Ingram, "Charivari and Shame Punishments," in *Social Control in Europe Volume I, 1500–1800*, ed. Herman Roodenburg and Pieter Spierenburg (Columbus: Ohio State University Press, 2004), 288–308.

26 Amussen and Underdown, *Gender, Culture and Politics*, 162.

27 Pamela Allen Brown, *Better a Shrew Than a Sheep: Women, Drama, and the Culture of Jest in Early Modern England* (Ithaca: Cornell University Press, 2003).

28 Jacques-Louis Ménétra, *Journal of My Life*, ed. Daniel Roche, trans. Arthur Goldhammer (New York: Columbia University Press), 1986.

29 The Ordinary of Newgate's Account, Old Bailey Online, 16 July 1714, 22 December 1721, 14 March 1726, 18 July 1722, 16 May 1750, https://www.oldbaileyonline.org/index.jsp.

30 Gerd Althoff, *Family, Friends and Followers: Political and Social Bonds in Early Medieval Europe* (Cambridge and New York: Cambridge University Press, 2004), 136.

31 Althoff, *Family, Friends and Followers*, 162.

32 Althoff, *Family, Friends and Followers*, 155.

33 Althoff, *Family, Friends and Followers*, 140; see also Martha Bayless, "Medieval Jokes in Serious Contexts: Speaking Humour to Power," in *The Palgrave Handbook of Humour, History, and Methodology*, ed. Daniel Derrin and Hannah Burrows (Cham, Switzerland: Palgrave Macmillan, 2021), 257–73, https://doi.org/10.1007/978-3-030-56646-3_13.

34 Jacques Le Goff, "Laughter in the Middle Ages," in *A Cultural History of Humour*, ed. Jan Bremmer and Herman Roodenburg (Cambridge: Polity Press, 1997), 40–53, 44; see also Stephen Jaeger, *The Origins of Courtliness: Civilizing Trends and the Formation of Courtly Ideals, 939–1210* (Philadelphia: University of Pennsylvania Press, 1985), 170–2.

35 Peter J. A. Jones, *Laughter and Power in the Twelfth Century* (Oxford: Oxford University Press, 2019).

36 Beatrice K. Otto, *Fools Are Everywhere: The Court Jester Around the World* (Chicago and London: University of Chicago Press, 2001).

37 Enid Welsford, *The Fool: His Social and Literary History* (Garden City, New York: Anchor Books, 1961), 157.

38 See Dorinda Outram, *Four Fools in the Age of Reason: Laughter, Cruelty, and Power in Early Modern Germany* (Charlottesville and London: University of Virginia Press, 2019); Norbert Schindler, "Ein bäuerlicher Münchhausen? Die Memoiren des Zillertaler

'Hoftirolers' Peter Prosch (1789)," *Österreichische Zeitschrift für Volkskunde* 72, no. 1 (2018): 85–110.

39 Sebastian Giustinian to the Doge, 28 February, "Henry VIII: February 1518," in *Letters and Papers, Foreign and Domestic, Henry VIII, Volume 2, 1515–1518*, ed. J. S. Brewer (London, 1864), 1220–236, British History Online, http://www.british-history.ac.uk/letters-papers-hen8/vol2/pp1220-1236. I should note a limitation of these diplomatic sources in that I am relying on the calendar synopses rather than the originals.

40 Eustace Chapuys to Charles V, 5 February, "Henry VIII: February 1532, 1–15," in *Letters and Papers, Foreign and Domestic, Henry VIII, Volume 5, 1531–1532*, ed. James Gairdner (London, 1880), 367–81, British History Online, http://www.british-history.ac.uk/letters-papers-hen8/vol5/pp367-381.

41 Federico Badoer, Venetian Ambassador at Brussels, to the Doge and Senate, 29 December, "Venice: December 1556, 21–31," in *Calendar of State Papers Relating to English Affairs in the Archives of Venice, Volume 6, 1555–1558*, ed. Rawdon Brown (London, 1877), 877–93, British History Online, http://www.british-history.ac.uk/cal-state-papers/venice/vol6/pp877-893.

42 Guzman De Silva to the King, 25 June, "Simancas: June 1565," in *Calendar of State Papers, Spain (Simancas), Volume 1, 1558–1567*, ed. Martin A. S. Hume (London, 1892), 432–42, British History Online, http://www.british-history.ac.uk/cal-state-papers/simancas/vol1/pp432-442.

43 Guzman De Silva to the King, 24 May, "Simancas: May 1568," in *Calendar of State Papers, Spain (Simancas), Volume 2, 1568–1579*, ed. Martin A. S. Hume (London, 1894), 26–40, British History Online, http://www.british-history.ac.uk/cal-state-papers/simancas/vol2/pp26-40.

44 Antonio De Guaras to Zayas, 1 February, "Simancas: February 1576," in *Calendar of State Papers, Spain (Simancas), Volume 2, 1568–1579*, 519–28, British History Online, http://www.british-history.ac.uk/cal-state-papers/simancas/vol2/pp519-528.

45 See Sharon L. Jansen, *The Monstrous Regiment of Women: Female Rulers in Early Modern Europe* (Palgrave Macmillan, 2002).

46 https://en.wikisource.org/wiki/1911_Encyclopædia_Britannica/Margaret_of_Austria_(1480–1530).

47 Quoted in Eleanor E. Tremayne, *The First Governess of the Netherlands: Margaret of Austria* (London: Methuen, 1908), 254.

48 André Joseph Ghislain, "Notice sur Marguerite d'Autriche, Gouvernante des Pays-Bas," in *Correspondance de l'empereur Maximilien Ier et de Marguerite d'Autriche* (Paris: J. Renouard, 1839), 2 vols., 2:430.

49 Wingfield to Wolsey, 19 January, "Henry VIII: January 1523, 17–29," in *Letters and Papers, Foreign and Domestic, Henry VIII, Volume 3, 1519–1523*, ed. J. S. Brewer (London, 1867), 1171–181, British History Online, http://www.british-history.ac.uk/letters-papers-hen8/vol3/pp1171-1181.

50 Fitzwilliam and Wingfield to Wolsey, 9 May, "Henry VIII: May 1525, 1–9," in *Letters and Papers, Foreign and Domestic, Henry VIII, Volume 4, 1524–1530*, ed. J. S. Brewer (London, 1875), 570–83, British History Online, http://www.british-history.ac.uk/letters-papers-hen8/vol4/pp570-583.

51 Lettres de Marguerite de Croÿ à Marguerite d'Autriche, 1509–1513, Archives Départementales du Nord, Lille, France. The pet name "trocquette" is one de Croÿ used repeatedly, but its meaning is uncertain—barterer perhaps, playing on Margaret of Austria's diplomatic activities; "troquet" was a also a term used for a hunting dog, a reference that would seem more brazen coming from a subordinate. In any case, it was clearly a playfully affectionate term drawn from their personal relationship. Another possibility, assuming variable spelling, would be a reference to "truc," implying trickster.

52 Tremayne, *First Governess,* 92–93.

53 For a recent discussion, see Carole Levin, *The Heart and Stomach of a King: Elizabeth I and the Politics of Sex and Power*, 2nd ed. (Philadelphia: University of Pennsylvania Press, 2013), 39–65.

54 The Bishop of Aquila to the King, 30 May, "Simancas: May 1559," in *Calendar of State Papers, Spain (Simancas), Volume 1, 1558–1567*, ed. Martin A. S. Hume (London, 1892), 64–78, British History Online, http://www.british-history.ac.uk/cal-state-papers/simancas/vol1/pp64-78.

55 Guzman to the King, 23 July, "Simancas: July 1565," in *Calendar of State Papers, Spain (Simancas), Volume 1, 1558–1567*, 442–58, British History Online, http://www.british-history.ac.uk/cal-state-papers/simancas/vol1/pp442-458.

56 Guzman to the King, 28 January, "Simancas: January 1566," in *Calendar of State Papers, Spain (Simancas), Volume 1, 1558–1567*, 511–17, British History Online, http://www.british-history.ac.uk/cal-state-papers/simancas/vol1/pp511-517.

57 Guzman to the King, 2 December, "Simancas: December 1566," in *Calendar of State Papers, Spain (Simancas), Volume 1, 1558–1567*, 598–606, British History Online, http://www.british-history.ac.uk/cal-state-papers/simancas/vol1/pp598-606; for more of Elizabeth's laughter in political maneuvering, see Estelle Paranque, *Elizabeth I of England through Valois Eyes: Power, Representation, and Diplomacy in the Reign of the Queen, 1558–1588* (Cham, Switzerland: Palgrave Macmillan, 2019), 34, 45.

58 Marie-Christine Pioffet, "Le rire de Paul Le Jeune: Du rire jaune à l'humour noir," *Nouvelles Études Francophones* 22 (2007): 122–34, https://www.jstor.org/stable/25702074.

59 Thomas Adams, *The Blacke Devil or the Apostate Together with the Wolfe Worrying the Lambes* (London, 1615), title page, 72, 76, Early English Books Online; spelling modernized.

60 Olaudah Equiano, *The Interesting Narrative and Other Writings*, ed. Vincent Carretta (New York: Penguin, 2003).

FIGURE 2.1   Benvenuto Cellini, drawing of a bearded man, possibly a self-portrait

Source: Wikimedia Commons, from original in Royal Library Turin

2

THE LAUGHTER OF AGGRESSION

Benvenuto Cellini

When Benvenuto Cellini was arrested in Rome in 1538, the courtroom rang with laughter—his own. In earlier days the gifted young goldsmith had literally gotten away with murder (more on that later). But this time he was hauled in for something he actually may not have done. It was a charge dredged up from years before, an accusation that he had looted some papal jewels during the sack of Rome in 1527. Cellini was indignant, especially given his heroism during the siege, which he recounted earlier in his autobiography. According to him, his spectacular gunnery was a highlight of the conflict. To show his contempt for the charge and seize control of the scene, he turned to laughter. On hearing the Governor of Rome make the accusation, Cellini "could not hold from bursting into a great roar of laughter [*grandissime risa*]."[1] This is some of the loudest laughter in his life story, in the face of officials who held him in their power, under arrest. Cellini describes it as irresistible laughter, welling up in him spontaneously in a way that could not be suppressed. But, of course, it was an expression of defiance, the strongest he could manage. Further, it did not end with the one great outburst; he continued laughing for some time, he tells us, before answering. His laughing bravado did not spare him from prison—and like much of Cellini's self-dramatization, it may not exactly be true—but it shows how his memories and portrayal of laughter were bound up with power and self-assertion.

No one could laugh better than Benvenuto Cellini. And in his own telling, few could beat him at anything else either. Author of one of the most vivid autobiographies ever written, he had an unshakable belief in his own greatness. When he wrote the story of his life in the mid-sixteenth century, hardly anyone had done so since the Confessions of St. Augustine around 400 CE—and no one in his racy, dramatic style. Augustine, of course, had a spiritual motive for writing about himself: it was the tale of conversion from a sinful life into a godly one that made the individual self worthy of attention. Cellini's self-absorption was far

DOI: 10.4324/9781003247517-3

more earthly. For those who see in the Renaissance a new surge of individualism and secularism, he could serve as a perfect example—although he thought he was on excellent terms with God, too! The brash self-promotion that so impressed or intimidated his contemporaries shines through on every page of his autobiography. Giorgio Vasari, the biographer of artists, who himself was no stranger to praise of worldly accomplishments, described the self-confident Cellini as "a real terror," an intimidating force.[2] Cellini did in fact possess tremendous artistic talents, which led the Florentine goldsmith to the courts of rulers, from the Pope to the King of France. Other artistic geniuses, such as his contemporaries Leonardo and Michelangelo, had to rely on a biographer like Vasari to heap them with public praise. Cellini did it for himself, or tried to; his plans for print publication were not realized during his lifetime. In his own story, laughter was only one of the many signs of his superior personality and achievements. We do not have to swallow all his claims whole. We have only his word for it that he laughed at the magistrates, after all. But the prominence he gave to laughter shows its importance to his own self-image.

It Isn't Necessarily Funny

Cellini's laughter has very little to do with humor. Of course, like anyone else, he and his contemporaries laughed when they were amused—or when they wanted people to think they were amused. But with one or two exceptions, the laughter he recounts was not about jokes; funny material was not really the point. What mattered to him, instead, was what the laughter signified about status and power. This is what made laughter worthy of memory—and, one suspects, what might lead to its invention or exaggeration in scenes where its meaning was needed. If his equals or, worse, people he considered inferior laughed at him, it was an insult not to be borne. Of course, he sometimes purposely promoted laughter among convivial companions: he excelled at this, like everything else (according to him). Even here, though, the laughter was often in triumph or defiance—such as triumph over hair-raising dangers, or defiance of the plague that had been killing family and friends on every side. When patrons laughed, especially if they were also rulers, it was usually a feather in Cellini's cap, showing the favor he received and his skill in interactions with the great. Cellini's own laughter was a celebration of his manhood and frequently an aggressive demand for recognition of it by others.

Cellini, then, offers a case study in the laughter of aggression, with insights into how it could be used to assert social power. There are various types of laughter in his autobiography, but the strain of self-promotion and contest with rivals infuses them all. The laughter of Cellini's story helps us understand the long anti-laughter tradition in Western Christian culture. Not only in masculine aggression, but in other ways as well, there were many who saw more harm than good in laughter. At the same time, he leads us into some questions of historical change. Did ridicule become more prominent during the Renaissance? How did laughter intersect with the new avenues of social advance that emerged as Italy, and gradually wider parts of Western Europe, developed a more complex society and economy? The competitive side of laughter and jest, which appears so strongly in his story, has a larger history.

Laughter and Male Rivalry

The laughter of aggression that besprinkles Cellini's account is largely male territory, just as the contests in which he constantly asserted his manhood were mainly a matter of beating other males. He had some female enemies, but to him women were too inferior to be rivals. His most bitter conflicts, as well as exchanges of hostile laughter, were with professional competitors. He had other enemies too—intriguers at various courts who were constantly badmouthing him to his patrons. In his telling, such backbiting was nearly always the cause of his failure, if a rival beat him out of an important commission. (He could not believe, or at least would not admit, that anyone genuinely preferred another's artwork to his own.) He readily expressed anger even to potentates, sometimes getting himself into trouble with patrons, such as the usually indulgent Pope Clement VII. Contemporaries complained of his arrogance, as he often reports. Laughter was more insulting than anger, however—which made his laughter at the governor on his arrest so daring. It made a good story, but it did not end well; he was still sent to prison. More commonly, aggressive laughter was exchanged among relative equals, while the laughter of superiors was a sign of indulgence to be cultivated.

Cellini recounts many instances of aggressive laughter in confrontations with male competitors, as a sign of defiance or contempt. As always, his account is a reconstruction designed to highlight his own greatness. The laughter, whether it actually occurred as described or not, is a signifier of meaning. An old master laughed on refusing Cellini's back pay for his work as a journeyman. Another goldsmith, again an older superior, laughed at Cellini's claim that he could out-earn him by creating settings for jewels rather than large silver vases for the papal palace. These were relatively harmless quarrels, and Cellini eventually triumphed in each; the men even became reconciled. The other men's status as his elders likely made the young Cellini somewhat more tolerant of their laughter, although he strongly asserted himself to show they were wrong.[3]

With serious rivals the laughter could quickly turn to violence. In one bitter quarrel in Florence, a competitor pushed a load of bricks over onto him. Cellini retaliated instantly: "Turning suddenly round and seeing him laughing, I struck him such a blow on the temple that he fell down, stunned, like one dead."[4] Charged with assault, Cellini accidentally hurt his case by calling his action a "slap" rather than a "blow," not realizing the slap carried a heavier punishment because it was a dishonoring insult. Luckily for him, he had a friend among the magistrates who portrayed his naivety as a sign of innocence. Let off with a modest fine, he made a joke of it: "I muttering all the while, It was a slap and not a blow, leaving the Eight [magistrates of Florence] laughing."[5] Cellini leaves readers of his life thinking he had the last laugh, and even got indulgent laughter from the magistrates—but in fact he got into major trouble for further aggression in the same quarrel. He was declared an outlaw and forced to leave Florence for Rome, only returning years later after his father managed a reconciliation for him.[6]

Laughter was the final insult from a longtime enemy in Rome, the jeweler Pompeo—after which Cellini tracked him down and killed him in the public street (not his first homicide; he had earlier killed a man in revenge for killing his brother in a quarrel). As Cellini was sitting with his friends, Pompeo came along with a following of ten armed men, implying a challenge. Already Cellini's friends foresaw violence and signed to him to draw his sword—but in contrast to his usual fiery aggressiveness, he refrained. The Pompeo crowd soon erupted in laughter: "When Pompeo had stood there time enough to say two Hail Marys, he laughed scornfully in my direction; and going off, his companions also laughed and shook their heads, with much flouting."[7] The laughter of scorn was an insult that required a response. Cellini's uncharacteristic restraint, he takes care to explain, was for the sake of his friends: he was willing to risk his own life but not the lives of others. But he was not about to let the matter rest, especially when, following Pompeo and his cronies, he heard the man boasting "of the insult he imagined he had put upon me."[8] Cellini tells us he actually meant to cut Pompeo's face rather than kill him, to inflict a dishonoring revenge, but when the man turned suddenly, the knife entered under his ear and killed him. Their enmity went much further back, of course. Pompeo had opposed Cellini's interests with the pope and had falsely accused him of another homicide. But the immediate spark was the public and insulting laughter. Cellini could not forget the scene until he had confronted the enemy and avenged his honor.

Matters of Honor

An important context for Cellini's laughter, as well as his violence, is the prevailing code of male honor—in early modern Europe, and in his own milieu in particular. Men and women across Europe were concerned to preserve the precious social capital of honor, a combination of reputation and self-respect. For women honor was conceived largely in terms of chaste sexual behavior, but for men the demands of maintaining respect and social standing were more complex. The terms of honor varied greatly, of course, according to class status and location. Those with pretensions to nobility might feel the need to cultivate a reputation for bravery and generosity, while urban merchants were developing a code of virtues that would come to be seen as bourgeois, such as honest dealing and industriousness. Both the terms of insult and responses to them varied with social place. In the Mediterranean region, a concept of aggression as central to the defense of masculine honor was widely shared across classes. Failure to avenge an insult to oneself or one's close associates was considered a shameful dereliction of masculine duty.[9]

In the city of Florence, there were shifting and competing notions of honor with time and social perspective.[10] At the same time, there were distinctive concerns about personal standing in such northern Italian cities. Historians have long pointed to the intensive competition among men of the Italian Renaissance.[11] Cellini's hair-trigger temper, bitter rivalries, and minute attention to the nuances of his treatment by others were the extreme of a more general environment of struggle for status and advancement. This was true especially for artists, whose position was in flux: rooted in their origins in the craft guilds, yet increasingly claiming new prestige as creative intellects or, as Vasari and Cellini would certainly assert, geniuses. Cellini had developed a finely pitched sense of his own personal dignity and honor as a craftsman, long before he began to hobnob with the great. The interaction with rulers and patrons was full of unresolved issues of protocol—how far could he push his assertiveness without losing the ability to make his patron laugh? The boundaries of behavior were shifting and dangerous.

The use of laughter as insult was hardly unique to Cellini or to his immediate environment, of course. Responses to the laughter of offense, especially laughter that touched on issues of honor, differed according to local culture, and also according to the availability of potentially face-saving remedies like lawsuits or formal rituals of reconciliation. In the Middle Ages, violence in response to insult was a widely accepted male prerogative, only shifting very gradually in Western Europe toward the use of legal processes as a means of redress. Governments had a long struggle with social elites in their attempt to ban feuds and dueling, and with lower classes in the curbing of brawls.[12] In Italy, the custom of vendetta—violence in defense of a family and its adherents against equally violent rivals—remained influential, even as legal settlement of disputes became increasingly common. Certain forms of insulting ridicule could be punishable by courts as offenses to honor, or could spark private violence in revenge.[13] But legal redress for a laughing insult might be uncertain. Peter Burke cites a case from sixteenth-century Bologna in which a plaintiff claimed he had been defamed in a sonnet. The court ruled against him, declaring that the words were merely "a joke, containing something laughable."[14] Culprits hauled before courts sometimes tried to downplay their violations of order with claims that they were only joking—though it is not always clear whether the claim helped their cause.[15]

Performance of Laughter

Cellini's exchanges of hostile laughter were charged with emotion—anger, indignation, even rage. Yet the spontaneous feeling was linked to particular forms of public display. The rituals of confrontation followed a script in which gestures and laughter had coded meanings that could be read, not only by the contestants, but also by observers. Just as in the governor's court, where he proudly describes how he was overcome by the urge to loud and prolonged laughter, Cellini traces the changes of both his inner emotions and his self-presentation. He recounts these layers of feelings and performance at length in a dramatic confrontation with his rival and enemy, Bartolommeo Bandinelli, a sculptor at the Medici court. The two shared a long history of hostility. But this particular moment in 1547 saw them at odds in the presence of Duke Cosimo I de' Medici and his entourage. The surrounding audience of both prince and courtiers was an integral element in the encounter. It was one of Cellini's proudest performances.

As Cellini tells it, he and the Duke were conversing pleasantly about the beauties of an ancient Greek statue, when Bandinelli entered and opened hostilities—with a laugh: "Breaking into one of his malignant laughs and shaking his head," he derided the art of the ancients: knowing nothing of anatomy, Bandinelli said, they had committed many errors in sculpting the human body. The Duke turned to Cellini for a rebuttal, listening happily as he disparaged his rival. If the Duke fostered this first exchange of hostilities, his courtiers extended it, bringing Cellini along when Bandinelli followed the Duke to another room. There the Duke's men stared at Bandinelli, "tittering among themselves about the speech I had made in the room above."[16] Cellini had succeeded in rousing semi-public amusement at the expense of his rival, and in the presence of the highest authority. The two traded verbal barbs again, and—if we believe Cellini—his opponent could tell he was getting the worst of the exchange from the expressions and gestures of the Duke and his men. Finally, driven to a frenzy, Bandinelli yelled at Cellini: "Be quiet, you great sodomite!"[17]

This was a cutting and well-grounded insult. Cellini had already been hauled before a Florentine court for "sodomy" in his youth, had fled town temporarily in 1546 when another accusation cropped up, and was to suffer punishment for the offense ten years later, even at the height of his fame.[18] The term "sodomy" applied to various forbidden sexual practices, but particularly anal intercourse. Despite the illegality of homosexual relations, widespread male–male sexuality was an open secret in Florence. Prosecution of sodomy was inconsistent and fluctuating during Cellini's lifetime. Cosimo's court was an especially fraught locale for such a scene; the Duke had introduced a stringent law against sodomy a few years before, in 1542, leading to a temporary upsurge in prosecutions.[19] In the autobiography, Cellini recounts multiple (but not all) accusations of sodomy against him, along with his own often ambiguous denials or deflections of the charge.

Enraged by the insult, Cellini was still mindful of his audience. His account turns to the reactions of the Duke and courtiers at all stages of the dispute to endorse his own interpretation of its course. When Bandinelli uttered the word "sodomite," Cellini tells us, the faces of the listeners showed their disturbance with furrowed brows and pursed lips. It was a tense moment: might this be seen as not merely an insult but a public accusation before the fount of justice, one to be taken seriously? And word of what passed would certainly travel through the ever-active networks of court gossip that figured so frequently in the tale of Cellini's fortunes.

Cellini describes his own fury and his turn to laughter as a resource. Instead of addressing the charge, he made fun of it. His remarkable account of his response and the result deserves to be quoted at length:

> "You madman! you've lost your senses. Yet I wish to God that I knew how
> to exercise such a noble art; for we read that Jove practiced it with Ganymede
> in paradise, and here on earth it is practiced by the greatest of emperors and

kings. I am but a lowly, humble little man, who neither could nor would understand anything so marvelous." At this no one could contain himself; the Duke and his attendants broke into the loudest laughter that one could imagine possible. And though I pretended to be amused, you must know, kind readers, that my heart was bursting in my body to think that a fellow, the foulest villain ever born, should have dared, in the presence of so great a ruler, to insult me so atrociously. But you must also know that he insulted the Duke, and not me; for had I not been in that august presence, I would have struck him dead. When the dirty, clumsy scoundrel saw that the gentlemen would not stop laughing, he tried to change the subject, and divert them from enjoying his chagrin.[20]

Clearly, Cellini took pride in the quick wit that enabled him to turn the matter into jest, and he likely embellished his clever riposte after the fact. The mock humility of his answer does not exactly deny the charge (like many of his answers in parallel situations). Instead, it deflects and disperses it. The success of his ploy was marked by the laughter of his distinguished audience, whom Cellini was always eager to impress. They laughed, and not only that, they could not restrain themselves, but raised a huge, extreme laughter—the greatest laughter one could imagine possible. Evoking such laughter as this, in a moment of extreme need and threat, ranked with his more violent exploits as a mark of his manly triumph— here, not only over his despicable rival, but with power to move his superiors as well in the direction he wanted.

And the laughter was not done. The duke and courtiers would not stop laughing. No longer merely laughter of amusement and release of tension, it turned to laughter of derision directed at Bandinelli, or that is how Cellini paints it. He claims this was the cause of Bandinelli's lame attempt to shift the subject, to the seemingly unrelated matter of Cellini's boasts about a promised block of marble. In the end, Cellini came through with the marble as well as the joke, a memorable coup indeed. But, as always, we only have his word for it, and his version of the laughter and its meaning.

Sodomy was a recurring issue in Cellini's life and in his autobiography. He tells about some of the accusations that arose against him, though he is silent about the cases in which he was convicted and punished. Perhaps not surprisingly, the instances he includes are ones in which he was able to dominate his opponent, either through wit or through violence. In contrast to modern concepts of homosexuality, involvement in sodomy was seen as an excess of lust rather than a separate or effeminate sexual identity. Cellini had many sexual relationships with women as well as men, siring a number of children both illegitimate and legitimate. Aside from the outburst from Bandinelli, at least two accusations of sodomy came from women—both of whom he denigrates as whores to discredit them. By seizing on moments of laughter in these conflicts Cellini showed his contempt, both for the women and for the official rules of sexual behavior.

Conflicts with Women

In Cellini's worldview women tended to be of little account unless they had power as patrons or could serve as sexual objects. When they were women who controlled patronage, he knew how to hide any resentment of their influence. But he was enraged when women tried to turn the law against him, particularly when he thought they ought to fall under his patriarchal authority. In 1543, during his sojourn as goldsmith to the King of France, his model Caterina formally accused him of sodomy. He states matter-of-factly that he "used" her for sexual as well as artistic services, but asserts that the legal summons came of spite after he had thrown her out. Arriving at the court with an armed following, he noticed Caterina and her mother laughing with their lawyer—undoubtedly fueling his rage, in a case where his life could be at stake, since sodomy was a capital crime in France. Cellini was immediately belligerent, demanding to hear the charge. He was accused of treating her "in the Italian fashion"—a euphemism for anal intercourse and a reflection of the reputation of Italian cities like Florence. (Germans even invented the verb "florenced" to refer to the practices of "sodomites.")[21] But Cellini boldly "retorted that, so far from being the Italian fashion, it must be the French method, since she knew it and I did not." In less serious circumstances, such reversal would have been the stuff of jest. He insisted on all the details, making her repeat them three times, and then turned the tables even more: the law imposed the punishment of burning on both parties, he said, and here she had admitted it, while he maintained his innocence. To the fire with both her and her mother! he thundered. It was no longer a laughing matter for them, and "the little whore and her mother fell to weeping."[22]

Cellini emerged triumphant from this encounter, yet full of resentment against Caterina for daring to accuse him, despite the fact that her claims were probably true. Cellini hints at this to his readers later, as he describes his continuing abuse of her—though he does not specify details of their sexual activities. After the court case, his fury was roused still further by finding her consorting with his young protégé, Pagolo Micceri. Near killing the man, Cellini instead dishonored him by forcing him to marry the "vicious whore." Then he called her back as a model, making her pose naked, and "I had sex with her in revenge, jeering at them both."[23] Out of malice he kept her for hours in uncomfortable positions and beat her when she talked back. He felt a few qualms about the beating of Caterina, mostly because the bruises on her body would interfere with her modeling. But she returned the next day, "laughed and fell upon my neck," and after a brief reconciliation received more of the same violent treatment. Cellini depicts her laughter as a sign of her submission and an attempt to placate his wrath. In his retelling of the events, he has turned her rebellious laughter first into tears, and then into an obsequious laughter that accepted his own jeering and violence.

In 1546, after he had returned to Florence to serve the Medici duke, he faced another charge: the mother of a young apprentice accused him of sodomizing the boy. Like Caterina, she was likely telling the truth. In Renaissance Florence sodomy nearly always took the pattern of an older male as the active partner of an adolescent. In the late fifteenth century this practice was so common among young men that it appears to have been the norm. It was rare for someone as old as Cellini (then in his forties) to be involved, however, and these were different days, with harsher laws in force.[24] Cellini laughed the mother's "whorish wiles" to scorn and, he says, refused to be blackmailed. With violent blows he threw both mother and son out of his house—assuming a right of patriarchal punishment over them both. However, since (he says) she was in cahoots with a powerful official, he quickly left town. Like his laughter before the governor, his laughter here was partly empty bravado: he knew that he could be in serious trouble. But as with Caterina, the scornful laughter was combined with physical violence and sexual insult. He saw the women as insolent subordinates, to be punished with beatings and abuse rather than battled like a rival.[25]

Among Friends

Cellini played with ideas of sexual transgression in his proudest moment of jesting merriment among friends. The occasion was from his youth, but remembered fondly as he composed his life story, even as he was under house arrest for sodomy. In the aftermath of a visitation of plague in Rome, a group of surviving artists formed a club, led by the Sienese Michelangelo di Bernardino di Michele, "the most delightful and amusing man ever known in the world."[26] They met at least twice a week to make merry. On one occasion the leader invited them all to dinner, with a decree that each man must bring his "crow," his mistress. Cellini is at pains to tell us that he could certainly have taken a beautiful woman if he had chosen, a courtesan who was "very much in love" with him, but he generously gave her up to a friend. Instead, "to add more laughter to the merriment," he substituted a handsome 16-year-old boy, dressing him up in female finery. The young Diego performed his role admirably. When the host bowed down to ask "her" blessing in mock adoration, "the charming creature laughed, lifted the right hand and gave him a papal benediction, along with many pleasant words." Seated among the women, Diego grew tired of their "silly talk." Seeing him fidget, one asked what the matter was. He replied that he thought he was pregnant, at which they felt his body and discovered the imposture. The women responded with gibes as "the whole room rang with laughter and astonishment." Cellini earned the kudos of his fellows, lifted up with cries of "long live the lord" for his fine prank.[27] The women appear to have been less pleased, but the men shared a joke about the interchangeable charms of boys and women that drew on their awareness of widespread homosexual practice.

Laughing Patrons

Arousing the laughter of friends enhanced his status among them, but the laughter of patrons could be even more essential to success. Relationships between patron and client, like those between rivals or enemies, had some predictable elements in the exchange of speech and action, yet also nuances of gesture that could be read for special significance. Cellini was constantly attentive to these—or possibly inventing them, years after the fact—as indicators of what each encounter meant. Like the furrowed brows and later laughter of the Duke at the contest with Bandinelli, the details of patrons' behavior are taken to reveal their underlying feelings and their relationship with Cellini. The often formalized patterns of social meaning are presented as spontaneous moments of emotion. More important than the question of whether people really felt the emotions imputed to them, or whether Cellini himself did and felt as he described, is the fact that he frames his memories in this way, with each raised eyebrow, blush, or titter carrying a special significance. He, the protagonist of his own story, was constantly on the alert for these signs and using them to calibrate his own reactions.

Such signals played a vital role in occasions featuring the laughter (or, indeed, the anger) of patrons. Like the laughter that Cellini cultivated with friends, the laughter here was non-aggressive laughter that still redounded to his own glory. His account of his relations with an early patron, the highborn and beautiful Madonna Porzia, illustrates both attention to nuance and the uses of laughter. Cellini even implies that she was flirting with him—which, of course, may well have been a self-promoting invention. They met when she noticed him studying and copying works by Raphael at her relative's house. She admired his artistry, but also his person, as she told her friend "with a smile: I am amusing myself by watching this worthy young man at his drawing; he is as good as he is handsome."[28] Cellini tells us that he blushed as he expressed readiness to serve her—and she, "slightly blushing" likewise, gave him jewelry to be reset, with 20 gold crowns for the work.

When Cellini presented her with his exquisite setting, Madonna Porzia was astonished at the wondrous work. She asked him to name his price but "added laughing that I must ask what lay within her power." The lady's favor was such, and Cellini's daring likewise, that he took her laughter as an invitation to his own rather arrogant joking. He answered, "laughing myself," that pleasing her was the only reward he wished. The lady admired this answer and proceeded to an exchange of quips:

> "Friend Benvenuto, have you never heard it said that when the poor give to the rich, the devil laughs?" I replied: "And yet, in the midst of all his troubles, I should like this time to see him laugh"; and as I took my leave, she said that this time she had no will to treat the devil so kindly.[29]

Like all of Cellini's anecdotes, this one ended in a way that enhanced his glory. He had a running competition with a master workman in his shop, who had laughed at him for wasting his time with trivial jewel settings when he could be producing large-scale pieces of silver plate for eminent patrons like the pope. Madonna Porzia—well understanding that Cellini's refusal of payment for his work was not serious—sent him a generous bag of gold, with a message recalling their shared jest about the devil's laughter. Cellini emptied it dramatically in the workshop, putting his rival's regular pay from the pope to shame.

Madonna Porzia's laughter signified her favorable outlook on her subordinate, a readiness to engage him in playful dialogue, and, for Cellini, a golden opportunity for self-advancement through wit and daring. The laughter of another patron, Pope Clement VII, likewise signaled favor and readiness to further Cellini's interests. Entrusted with some of the pope's jewels for setting, Cellini suffered a robbery in his shop and was tormented by the idea that if any were missing, people would accuse him to the pope of dishonesty. Fortunately, his dog had driven off the thief before he could get to the gems. Benvenuto sped to His Holiness to tell at length of the robbery and his anxiety; "At last, breaking into laughter at the long tale I was telling, he sent me off with these words: 'Go, and continue to be the honourable man I knew you to be."[30] Pressing his advantage, Cellini asked and received a lucrative office as macebearer, again with papal laughter.[31] He later clashed with Clement, in angry exchanges of which Cellini appears just as proud. The laughter of a patron was valued for the tangible good it brought. For Cellini, the advancement was key and he would demand it when it wasn't forthcoming.

Cellini loved it when he could get the King of France laughing. In glowing terms, he describes the delight of Francis I on first seeing his design for a grand new fountain at Fontainebleau. He called Cellini "my friend," he laid his hand on his shoulder, he spoke of his good fortune in finding such an artist "after his own heart." When Cellini spoke gratefully of his own good fortune, "He answered laughingly: Let us agree, then, that our luck is equal! Then I departed in the highest spirits, and went back to my work."[32] If only, he complained, people did not speak to the King against him behind his back, when he could not exercise his charm!

The laughter of a patron was worthy of memory for the way in which it signified favor, with a promise of fat commissions and enhancement of Cellini's social and professional standing. Getting a patron and especially a ruler to laugh was a coup. In his stories of favor and patronage won and lost, the script frequently follows a predictable pattern. Left to his own devices, one-on-one with the patron, his charm and wit enhance the impression already created by his artistic skill, leading to cordial relations and often laughter. Discordant notes arise when the patron becomes stingy or otherwise lacking in support, in which case Cellini displays his arrogance—or when, as so often happened, his enemies influence the patron against him.

Laughing at Devils

Cellini's self-image of glorious success was enhanced by his many uses of laughter. Even when not aggressive, it was instrumental, used to advance an agenda of competition and contest. One final instance hints at his ability to outface not only men but even unearthly powers. In the early 1530s Cellini became fascinated with necromancy—the summoning of demons. His adventures in this dark art created an occasion for laughter that signaled his superiority to dangers and fears that tormented others. He even brought in scatology—bathroom humor—to turn a scene of supposed demonic terror into one of broad comedy. Necromancy was condemned by both church teachings and law, but Cellini found a learned priest who was known for his skill in conjuring demons. Because the summoning of demons required secret book-learning and encounters with spiritual forces, many of the underground practitioners were clergy. Cellini sought reunion with a lost lover and was told he must bring a virginal boy along if he wanted a response. So, with a friend and a young lad from his shop, he went to the Coliseum in the dead of night, where the necromancer conjured with magic circle, perfumes, and incantations. But the spells drew thousands of demons—far more than desired, the most dangerous in hell, who resisted all the summoner's attempts to dismiss them. Everyone was petrified with terror, except Cellini. When the necromancer called for asafetida—a foul-smelling plant extract—to be thrown on the fire to drive the demons off, Cellini quickly relayed the instruction to his friend, who was minding the fire. But the friend was so terrified that he beshat himself and gave off a smell that was

> far more powerful than the asafetida. The boy, roused by that great stench and noise, lifted his head a little and when he heard me laughing, took a bit of courage, and said the devils were taking to flight tempestuously.[33]

Laughter here highlights Cellini's exceptional bravery, in contrast to those trembling around him. The joke also serves as a reminder of the license he likely took to invent and embellish in the story of his life.

Other Aggressors

Cellini was one of a kind, but similarly aggressive uses of laughter can be found in many milieux. Laughter as insult was taken seriously by courts in seventeenth-century England. The Court of Chivalry, active in the 1630s, handled mainly matters of honor and insult for people who could claim to be "gentlemen"—a status just below nobility in rank. This court was supposed to curb violence by offering the elite an honorable alternative to dueling. In fact, though, much of its business was brought by upper-class plaintiffs demanding respect from social inferiors, even in the face of abuse (cases which the gents nearly always won). The question of jest was a serious one here, with litigants at times in dispute about whether words were spoken "in jest and merriment" or "maliciously."

In the case brought by Thomas Bowen in 1635, the defendants had treated him with derision. They ridiculed his red face, but mainly they jeered at him for having hauled one of them before the Court of Chivalry for a prior insult. Bowen's questions for the defendants demanded: "Did you not laugh at Bowen because he had applied himselfe to my lord for justice against those abuses & affronts done to himselfe & friends?" The laughers were called back into court and charged with contempt.[34]

The court frowned very much on those who laughed at a successful litigant; here the laughter was not only personal insult but insult against the court itself. Abraham Comyns, ordered to make a public "submission" (a public apology with promise of good behavior) to George Badcock, turned the occasion into one of public ridicule. Before the congregation in church, he read the words of apology in "a jeering and fleering manner." Later he made a mocking bow "in way of derision to Mr Badcock, laughing in his face which moved a great part of the congregation to laughter." Comyns was called back into court, fined and imprisoned.[35]

Cases before the Star Chamber, another elite site of English justice, also treated laughter as potential evidence of an offense. Complaints lodged with the court accused defendants of having composed libelous ballads and sung them "by way of jest and merriment, scoffingly," or asserted that they would "rejoice and laugh thereat in scornful, deriding and infamous manner."[36] Like the Court of Chivalry, the Star Chamber aimed to curb ridicule by ordinary people against those considered their superiors. Far from being considered harmless, such scurrilous jesting could be punishable as libel, even if its contents were true. Defamatory libels prosecuted at the Star Chamber typically joked about the sexual peccadilloes of socially powerful people. In contrast to the largely masculine contests of Cellini, libelous laughers here included women as well as men. Similarly, in defamation cases at church courts, an arena more open to plaintiffs of humble background, defendants who tried to claim that they were only joking appear to have had little success in averting punishment. These cases, largely focused on sexual reputation of both men and women, will concern us in a later chapter.

Dangerous Laughter

The broader history of aggressive laughter takes us backward and forward in time. This type of laughter has dominated many laughter theories, in a long tradition of negative views among philosophers and theologians. Plato criticized laughter partly for its lack of self-control, but also saw it as largely malicious.[37] Although Aristotle can be cited on the side of the genteel use of wit, there is little praise for laughter in classical Western thought. Among the Christian fathers there was still more hostility, with multiple reasons for disapproval. Laughter was a worldly pleasure that could distract the soul from holy things, as well as an irrational loss of control. Especially, though, it was associated with mockery and scorn. The laughter in the Bible is nearly all of this variety. Some made an exception for the joyful laughter of Abraham on learning that his aged wife Sarah was pregnant—but others, such as St. Jerome, condemned even this laughter as showing disbelief, a lack of faith in God's ability to bring about the miraculous birth. Nearly all Christian authorities agreed that Sarah's laughter on this occasion was out of line for doubting God.[38]

Although some Christian thinkers were more favorable toward laughter than others, its association with derision made it widely suspect. There was a place for positive laughter in the thinking of the great medieval authority Thomas Aquinas— more on that in the next chapter. But the dangers of laughter loomed large. In particular, laughter could be directed against true religion itself. The ungodly were the quintessential scoffers: they made fun of the prophets of the Old Testament, they mocked and derided Jesus, and they appeared regularly in the lives of saints to ridicule the unworldly doings of holy men and women. On the other hand, it was permissible or even good for the faithful to laugh at their enemies, at least according to some Christian authorities.[39] In the Bible, even the laughter of God was this hostile variety, laughing his enemies to scorn before turning his wrath upon them.[40] The nature of laughter makes mockery challenging to answer, however: it is not responsive to argument. One can perhaps turn the tables and laugh back; but what made the laughter of God effective was its backing by real power to punish. When the prophet Elisha triumphed over mockery, the scoffers were mauled by bears, not outwitted by better laughter.[41] More ordinary Christian authorities tended to take laughter at religion seriously, as a prelude to damnation if not repented.

Christianity was the official, prescribed religion of Western Europe, and the main source of negative voices about laughter. But one can also find suspicion of laughter's dangers among Jewish religious authorities, some of whom saw laughter as incompatible with religious study. Frivolity, they warned, would lead to licentious behavior. In fact, an early source for the Jewish custom of breaking a glass at weddings goes back to a rabbi who, disturbed by excess gaiety at a wedding, put a stop to it by breaking a glass. With marvelous and creative irony (and despite more somber theories about the custom's meaning), later practice has turned the glass-breaking into a signal for joyous celebration. On the other hand, there were also joking rabbis and a long tradition of Jewish humor. Both Christian and Jewish teachings were marked by ambivalence about laughter, in theory if not in practice.[42]

One can find the laughter of derision in any time and place, but its power was increasingly recognized during the Renaissance, at least among the educated. Jacob Burckhardt famously identified a new, self-conscious individualism in Renaissance Italy. Along with it, he said, came a new, modern form of wit: there were medieval forerunners, but "wit could not be an independent element in life till its appropriate victim, the developed individual with personal pretentions, had appeared."[43] Note here the assumption that wit is aggressive, directed toward making someone else a ridiculous target of laughter. Of course, Burckhardt's view of a new individualism has been challenged, particularly by medievalists, who so often see their period used as a foil for theories of modern development. But certainly there were growing possibilities for "self-making" in paths of social ascent outside the traditional elites of church and nobility.

Burckhardt found many examples of aggressive wit in Renaissance Italy. One could start with the earliest of Renaissance men. In seeking to revive the brilliance of Greece and Rome, the early humanists admired the eloquence of classical Latin, so different from what they saw as the stilted language of the medieval church. The fluid and subtle language of ancient days had power—to rouse people's emotions, to persuade them to action, and—yes—to get them to laugh. Among the Roman classics the humanists discovered biting satire (Juvenal's being the most famous) that provided them with an effective weapon. In advancing their call for change, humanists loved to make fun of their intellectual predecessors, the medieval scholastics, and anyone else who used poor Latin or didn't know his classics.

Francesco Petrarca or Petrarch, often called the "father of humanism," was a pioneer in the revival of satirical writing. His letter to "a certain famous man" is a masterpiece of mock politeness, even as he skewers the man for his ignorance. Petrarch's "Letters on Familiar Matters" were modeled on the newly rediscovered personal correspondence of Cicero. Although addressed to individuals, these were gathered and edited by the author with a clear intention of publication—which, in this pre-printing era, meant circulation in manuscript. Petrarch, showing how his correspondent misidentified the philosophers Plato and Cicero as poets, and also displayed ignorance in various other ways, asserts disingenuously that he wants to protect the man's reputation: "Certain unjust judges of such matters would measure your abilities by such small things as you playfully include through the oversight of the wandering mind."[44]

Such ridicule of the less intelligent, less learned, or otherwise vulnerable reached an extreme by the sixteenth century in the satires of Cellini's contemporary, Pietro Aretino. Petrarch's sallies at the expense of inferior scholars could circulate in manuscript, but by Aretino's day the printing press had made the potential power of vicarious laughter still more formidable. And, by all accounts, he was both ruthless and well-connected. His biting pen was said to strike fear even into the hearts of rulers, earning him the nickname the "scourge of princes."

Outside the realm of literature, Burckhardt pointed to actions, in particular the cruel practical jokes of Pope Leo X (r. 1513–1521). Leo liked to make people objects of ridicule by convincing them, through elaborate subterfuge, that they had exceptional talent in music or poetry.[45] If aggressive joking had reached a crescendo in Italy by the sixteenth century, that may explain as well the rising chorus of voices seeking to curb such excess. Giovanni della Casa, in his influential 1558 treatise on manners, declared that he "wishes to see the desire of triumph banished altogether from jokes and *burle* [pranks]."[46] It was fine to laugh, but not in an aggressive manner. Della Casa, a close contemporary of Cellini and a Florentine, advocated good manners as a means of avoiding offense to others—the last thing on Cellini's mind!

As we will see, Baldassare Castiglione, in his equally famous book of courtly manners, had even more to say about laughter. Here he can definitely be counted among the Renaissance voices raised against excess and aggression in laughter. Indeed, the essential function of laughter for Castiglione was quite different. While della Casa wanted to avoid giving offense, Castiglione praised the positive value of laughter. The ideal courtier "should know how to sweeten and refresh the minds of his hearers, and move them discreetly to gaiety and laughter with amusing witticisms and pleasantries, so that, without ever producing tedium or satiety, he may continually give pleasure."[47] Witty sayings, it's true, might need to "sting a little" (Book II, chap. 43). The courtier may use ridicule judiciously, but "must take care not to appear malicious and spiteful" (Book II, chap. 57), laughing at people's absurd vices but not at the unfortunate or the truly wicked. Both della Casa and Castiglione were reprinted across Europe, spreading courtly ideals of polite behavior.

In practical joking, too, there were attempts to curb excess, or rather, a shifting conception of what constituted excess. Peter Burke has pointed to increased restrictiveness about joking in Italy by the second half of the sixteenth century:

> What we find in the period 1550–1650 in particular are increasing restrictions on the public participation of clergy, women, or gentlemen in certain kinds of joke, a reduction of comic domains, occasions, and locales; a raising of the threshold; an increase in the policing of the frontiers.[48]

Strictures included increasing attempts to suppress excessive laughter in church, joking in sermons, and comic Easter plays. Such initiatives were part of counter-Reformation moves to raise the moral tone of Catholic practice. At the same time, manners at the level of courtiers and gentry were shifting across a range of behaviors, as Norbert Elias found in his work on the "civilizing process." Along with more curbing of violence and control of bodily comportment, upper-class tastes moved away from physical joking toward more verbal humor (although, of course, such verbal humor could still be aggressive).[49] Chris Holcomb has traced this trend in his study of advice about jesting in sixteenth-century England.[50]

The Renaissance reputation of laughter was largely a negative one, even though Renaissance humanists were often enthusiastic laughers themselves and were pioneers of the jestbook tradition. Like Burckhardt, Quentin Skinner finds keen awareness of laughter's aggressive power among early modern commentators. Raising the profile of laughter with increasing recognition of its significance, the writers of the sixteenth and seventeenth centuries typically gave it a hostile tinge. The long strain of anti-laughter thought was amplified in the discussions of laughter that emerged in these years.[51]

Examples of disapproval of aggressive humor could be multiplied. Robert Burton, whose *Anatomy of Melancholy* went through multiple editions after its initial publication in 1621, was far from an enemy of laughter. But he had a sharp sense of the harm it could do. Abusers of laughter could inflict cruel torment: "A bitter jest, a slander, a calumny, pierceth deeper than any loss, danger, bodily pain, or injury whatsoever."[52] For sensitive souls—the "melancholy" who were Burton's chief concern—the harm could follow even without malice on the jester's part: "Although they peradventure that so scoff do it alone in mirth and merriment, and hold it . . . an excellent thing to enjoy another man's madness; yet they must know that it is a mortal sin."[53] Burton himself knew how to wield laughter's power, and he threatened to laugh down his critics—but only in self-defense. He calls himself Democritus Junior, in homage to the philosopher of ancient Greece who purportedly laughed at the whole world. He issues this warning in Latin:

> To the reader who employs his leisure ill[:] Whoever you may be, I caution you against rashly defaming the author of this work, or cavilling in jest against him. . . . For, should Democritus Junior prove to be what he professes, even a

kinsman of his elder namesake, or be ever so little of the same kidney, it is all up with you: he will become both accuser and judge of you in his petulant spleen, will dissipate you in jests, pulverize you with witticisms, and sacrifice you, I can promise you, to the God of Mirth.[54]

A few years later, Thomas Hobbes put forward his often-quoted description of laughter as "sudden glory" in a feeling of superiority: "The passion of laughter is nothing else but a sudden glory arising from sudden conception of some eminency in ourselves, by comparison with the infirmities of others, or with our own formerly."[55] His full treatment of the subject is more complex than it is sometimes painted. It included the possibility of laughing at oneself (feeling superior to one's own former failings) or of more benign laughter in which people laugh together at some abstract absurdity. But Hobbes was no fan of laughter, and his objection was based largely on its role in claiming superiority over others—a claim that Hobbes found pathetically weak. People with genuine superiority did not need to laugh. Laughter was commonest among those "that are conscious of the fewest abilities in themselves; who are forced to keep themselves in their own favour, by observing the imperfections of other men."[56] That great laugher Cellini would have been incensed. In any case, at least for Hobbes, the smoothing efforts of polite manners had not changed the essentially aggressive nature of laughter.[57]

But the aggressive laughter of Hobbes and Cellini is only part of the story. We will meet more conflict in the chapters ahead, but first, to happier memories of laughter.

Notes

1 Cellini, *Vita*, 1:103. I give citations by book and chapter because quotations are a composite drawn from consulting the following editions: Benvenuto Cellini, *My Life*, trans. Julia Conaway Bondanella and Peter Bondanella (Oxford and New York: Oxford University Press, 2002); Benvenuto Cellini, *La Vita*, ed. Lorenzo Bellotto (Parma: Fondazione Pietro Bembo, 1996); *The Life of Benvenuto Cellini*, trans. John Addington Symonds (New York: Brentano's, 1863), https://en.wikisource.org/wiki/The_Life_of_Benv enuto_Cellini. The Bondanella translation is the most recent and authoritative English version; the Symonds translation is old but has a nice feel for the verve and bravura of the original. In some instances I have also consulted *The Autobiography of Benvenuto Cellini*, trans. George Bull, rev. ed. (New York: Penguin, 1998). Many thanks are due to Thomas V. Cohen for consultation on some sticky issues of translation (naturally he is not responsible for any of my errors).
2 Giorgio Vasari, *Lives of the Most Eminent Painters, Sculptors and Architects*, trans. Gaston du C. De Vere (London: Medici Society, 1915), 10:22, https://archive.org/stream/livesof mostemine10vasauoft/livesofmostemine10vasauoft_djvu.txt.
3 Cellini, *Vita*, 1:14, 20.
4 Cellini, *Vita*, 1:16.
5 Cellini, *Vita*, 1:17.
6 See Paolo L. Rossi, "The Writer and the Man. Real Crimes and Mitigating Circumstances," in *Crime, Society and the Law in Renaissance Italy*, ed. Trevor Dean and K. J. P. Lowe (Cambridge: Cambridge University Press, 1994), 157–83, 161–65. On assaulting

the face as dishonor, see, for example, Thomas V. Cohen and Elizabeth S. Cohen, *Words and Deeds in Renaissance Rome: Trials before the Papal Magistrates* (Toronto: University of Toronto Press, 1993), 25.

7 Cellini, *Vita*, 1:72.
8 Cellini, *Vita*, 1:73.
9 See Edward Muir, *Mad Blood Stirring: Vendetta in Renaissance Italy* (Baltimore: Johns Hopkins University Press, 1998), 32.
10 See Paul Douglas McLean, *The Art of the Network: Strategic Interaction and Patronage in Renaissance Florence* (Durham, NC: Duke University Press, 2007), 59–89.
11 See, for example, Peter Burke, *The Italian Renaissance: Culture and Society in Italy*, 2nd ed. (Princeton, NJ: Princeton University Press, 1999), 198–99.
12 See, for example, Pieter Spierenburg, *A History of Murder* (Cambridge: Polity Press, 2008), 12–64.
13 See Muir, *Mad Blood Stirring*, 33–34.
14 Peter Burke, "Frontiers of the Comic in Early Modern Italy," in *Varieties of Cultural History* (Ithaca, NY: Cornell University Press, 1997), 77–93, 85.
15 See, for example, Thomas V. Cohen, "The Lay Liturgy of Affront in Sixteenth-Century Italy," *Journal of Social History* 25, no. 4 (1992): 857–77.
16 Cellini, *Vita*, 2:70.
17 Cellini, *Vita*, 2:71.
18 See Bondanella, "A Chronology of Benvenuto Cellini," in Cellini, *My Life*, xxxiv–xxxv.
19 Michael Rocke, *Forbidden Friendships: Homosexuality and Male Culture in Renaissance Florence* (New York and Oxford: Oxford University Press, 1996), 6–14, 231–34.
20 Cellini, *Vita*, 2:71.
21 Helmut Puff, *Sodomy in Reformation Germany and Switzerland, 1400–1600* (Chicago and London: University of Chicago Press, 2003), 13.
22 Cellini, *Vita*, 2:30. On Cellini's use of humor in this encounter see Margaret A. Gallucci, *Benvenuto Cellini: Sexuality, Masculinity, and Artistic Identity in Renaissance Italy* (New York: Palgrave Macmillan, 2003), 33.
23 Cellini, *Vita*, 2:34.
24 Rocke, *Forbidden Friendships*, 12–13, 114, 231–34.
25 Cellini, *Vita*, 2:61.
26 Cellini, *Vita*, 1:30.
27 Cellini, *Vita*, 1:30.
28 Cellini, *Vita*, 1:19. Bondanella identifies her as Porzia Petrucci; Cellini, *My Life*, 390.
29 Cellini, *Vita*, 1:20.
30 Cellini, *Vita*, 1:52.
31 Cellini, *Vita*, 1:55.
32 Cellini, *Vita*, 2:22.
33 Cellini, *Vita*, 1:64.
34 Richard Cust and Andrew Hopper, "59 Bowen v Moulsworth and Gartfoote," in *The Court of Chivalry 1634–1640*, ed. Richard Cust and Andrew Hopper, British History Online, http://www.british-history.ac.uk/no-series/court-of-chivalry/59-bowen-moulsworth-gartfoote.
35 Richard Cust and Andrew Hopper, "20 Badcock v Comyns," in *The Court of Chivalry 1634–1640*, ed. Richard Cust and Andrew Hopper, British History Online, http://www.british-history.ac.uk/no-series/court-of-chivalry/20-badcock-comyns.
36 Adam Fox, "Ballads, Libels and Popular Ridicule in Jacobean England," *Past & Present* 145 (1994), 47–83, 53, 67.
37 John Morreall, "Philosophy of Humor," in *The Stanford Encyclopedia of Philosophy* (Winter 2016 Edition), ed. Edward N. Zalta, https://plato.stanford.edu/archives/win2016/entries/humor/.

38 See M. A. Screech, *Laughter at the Foot of the Cross* (London: Allen Lane, Penguin, 1997), xix–xxii, 48.

39 Screech, *Laughter at the Foot of the Cross*, 40.

40 Morreall, "Philosophy of Humor."

41 2 Kings 2:23, cited in Morreall, "Philosophy of Humor."

42 Jeremy Dauber, *Jewish Comedy: A Serious History* (London and New York: W. W. Norton & Company, 2017), 190–91; for more on the history of the glass-breaking custom and its connection to mourning for Jerusalem, see Ari Z. Zivotofsky, "What's the Truth About . . . Breaking a Glass at a Wedding?" *Jewish Action* (Winter 2020), https://jewishaction.com/religion/jewish-law/whats-the-truth-about-breaking-a-glass-at-a-wedding/.

43 Jacob Burckhardt, *The Civilization of the Renaissance in Italy*, 2 vols., trans. S. G. C. Middlemore (New York: Harper & Row, 1958), 1:163. Peter Burke draws attention to this feature of Burckhardt's argument in his "Frontiers of the Comic in Early Modern Italy."

44 Francesco Petrarca, "Letters on Familiar Matters," in *University of Chicago Readings in Western Civilization 5: The Renaissance*, ed. Eric Cochrane and Julius Kirshner (Chicago and London: University of Chicago Press, 1986), 40.

45 Burckhardt, *Civilization of the Renaissance*, 1:166.

46 Burckhardt, *Civilization of the Renaissance*, 1:168.

47 Baldesar Castiglione, *The Book of the Courtier,* ed. Daniel Javitch, trans. Charles S. Singleton (New York: Norton, 2002), 103 (Book II, chap. 43).

48 Burke, "Frontiers of the Comic," 93.

49 Burke, "Frontiers of the Comic," 91.

50 Chris Holcomb, *Mirth Making: The Rhetorical Discourse on Jesting in Early Modern England* (Columbia, SC: University of South Carolina Press, 2001).

51 Quentin Skinner, "Hobbes and the Classical Theory of Laughter," in *Visions of Politics: Volume 3, Hobbes and Civil Science* (Cambridge: Cambridge University Press, 2002), 142–76, ProQuest Ebook Central.

52 Robert Burton, *The Anatomy of Melancholy*, ed. Holbrook Jackson (New York: Vintage Books, 1977), part 1, sec. 2, mem. 4, subsec. 4, p. 341.

53 Burton, *Anatomy of Melancholy*, 341.

54 Burton, *Anatomy of Melancholy*, "Democritus to the Reader," part 1, p. 124.

55 Thomas Hobbes, *Humane Nature, or, the Fundamental Elements of Policy* (1650), chap 9, sec. 13.

56 Thomas Hobbes, *Leviathan,* ed. J. C. A. Gaskin (Oxford: Oxford University Press, 1996), 38 (chap. 6, sec. 42).

57 See David Heyd, "The Place of Laughter in Hobbes's Theory of Emotions," *Journal of the History of Ideas* 43, no. 2 (1982), 285–95, 286.

FIGURE 3.1 Felix Platter as a young man, portrait by Hans Bock

Source: © Artokoloro/Alamy Stock Photo

3

THE LAUGHTER OF SOCIAL BONDING

Felix Platter

Felix Platter was a very different kind of laugher from Benvenuto Cellini. The funniest event of his life—which made him lose control and laugh till he nearly burst—was an occasion when he himself was fooled, along with a bunch of his fellow medical students. Other high points of hilarity came during his courtship and wedding, with laughter that cemented and celebrated new social bonds. He tells of making a fool of himself in an episode that ended in shared laughter and lifelong friendship. There were times when he was embarrassed at being laughed at—but they left no lasting resentment. The times when he laughed at others were times when they were trying to be funny. There could hardly be a greater contrast with the aggressive laughter of Benvenuto Cellini's story. Just as Cellini offered an entry point to the long tradition of negativity about laughter, Platter opens a window into the broader picture of "good" laughter.

The two men were near contemporaries, Felix Platter born in 1536, when Cellini had already worked for several years at the papal court in Rome. As writers of autobiography, both men reflect the growth of secular literacy and the new interest in recording one's life. Both also benefited from the era's expanding opportunities for social advancement through education and professional skill. But Felix—aptly named by his humanist father with the Latin word for happy—had no stories to tell of enmity, conflict, derision, and triumphant laughter. Instead, the laughter in his world bound people together. It nurtured him as he grew, forged bonds with his fellow students and future wife, and even could ease social relations across differences of religion and status. His story highlights the ways in which laughter could disperse the tensions associated with situations of anxiety and stress, from courtship to the potential threat of strangers and rivals.

Besides offering an entry point into the positive social uses of laughter in his personal account, Platter also represents an important strain of vindication for laughter: the view of doctors. In the development of secular professional identities

DOI: 10.4324/9781003247517-4

in the late Middle Ages, medicine and law were the two main fields of advancement outside the priesthood. The increasing prestige of medical degrees promoted
the spread of ideas about laughter that diverged from the suspicion or disapproval
that prevailed among many church authorities. Physicians, with their interest in the
human body, asked different questions about laughter than did theologians. They
did care about moral questions—because health of the spirit was connected to that
of the body. Mainly, though, they wondered about the physiology of laughter, and
they largely found it beneficial. Platter was not just a doctor, but one who studied
at the historic medical school of Montpellier in France—a hotbed of laughter
theory and practice, as we shall see!

Felix Platter, physician and professor of medicine at the University of Basel
in Switzerland, was in the second generation of a family with an extraordinary
rise into the ranks of the intelligentsia. It is not enough to say that Thomas, the
elder Platter, was born a peasant. The term "peasant" often conveys an exaggerated notion of poverty to modern readers; in fact, many peasant farmers held
substantial property and had their own brand of prosperity. (The famous family
of Martin Guerre is a good example; Martin was worth impersonating because
of his property and standing in his village.[1]) But Thomas Platter's status was much
lower, his family without the means to support him and his brothers after his father
died. He worked early as a shepherd, traveled with wandering students who supported themselves by singing and begging, and later learned ropemaking. Thomas
was drawn irresistibly to books, learning and studying at every spare moment. He
was swept up by enthusiasm for the new learning—the humanist movement—in
which study of ancient languages offered a different path from the hidebound and
church-dominated universities. Eventually, he became skilled not only in Latin,
the standard language of learning, but also in Greek, the language studied by more
zealous humanists, and even in Hebrew, a still rarer accomplishment that put him
in demand as a teacher of others. Through teaching, ropemaking, and eventually
printing, he and his wife worked their way to a degree of wealth that enabled them
to send Felix to medical school. In his own autobiography, Thomas gave his wife
a substantial share of the credit for their economic success. The family thrived by
applying their individual initiative in an age of unprecedented opportunity. It was
likely awareness of this remarkable achievement and transformation that sparked
the impulse to autobiography. When Felix took his doctoral degree in 1557, it
was a financial as well as an intellectual hurdle. This highest of academic degrees
conferred an honorary status that could approach that of nobility. It was a proud
moment for a father who had started life near the lowest of social ranks.[2]

Felix Platter was far from a tireless self-promoter like Cellini. Still, he thought
it was important to keep a written record of his own life. He kept daily journals already as a teenager, from which he reconstructed events when composing his autobiography late in life. He also urged his father and brother to write
autobiographies—making the Platters an unusually well-documented family. He
saw his life story as one with value for others, writing to a friend of how it would

contain the "many rare and wonderful things that I have seen." Though likely not seeking the printed publication and wide fame that Cellini hoped for, Felix envisioned readers in his circle of family and friends. He circulated his father's autobiography in manuscript and wrote to the same friend of his pleasure at hearing "that it has so moved you to read my late father's *Life*."[3] The writing of a life was a social as well as a personal endeavor, a story to be shared.

The Freedom of Youth

Occasions of laughter were especially common in the early years of Felix's story. He saw youth as an especially appropriate time for hilarity, and in this he was echoing common wisdom. Commentators on laughter frequently noted the greater readiness to laugh of children (and, they sometimes said, women and the uneducated as well). One of the few contexts in which even those hostile to laughter tended to loosen up was in relation to children. Platter relates some incidents from his childhood that show the indulgent amusement of adults at a child's foibles. In these episodes he himself was not laughing, but he provided the spur to adult laughter or joking. When he was four or five years old he found eggs in the straw near his neighbor's dog, named Canis. He thought the dog had laid them and told people so. After that the neighbor often gave him eggs "that his wife said Canis had laid."[4] Some years later, at the urging of his aunt, his father gave him money for his mother to buy him a dagger he had craved. But he couldn't wait for his mother, ran on ahead, found the daggers too expensive, and bought toys, including puppets "and other silly things." The household's group of young boarders teased him, but "when my mother came home, complained of my foolishness and scolded me, my aunt as well as my father laughed and made peace."[5] The everyday amusement and shared laughter over children's doings held a very low profile in intellectual discussions of laughter, seeming perhaps too trivial—but may have been among the most common experiences of it.

The adolescent boarders were a frequent source of frivolity in Platter's early life. Besides their teasing, they delighted in mummery. On festive occasions they loved to dress up as devils or fools.[6] Platter especially remembered a wedding where they set up a play in the garden. The laughter there was so strong as to challenge physical control. One of the youths "in fool's costume played so many funny tricks that [Platter's friend and fellow scholar Jacob] Myconius later confessed, he almost pissed his pants with laughter."[7]

Although writers of advice about laughter often stressed moderation, Platter and his friends valued laughter that caused powerful physical reactions. He does not mention rolling on the floor, but losing control of one's body, or nearly losing control, meant especially successful joking and especially memorable laughter. How hilarious were the antics of his friends the wedding mummers? Myconius nearly wet his pants—an experience he recounted to Felix as testimony of the laughter's intensity. Similarly, the very best joke Platter remembered from his student days made him nearly burst with laughing. This was a practical joke that emerged from the students' well-lubricated culture of jest and raillery at the tavern. Two of his friends, Ludovicus Hechstetter and Melchior Rotmundt, celebrated one Three Kings Day (the post-Christmas holiday also known as Twelfth Night or Epiphany) with drinking that led to a quarrel. Hechstetter taunted Rotmundt with the insult "milchmaul [milkmouth]." Vowing, "I'll make you a milkmouth!" Rotmundt took Hechstetter to a barber and had his bushy beard shaved clean off. Obviously it was a good-natured squabble, since Hechstetter cooperated with the stripping of his beard—and it gave them both an opportunity to put one over on their other friends, when they saw how completely it changed Hechstetter's appearance. Rotmundt told the others that Hechstetter was a new German student just arrived in town. The German students at Montpellier had a custom of welcoming fellow countrymen with some ceremony, so they invited him to a meal at the tavern, extending every courtesy. Just as they were about to sit, "Hechstetter threw off his cloak and said, 'you fools, don't you know me, it's Hechstetter!' at which we all fell into such laughter, that for my part I thought I would burst."[8]

The pranks of young males were often recognized and ritualized in early modern Europe, as we saw in the activities of youth groups who staged public mockery (see Chapter 1). There were opportunities for individual license as well, including mixed-gender play, as in a daring episode from the personal account of Johann Dietz, a barber-surgeon in seventeenth-century Saxony. Traveling from his native Halle to Berlin, Dietz reveled in the vibrant youth culture of music and play. One night he sneaked into the bedroom of a magistrate's daughters, with the girls actively colluding by lowering a bedsheet to enable him to climb up. It was a scene of riotous fun: "I need not tell you how we laughed and diverted ourselves. Now I was lying in this bed, now in that; and this was not done without laughter, shrieks and a general uproar." When the old father came to investigate the noise, the daughters hid the young man in a bed and covered up the mischief. All ended well, but Dietz was aware that he took a dangerous risk: "To me, however, the matter was not entirely one for laughing. The pastime might so easily have changed into something more serious."[9] There is no way to know how much Dietz may have embellished his story. Was the father really a high official, far above Dietz's own social station? Was there really a dramatic moment of breathless hiding beneath the bedclothes, fearing the powerful father's wrath? Was there sexual contact involved, or mere highjinks? He seems unlikely to have invented the whole story, however. Dietz's account points to the subversive potential of play—clearly a reason for moralists' suspicion. But it also underlines the divergence between rules and lived experience, and the space for laughing relations in mixed company, especially for youth.[10]

Perhaps Felix Platter really did laugh more in youth, adopting a more sober demeanor in later life. But there is another reason for the concentration of his remembered laughter in youth: that is, its significant role in social bonding, the formation of new relationships. These were moments of potential anxiety in which laughter could shift the ground from danger to safety. Platter tells, for instance, of a warm friendship that began in his student days, with a gaffe that made him the butt of laughter. Fancying his own abilities as a Latin poet, he proudly read his verses to a new fellow student, Peter Lotichius. He even offered to teach him— little knowing that Lotichius was already a recognized and published poet. His other peers laughed when they learned of how he had behaved in his ignorance. Platter immediately went to Lotichius to complain of how he had let him make such a fool of himself. Trading quips, the two soon became good friends, addressing each other ever after in terms of jesting kinship that recalled this early encounter.[11]

No one's experience of laughter is all of a piece. It has too many different modes for that. Even as Benvenuto Cellini shared some companionable laughter with friends alongside his aggressive uses of it, Felix Platter knew some bad laughs. In general he does not shy away from occasions when he himself was the target of laughter, and they usually were not laden with much angst. He made a fool of himself over poetry with Lotichius, for example, but they made it up and became fast friends. People laughed at him on his youthful journey into France when, unfamiliar with the local custom of kissing on greeting, he resisted being kissed by the innkeeper's daughter.[12] One occasion made him really ashamed, though. As a student in Montpellier, he was escorting a girl to a dance when they encountered a nasty "mistlachen"—a puddle of dung. Attempting to leave her a clear path, he stepped in the puddle and sprayed the stuff all over her. He was mortified not only by the mishap itself, but even more because someone went by and mockingly said, "he's given his darling holy water."[13]

Courtship and Bonding

Many incidents of recorded laughter cluster around Platter's courtship and wedding in 1557. Not only the wedding celebration itself, but the beginnings of personal relationship between the two shy young people were eased by shared jest and play. Felix and Magdalena Jeckelmann, daughter of a Basel surgeon, had limited opportunities for conversation before their betrothal. Once accepted as future bridegroom, however, Felix was given free access to the house where they "conversed and jested honorably about all sorts of things." In fact, in retrospect he was somewhat surprised at how much latitude he had been given, since it "was not yet a completed marriage and could easily have fallen through." Felix joked at his own expense, pretending that he had run up lots of debts as a student in France. Finances were in fact a touchy subject in the bargaining over this wedding—Felix did not yet have an established income, and the couple actually lived for a couple of years with his parents before they were able to set up housekeeping on their own. Laughter could both acknowledge and deflect the problem. He also liked to tease Magdalena's young brother about his own future bride. His emphasis on the honor as well as the jest suggests how much shared laughter was an accepted (and perhaps even expected) element of respectable courtship.

Felix recorded in detail one special episode of hilarity, a game of hiding in which the first to surprise the other would be owed a gift. He sneaked into Magdalena's house and hid in the cold for hours, then burst out to claim his prize—but she wasn't there. The maid claimed she had gone out, but really she was hiding under the stairs, awaiting her own opportunity to leap out and surprise him first. Always a good sport, Felix wanted to give her a gold necklace brought from Paris—but she would only accept a nicely bound New Testament. In his account of the incident, Felix explicitly invokes the joys of youth: "So we had our play for a while, as young folks do."[14]

The laughter surrounding courtship may come as no surprise to modern readers. After all, people today laugh with their partners and often consider the laughter as an important aspect of their mutual bond. Dating profiles, and before that personal ads seeking romantic connection, regularly highlight a sense of humor as a desirable characteristic. (This is a modern development, by the way—a change from the earlier personal ads of the nineteenth century, which focused on concerns like economic resources and moral character.[15]) The familiarity of courtship laughter should not blind us to the different nuances of the early modern version, however. It's true that the pursuit of a mate is still fraught with tinges of anxiety, but the stakes were much higher for couples entering marriage in the sixteenth century. The early modern household was the nucleus of economic life, with livelihood and personal relationships bound up together. Marriage also formed new kin ties that could determine one's economic as well as emotional future. It's likely that Magdalena did not become as involved in her doctor-husband's work as her mother-in-law, who had been an active and recognized partner in building the family fortune. Still, one might think of early modern courtship as a combination of dating and job interview. The laughter of courtship was playing with very serious business—making its role in confronting anxieties all the more striking.

Courtship and wedding combined two privileged sites for laughter, the license of youth and the celebration of new social and sexual bonds. Felix's father threw a grand party for 150 guests, with feasting and dancing continuing for two days. (In fact, he spent the bride's dowry on the wedding—part of the reason for delay in the couple's ability to live independently.) According to tradition, the young folks, particularly the groom's young male friends, would joke and play tricks—customs that have their echo in modern times with such practices as the tying of noisemaking cans to the bridal car. Felix hoped to avoid the noise and highjinks by sneaking into private spaces. His mother, always a lover of fun, offered to help: the young merrymakers were looking for him, but she could lead him and his bride up to their chamber by the back stairs and through the maid's room. Happy that the rowdy crowd could not find them, they went to bed. A little later they heard his mother come up to the privy, where she "loudly sang out, like a young girl, though she was already very old, at which my bride laughed heartily."[16] The 60-year-old mother seized on the youthful privilege of wedding hilarity to mark their sexual union. The bride's heartfelt laughter formed a happy counterpart to the tears she had shed shortly before, at parting from her father. Both here and in courtship, laughter served to form and strengthen the new social bonds.

Felix's description highlights both gender mutuality and gender difference in laughing relationships. It is the male youth who stir up noisy joking at the wedding. Felix appears as the more active jester in the courting conversations, teasing Magdalena's brother and talking facetiously about himself. Early on Magdalena was shy, but as the wedding approached Felix enjoyed the mutuality of their conversations. We know she had a hearty laugh at his mother's comic initiative in the privy. And there was more jesting the following day from the maid who came to bring Magdalena's things from home: a fun-loving young woman, she "made many rare jokes."[17] (He does not tell us what they were.)

While memorable laughter could be powerful in forming or cementing social bonds, failed jokes also failed in relationship-building. Some incidents of unsuccessful joking form the flip side of Platter's positive laughter, and—no accident, surely—he does not record people laughing at these. He heartily disapproved of one practical joke, played in a courting context but without good humor. A woman secretly hid a hackle (a comb with long metal teeth for straightening textile fibers) in the bed of a man she wanted to marry. Platter condemned this "coarse joke" (*grober schimpf*)—the man might have been hurt, he said, if he had not noticed it. He did not comment directly on the sexually suggestive aspect of vicariously invading the man's bed, although this could have been another reason he found it rude. The potential swain was repulsed by her shrewishness. Besides, she was skinny and a widow, probably older than the target of her prank. But as a widow with property, she was able to find another husband.[18]

Another courtship-related jest was inadvertently spoiled by Platter himself. Not long after his marriage, he visited a doctor in Strasbourg, where he was handsomely entertained with a banquet, music and dancing. The doctor's pretty sister-in-law was told that Felix had come to court her—a practical joke that moved her to treat him with friendly attention all evening, until—"when at midnight I said to the company, 'if my wife at Basel knew that I was banqueting so late, she would worry,' I completely spoiled the game and was no longer so valued."[19] Platter does not express a judgment of the joke, and he was not in on the deception—but the pretty sister clearly was not laughing.

Laughter and Religious Division

Felix Platter lived in an age of intense religious conflict, as the movements sparked by Martin Luther and other reformers shattered the former unity of Christendom. The Platters were Protestants of the Reformed variety. Their hometown of Basel had been open to Protestant worship as early as 1527, while there remained substantial Catholic presence in the region also.[20] Basel was an area of relative religious peace and coexistence in the mid-sixteenth century, although Protestants like the Platters were keenly aware that this was not the case everywhere, and that mockery across confessions could include violence and cruelty. In France, when Felix was there as a medical student, two Protestant "heretics" were executed by burning, events which he recounts in detail, with admiration for their steadfastness as martyrs. On the day of the first execution there was prodigious thunder, which Platter clearly saw as a sign of God's displeasure; but "the priests jokingly said that the smoke from the burning heretics had caused it."[21] Obviously, not all religious humor was benign.

Nevertheless, laughter's role in easing social relationships could extend across religious difference, in a striking episode from Felix Platter's remembrance. He was able to enter into relations of pleasant banter with the Catholic abbess of Olsberg, Katharina von Hersberg. She, like Felix's mother, was described as "merry [*frölich*]," a woman who loved a jest. As Felix established his medical practice in Basel, his acquisition of elite clients like the abbess was a marker of his success. Not only did difference of faith not hinder her patronage of a Protestant physician, but the jesting exchanges he records show that they even played with some of their points of religious divergence. Platter was likely proud of both the professional relationship and the sociable relationship across lines of religion and social class. His doctorate gave him honorary elite status, but he would always be at a humbler social level than the abbess, a born noblewoman. Still, he felt free to joke. The Catholic worship of saints—rejected by Protestants—figured in a quip he recalled fondly (I say fondly because it was quite rare for him to record a witticism of his own). A relative of the abbess had commissioned a painting for the abbey which had his own portrait depicted among the saints—a fairly common practice among Catholic patrons of art. Platter laughingly suggested to the abbess that this saint got more of her attention in prayer than the others.

The abbess was not offended in the least, and she played a still more daring joke herself. Besides their theological objection to the worship of saints, Protestants harshly criticized the purported immorality of convents; countless Protestant satires posed as exposés of the rampant concealment of illegitimate births among nuns. Whether this critique was in Katharina von Hersberg's mind as she planned her practical joke, it is impossible to say; but it certainly entered Platter's. He and his wife were frequently invited to the abbey for sociable merriment, including music and mummery. On one occasion—possibly at carnival time—the abbess said she had a foundling infant in another room and asked Felix's wife to fetch it from its cradle. It took Magdalena Platter some time to realize that it was actually an amazingly lifelike doll—"a naked baby most delicately carved, as if it lived and slept." When the trick was discovered, they all laughed—but Platter could not help thinking of those Protestant critiques: "I thought, in some cloisters it was a custom to hide real children this way."[22] As I say, we have no record of what Abbess Katharina thought. It is hard to believe that these undertones of the episode could have escaped her, though. As the first abbess appointed at Olsberg after a period when nuns there had turned to Protestantism, she was well aware of Protestant ideas.[23] She may have been poking sly fun at the Protestant prejudice about nuns and babies (although genuine foundlings did find their way into religious houses as well). In any case, she was ready to go a long way for a joke and was not at all squeamish about the confessional divide.

Laughing Doctors and the Body

The medical school at Montpellier in France, where Felix Platter studied in the 1550s, was one of the oldest and most respected in Europe. It was also a center of laughter, to judge by the laughter interests and practices of a number of its sixteenth-century students and professors. Felix Platter himself (like Benvenuto Cellini) has not been especially noted for laughter until the present study. François Rabelais, who studied at Montpellier in the 1530s, some twenty years before Platter arrived, is possibly the most famous laugher of the age. Also in the 1530s, the Englishman Andrew Boorde studied there. A somewhat shadowy figure, Boorde penned popular medical works. More popular still were the two jestbooks—"Scoggin's Jests" and the "Mad Men of Gotham"—of which he was the reputed author. Laurent Joubert, author of the leading Renaissance medical treatment of laughter, was closer in age to Felix Platter. The two seem not to have crossed paths as students at the school—Joubert was a bit older and had left to practice and study in Italy when Felix arrived, though he returned to Montpellier to teach, and received his doctorate the year after Felix had left. Joubert went on to become a leading professor and member of the school's ruling board of administrators.[24] He wrote many medical works, including vernacular writings that spread his fame beyond the academy.

It was doctors, as promoters of health, who had the most positive things to say about laughter in the sixteenth century. Joubert, in his influential *Treatise on Laughter*, cited with approval the dictum of philosophers that "laughter is proper to man, that is, that it is natural for every man and for each man."[25] For each woman too: in fact Joubert thought that women, like fat people, were more easily moved to laughter than men. In his preface to the 1579 French edition, dedicated to Marguerite de Valois, he praised the beauty that laughter imparted to the female face: woman generally exceeds man in facial beauty,

> and since her constitution is more delicate, softer, and more passionate, her manners gentler, more benign and amiable, her condition gayer, more joyous and sweet, laughter in her is also more proper, more fitting, and more gracious, expressing her great gentleness and humanity.[26]

Of course, this passage expresses flattery rather than medical expertise. But laughter (in moderation) was good for you too. Joubert asserted that laughter for man is "the means to refresh his mind from time to time, overworked and tired due to serious occupations, such as study, contemplation, affairs of business, public administration, and others proper to man."[27]

Joubert's aim was a comprehensive scientific treatise, and he explores many aspects of laughter. His central focus was on physiology and health, however, with extensive discussion of the various movements and body parts involved in this physical phenomenon. Overall, he was favorable toward laughter's benefits for health: "Since being joyful and ready to laugh indicates a good nature and purity of blood, it thus contributes to the health of the body and of the mind, as experience coupled with reason shows us."[28] As a conscientious scientist, however, he felt bound to point to the dangers of excess as well. According to the humoral theory then prevailing, health depended on proper balance of the four humors: blood, phlegm, black bile, and yellow bile. Excess in any of them would be harmful to the system, and Joubert saw the same principle applying to laughter as to other matters of health: "There is nothing so useful and so pleasant that it cannot become harmful and dangerous if continued for too long a time."[29] He is somewhat doubtful about reported cases of death from laughter, which he finds not impossible because one might stop breathing, but certainly extremely rare.

Positive views of laughter appear also in the work of the sixteenth-century surgeon Ambroise Paré, who attributed laughter to the passion of joy and described its beneficial effects on the body.[30] Paré is famed for promoting innovations in surgical technique that reduced bleeding and infections, improving successful cures and survival. He gained extensive surgical experience with battle wounds of the French army, and his skills led to his employment by kings of France. He also published books on his surgical methods. Laughter gained praise in an account of his work that otherwise is taken up with much more gruesome subjects. In response to criticism in print by a conservative physician, Paré wrote his *Apologie and Treatise*, detailing his surgical experience to demonstrate how much more he knew about the body than his book-learned opponent. In the course of his successful cure of the Marquis d'Auret's leg wound, which had baffled a crew of physicians and surgeons for months, Paré recommended music and "a jester to make him merry." As the nobleman's health improved, the peasants of the district feasted and celebrated with "good laughing and drinking."[31]

The description of another incident in 1543 expresses Paré's positive view of laughter indirectly. The French army had driven the English out of Brittany. Among the sports they enjoyed afterward was a wrestling match, in which a highly skilled short wrestler was challenged by a very tall one. They seemed equally matched in skill, and for a while neither could get the advantage. Then the short man made a sudden move that threw his opponent, "on his Kidneyes spread abroad like a frogge, and then all the company laught at the skill and strength of this little fellow."[32] The large man "had a great spight, for being cast by so little a man" and took revenge by falling on the other with his elbow, bursting his heart and killing him. This serious end to the incident is what got Paré involved, as he performed an autopsy to determine the cause of death. It is notable, though, that while he describes the large man's fall as a comic sight, with the man "spread abroad like a frog," the laughter is presented not as derision, but as admiration of the coup performed by the underdog. The furious tall wrestler may have viewed it differently, of course.

François Rabelais had a more adventurous life than either Platter or Joubert. Like many intellectuals of the time, he began his career as a churchman, a member of the Franciscan order and later a Benedictine monk. As the son of a lawyer, he was already the product of a rising professional class that gained its status through education. He was an accomplished scholar in the humanist realm of languages, especially ancient Latin and Greek, and close study of texts, before he arrived at Montpellier for medical study in 1530. During his time at Montpellier, Rabelais was part of a merry troupe of medical students who staged a farce about a man married to a mute woman. A doctor cured her, but then had no remedy for her excessive talking except to make the husband deaf. After a few more turns in the plot, the enraged couple beat up the doctor for his malpractice. Rabelais reprised this comic plot in his famed *Gargantua and Pantagruel*, having Pantagruel remark that he had never laughed harder in his life.[33]

After his study at Montpellier Rabelais practiced medicine in Lyon and else-where, returning to teach at Montpellier in 1537. Meanwhile, he was writing the fiction that has made him famous. Rabelais's novels, which together make up the five books of *Gargantua and Pantagruel*, were published under a thinly veiled pseu-donym in a series between 1532 and 1552. Full of comic excess and grotesque buf-foonery, they sold rapidly but were condemned by church authorities. Rabelais's characters eat, drink, vomit, copulate, excrete, give birth—all in exaggerated comic physicality that was very far from the concepts of civilized decorum that were spreading in other circles of humanist and courtly society.

Rabelais's works inspired the most influential book ever written on the history of laughter, *Rabelais and his World* by Mikhail Bakhtin. As we have seen, Bakhtin viewed the rollicking physical comedy of Rabelais—full of unruly bodies eating, drinking, farting, defecating, coupling, and of course laughing—as an expression of the liberating comic worldview of carnival. It was a recognition of the shared human condition—grounded in the physical imperatives of birth, life, and death—that overturned the pretensions of authority by bringing them down to earth. Laughter was an antidote to oppression, maintaining a space of symbolic freedom. The carnival laughter of the world upside down could mock the powerful, but it was far from the personal derision of Renaissance polemics. It was pomp itself that was absurd. Bakhtin saw this shared celebration of laughter and community as something that would be lost with the growth of an individualistic, bourgeois society in the coming centuries. Rabelais, in this view, was both the last hurrah of medieval laughter and the representative of a unique Renaissance moment when the literate humanist could still have his feet firmly planted in the fertile mud of popular culture.

Platter's world was obviously much tamer than the imagination of his Mont-pellier fellow Rabelais. Platter did enjoy physical humor and laughter, including the kind that made you nearly burst or piss. However, his accounts of laughter are remarkably free of scatological references (bathroom humor), especially in com-parison to the sixteenth-century norm. One does not have to look far to find excrement in both public and private. Reformation polemics were famously crude, with, for instance, images of peasants shitting into the papal tiara. Martin Luther talked about lower body parts and so did his opponents, with an implication of lowering and casting derision on their targets.

Why was Platter so comparatively pristine? There are hints of a development in his story that Bakhtin would likely consider a move toward bourgeois values. Perhaps even the distancing of his elder self from the frivolities of youth points in that direction, but it emerges more clearly from his treatment of a "nasty [*wiest*]" custom he remembered from his early days in Basel: the groping of women's breasts. Platter describes this practice as "so general, even in distinguished houses, that seldom a maid left the house without the master having done her this honor."[34] Note the "even," implying that such behavior among lower classes might be no surprise; but it was pervasive among elite masters. He also describes it as a relic of the past, something no longer done. But it recurred on a later occasion, when he traveled with his father to visit Thomas's homeland in the Valais region. When they stopped at an inn kept by a kinswoman of theirs, "There was also a pretty woman there in the inn, whom a Platter grabbed very rudely, which made her angry."[35] Probably it was the elder Platter, following a custom he may have seen as fun, while his son (and also the woman) viewed it as an offensive assault. Some things, it seems, were no longer funny.

The friendly face of laughter that appears in Platter's life story had a relatively low profile in the public discourse of his time. The negatives of aggressive and irresponsible laughter, as discussed in the last chapter, tended to color its public image more darkly. Even the doctors who favored laughter, like Joubert, were worried about the dangers of excess. And although Christian criticisms of laughter dated back many centuries, the spread of print amplified aggressive laughter in ways that benign interpersonal laughter could not compete with. Renaissance invective in the style of Pietro Aretino, full of biting mockery, had value in the public market. So did jokes, extracted from their social surroundings and converted into commodities in the expanding genre of print jestbooks. The laughter materials of popular print, such as the pranks of Till Eulenspiegel or the violence of comic shrew-tamings, roused laughter that seems cruel to modern sensibilities. Platter's laughter, on the other hand, is very short on retailable jokes. Instead, the laughter was meaningful to him for the way it infused his social relationships, fostering connectedness and even joy.

This type of private laughter is the least likely to be reflected in written sources, yet was surely its most historically pervasive form. Laughter at the antics of children, laughter in the forming of youthful friendships, laughter amid the anxieties of courtship, laughter of celebration, the laughter of camaraderie—Felix Platter remembered them all. He is unusual not in these experiences but in his retention and recording of them, giving us a glimpse of everyday laughter.

Laughter of the Good Christian

The Christian tradition did include some recognition of benign laughter, although it was full of ambivalence about the subject. As we have seen, there was no doubt about what the ungodly would do: they would laugh without restraint, getting their comeuppance only in the afterlife when they finally learned that the joke was on them. Among pious Christians there was doubt and division, with authorita- tive early church fathers like St. Ambrose, St. Jerome, and St. John Chrisostom taking a strong position against frivolity. The lovers of fun could take comfort from St. Thomas Aquinas, however. His monumental *Summa Theologica* was the leading theological authority of the Middle Ages, and in his effort to encompass every aspect of Christian life and teachings, he found a respectable place for laughter. In addition to Christian learning, he cited the opinion of Aristotle on the value of pleasant wit in sociability. Play was necessary for relief and relaxation to the soul; recreation was even virtuous if exercised moderately, with care to harm no one and to refrain from obscene or irreligious jest. In fact, there could even be sin in failing to laugh: "a man who is without mirth, not only is lacking in playful speech, but is also burdensome to others, since he is deaf to the moderate mirth of others."[36] The reasonable Christian would take care not to put a damper on others' enjoyment.

On the Protestant side, Martin Luther was an enthusiastic laugher, though not a laughter theorist. For him laughter, like the body with its sexual urges, was part of God's creation of human nature and therefore not to be despised. Of course, like other polemicists of the age, he used humor as well as argument in sermons and writings to disparage what he saw as false religion. In private life, much of his hilarity was preserved by the boarders and guests who hung on his every word and took the notes that became known as his "Table Talk." Some of the note takers carefully labeled portions of the talk as "joke"—distinguishing them from the seri- ous theological content that fell from the master's lips. But they still wrote them down. There were some misogynistic quips, sprinkled into the conversation to tease his wife (more on these in a later chapter). There were jokes about Catho- lics, of course—such as about the delicacies served at a bishop's table during a fast, and about a priest chiding a dog for being Lutheran when the animal fouled the holy water.[37] There was a joke about the long sermons of his colleague Johannes Bugenhagen.[38]

Not all Protestant theologians were as sanguine about laughter as Luther.[39] John Calvin has an especially humorless reputation, often seen as confirmed by the pun- ishment of a man in Geneva for naming his dog Calvin. In 1554, during a period of controversy over Calvin's authority, a man was disciplined because he had said "he would rather return to the papacy to live joyously, because here no one ever laughs."[40] In the pursuit of godly discipline, such promoters of hilarity as dances and festivals were banned in Geneva. Reformers influenced by Calvin were among the chief critics of popular merriment, and their ideas gained increased traction in the seventeenth century with what Peter Burke has dubbed "the triumph of Lent."[41] Authorities in Protestant areas increasingly stepped in to curb rowdy celebrations of holidays like carnival, May Day, and Twelfth Night, with their opportunities for drinking, sexual play, and violence.

Still, among Calvinists broadly, lampooning of religious antagonists was accept- able. Calvinists in the Netherlands made fun of Catholics and their symbols during the Dutch revolt in the late sixteenth century.[42] Such mockery was a potential source of social power and also of social bonding among those who shared a common view of piety. They could even laugh at ungodly ways of having fun. In early seventeenth-century England, the puritanical Lady Grace Mildmay praised her governess for her moral strictness, but also for her jokes: "her mirth was very savoury and full of wit. . . . She scoffed at all dalliance, idle talk, and wanton behaviour appertaining thereto, with a touch of a caveat to take heed thereof."[43] The strictness of Mildmay's scruples kept her away from courtly pleasures such as feasts and plays, but she and her friends found their own sources of laughter. Later in the seventeenth century, the Puritan-leaning shopkeeper's apprentice Roger Lowe liked to tell comic stories, even at the minister's house, and proudly recorded them in his diary.[44]

Laughter of the Good Humanist

There were two major strains of new (or enhanced) endorsement of positive laughter in the Renaissance era, both from elite milieus. One came from the humanist intellectuals, the other from the partially overlapping world of the Renaissance court. We will explore the tradition of courtly laughter later, in Chapter 5. Humanists, as seen in the last chapter, were skilled at skewering their opponents with the rhetoric of ridicule. At the same time, they cultivated an ideal of sociability that echoed Aristotle's endorsement of jest for the cultured gentleman.

In theory, civilized jesting should be moderate, with its limits drawn by norms based on both class and gender. The playful Dutch humanist Erasmus, author of the *Praise of Folly* and other witty works, noted that laughter must be kept within bounds of decorum: "Just as it is ugly for a grave man to cry out like a woman if he is hurt, so too it is indecorous for him to burst out into guffaws from immoderate joy."[45] He drew the line at physical tomfoolery, as well as jokes that might target or shame a living person. Erasmus's manual *On Good Manners for Boys*, with its advice on civilized laughter, was widely used in schools in the sixteenth century and on into the seventeenth, both in Latin and in vernacular translations. Whereas Platter liked to remember occasions when he or his friends were completely overcome with laughter, to the point of losing physical control, for Erasmus these were precisely the types of laughter that needed to be curbed. The boy or man aspiring to wisdom should suppress such eruptions or, if that is not possible, at least hide them:

> Only fools use expressions like: "I am dissolving with laughter", "I am bursting with laughter", "I am dying with laughter". If something so funny should occur that it produces uncontrolled laughter of this sort, the face should be covered with a napkin or with the hand.[46]

This advice came in the context of controlling the bodily symptoms of laughter so that they would not create rude distortions of the face and body, nor unseemly sounds: "The face should express mirth in such a way that it neither distorts the appearance of the mouth nor evinces a dissolute mind." In Platter's account there is no mention of what people looked or sounded like when they laughed; it was simply not a concern for him. What mattered was the memorably delightful experience of laughing, and the social connections that nurtured and enhanced laughter (and vice versa).

Other humanists also recognized the positive side of laughter while seeking to curb excess. Juan Luis Vives, author of numerous works on philosophy, education, and morals, devoted a small portion of his treatise on the soul to the subject of laughter. "Laughter," he said, "is caused by joy and pleasure."[47] This pleasure had many possible causes and could be a good thing in moderation. People might laugh even at their own thoughts, and Vives himself could not help laughing when he ate something after a long fast.[48] Like many other commentators, Vives believed that children, women, and the unschooled were the loudest laughers. Laughter was a natural human response to pleasure, but the intelligent man could learn to control the reaction so that it did not lead to unseemly convulsions. This may seem a grudging sort of approval, but as we shall see, Vives could also recommend that women seek to please and refresh their husbands by telling them funny stories. In other social settings, however, laughter quickly became associated with the dubious morality of such pleasures as "wine, games, sex, jokes, song, [and] licentiousness."[49]

The English humanist Robert Burton, who had a keen sense of the stings of aggressive laughter, had a great deal to say about its positive side as well. In fact, laughter was a central theme in his writings. In addition to his most famous work, the *Anatomy of Melancholy*, Burton authored a highbrow jestbook, *Versatile Ingenium, The Wittie Companion, or, Jests of All Sorts*. But laughter was important even when he dealt with melancholy, the early modern version of depression—no laughing matter, one might think. Yet, as we have seen, he cast himself as the offspring of Democritus, the ancient Greek philosopher famed for his laughter. It was Burton's witty and amusing style, not merely his subject matter, that made the book a best seller. Of course, Democritus was laughing at the folly of the world, and Burton too felt free to ridicule its absurdities; it was personal derision that would harm. Full of his own ripe wit and comfortable with the paradoxical human combination of tragedy with absurdity, Burton adopts the persona of the retired scholar, able to laugh at the world's folly from his peaceable retreat. Yet he is able to laugh at himself as well, knowing that everyone thinks himself wiser than the fools around him: "So thou laughest at me, and I at thee, both at a third. . . . We accuse others of madness, of folly, and are the veriest dizzards ourselves."[50]

Laughter, in fact, was a powerful specific against melancholy. Burton cites the endorsement by physicians of merriment "as a principal engine to batter the walls of melancholy, a chief antidote, and a sufficient cure of itself." In contrast to damaging laughter, the cure is "honest" mirth, such as "pleasant discourse, jests, conceits, merry tales." An adept popularizer of humanist learning, Burton drew on a wide range of pro-laughter sources both ancient and modern. He approvingly quotes the fifteenth-century Italian humanist Marsilio Ficino, who linked health, religion, and philosophy, all for laughter:

> Live merrily, O my friends, free from cares, perplexity, anguish, grief of mind, live merrily, Heaven created you for mirth. . . . And this I enjoin you, not as a divine alone, but as a physician; for without this mirth, which is the life and quintessence of physic, medicines, and whatsoever is used and applied to prolong the life of man, is dull, dead, and of no force.

The only danger, in fact, was that men [*sic*] would become so attached to laughter as a banisher of melancholy that they would "neglect their business, and, in another extreme, spend all their days among good fellows in a tavern or an ale-house."[51]

Ficino here reminds his readers of his credentials as a cleric as well as a physician, and in fact professional religious training was not unusual among the leading proponents of laughter. Rabelais and Boorde, those merry doctors of Montpellier, both began their careers in religious orders, Rabelais as a Franciscan, Boorde as a Carthusian monk. Boorde was eventually freed from his vows. Rabelais maintained his religious calling even after his medical training, despite church condemnation of his books and the threat of charges of heresy. Ficino took up the priesthood later in life, after his fame as a philosopher was well established. In an age when theology still ruled the leading universities as queen of the sciences, religious training was common ground for intellectuals. The clerical fold could include not only the measured approval of Aquinas but also some bolder champions of laughter.

Besides theoretical discussions of laughter, humanists were early producers of jestbooks—starting in Latin with the *Facetiae* of Poggio Bracciolini and quickly moving into vernacular collections.[52] Jokes were often repeated from collection to collection; they were mined by preachers looking to spice up their sermons, as well as secular readers. Jestbook humor did not always keep to the high-minded standards of theory, especially as the genre spread; it included jokes that would strike the modern reader as cruel or tasteless, such as antisemitic, misogynistic, snobbish, or violent humor. In fact, in extracting the materials of laughter from social relationships into exchangeable bites, the jestbook form promoted the solidification of stereotypes that would get a reliable laugh. Still, jestbook jokes might make their way into sociable situations, in contexts of friendly camaraderie.

The sixteenth-century cloth merchant Johannes Rütiner, of St. Gallen in Switzerland, kept a "Diarium" where he recorded dozens of jokes, often with an indication of where he heard them or who told them. Rütiner socialized with fellow merchants as well as local intellectuals. His collection was written in Latin—a sloppy Latin that would not have passed muster with humanist purists—but it captured scenes of vernacular sociability. Rütiner records one tale told by an innkeeper that appears to have been cobbled together from conventional "bad wife" jokes in the widely read jestbooks of Heinrich Bebel and Johannes Pauli. In the midst of a terrible storm on shipboard, the protagonist of this story threw his wife overboard. Why? to jettison his heaviest burden. Then, searching for her body, he looked everywhere but where she had been thrown—because she was so contrary. (In most versions of this joke, the husband searches for his drowned wife upstream instead of down; the concept doesn't work quite as well for a storm at sea, but the teller was conflating different jokes.) Finally, executed for killing her, the man approaches the gates of heaven, but when he learns from St. Peter that his wife is there, he refuses to enter: she would totally spoil it for him, and he'd rather be in hell. It is worth noting that the joke teller here was an innkeeper, presumably entertaining his customers and perhaps especially likely to seek out and repeat humorous material from commercial sources.[53]

Rütiner's circle enjoyed many kinds of jokes, including obscene ones, and their humor was aligned with Platter's in its aim of giving pleasure and easing social relationships. As Carla Roth has pointed out, they wanted the target of a joke to be able to laugh along.[54] Rütiner and his Protestant friends enjoyed laughing both with and at the elderly Catholic cleric Adam Weckerli. Once they placed a raw egg on his seat—a practical joke that, as Roth notes, had sexual and scatological connotations. Yet Weckerli was the first to laugh when he sat on the egg, despite the stain to his clothing in a spot that might suggest inability to contain semen or urine. A rather charming anecdote of non-competitive laughter appears in the jests of the guildsmen inspecting cloth for defects. This was serious business, of course, a standby of guild activity in maintaining standards for quality goods. The status of the whole craft was at stake, along with the fortunes of individual weavers. Only responsible masters were entrusted with this task; but Ulrich Haniman liked to inject levity. When a flaw appeared in the cloth, he would say jokingly, "Oh, let it go, maybe it will fall in the quilting, and then it won't matter so much." When a piece of cloth was to be rejected, he said, "I'll crush it!"—leading a companion to threaten him wryly with harm. A third twitted Haniman whenever a serious flaw appeared: "Do you want to let that one pass too?" Since Rütiner's notes do not specify tones of voice or laughter, it is just possible that the jester's colleagues were annoyed rather than amused. But the retelling of the story to Rütiner, immediately following another joke of Haniman's, suggests enjoyment, at least among those who heard about the exchanges later.[55]

It may have been the growing jestbook genre in print that inspired the manuscript compilation of the English gentleman Sir Nicholas Le Strange, which he titled *Merry Passages and Jests*. During the 1630s and 1640s, he collected over 600 laughable sayings from among his family, friends, and acquaintances. His mother, Dame Alice, was an especially rich source, followed by his father and other relatives. The collection is a remarkable hybrid between the relational type of laughter recalled by Platter—laughter that occurs from being with the right people—and laughter that is abstracted from social relations into an exchangeable joke. Le Strange heard these jokes because of his relationship with the tellers, especially his most intimate relationships, and in scenes of convivial sociability. He attributed each quip to its speaker, perhaps as a reminder of the context and the relationship, or from a feeling that authorship deserved credit. Yet he also numbered his entries, giving each an abstract identity as a separate item in the sequence of comic utterances. Le Strange was not writing for publication in the laughter market, but his preservation of jokes as items of exchange moves in that direction.[56]

Of course, convivial laughter was a staple of sociability all along the social scale, not just among elite commentators and those with humanist education like Platter himself. We have noted the ritualized hilarity of the eighteenth-century Parisian printers in Chapter 1, and the scattered evidence of everyday interactions at all social levels captures moments of laughter, and valuing of laughter, in taverns, streets, and homes. Somewhat ironically, recorded evidence of such laughter comes largely of occasions when the merriment took a wrong turn and ended up before courts whose job was to maintain order. Thus, in Chapter 4 we meet people like the seventeenth-century English butcher Edward Peckett, who apparently reveled in his character as "a very merry and a jesting man" but wound up in trouble for what he thought was a harmless jest.

★★★

The adept Renaissance courtier, like the sophisticated humanist, would know how to pepper his conversation with jest for the pleasure of his companions. There will be much more to say about this in Chapter 5. It is important to note here, however, that the laughter advocated by both humanists and courtiers differed in significant ways from what we see in Platter's account. Platter showed no anxiety about bodily decorum in laughing, unlike Vives or Erasmus. Even though Platter himself was well educated, there is none of the competitive edge found in both courtly and humanist circles, where each strove to be recognized and admired for his (or, at court, sometimes even her) wit. Platter was not averse to laughter that the more fastidious would have seen as excessive. The mummers roused laughter with comic performances, the successful tricksters with hiding or disguise, but this laughter was not about excelling. Laughter that moved the body to near-bursting point was fine—in fact, it was the best.

These points highlight a persistent disjunction between laughter theories and the kind of everyday laughter that Platter shows us. Even the pro-laughter commentators like Thomas Aquinas, who recognized its importance to sociability, did not take this concept further to explore its role in building and sustaining relationships. For Aquinas, pleasantness and fun refresh the mind and enhance the enjoyment of the people one happens to be with. But as the example of Platter shows, the laughter he remembered, the laughter that mattered in the experience of a life, was much more about who he was laughing with than about funny content. It could not well be separated from its particular scenes and participants in relation to each other. Platter's laughter was different from theoretical laughter, and also from the growing body of commercial laughter materials in print. Even when jestbooks drew from real-life laughter, or claimed to do so, they bleached out the relationships while mining for their nuggets of mirth. As modern studies have shown, most real-life laughter responds not to humor but to particular contexts of social interaction and relationship.

The relational core of laughter is clear in Platter, and—despite the very different aim of aggressive self-assertion—it is central to Cellini's laughter also. In derisive laughter one laughs, not just because something or someone is funny, but because of hostile intent, enmity, a negative relationship. We will see in future chapters how both positive and negative laughter worked through relationships to inflect and negotiate power dynamics.

Notes

1 See Natalie Davis's classic *The Return of Martin Guerre* (Cambridge, MA: Harvard University Press, 1983), as well as the 1984 film *Le Retour de Martin Guerre*.
2 Thomas Platter, *Thomas Platter: Ein Lebensbild aus dem Jahrhundert der Reformation*, ed. Horst Kohl, Voigtländers Quellenbücher Bd 21 (Leipzig: R. Voigtländers Verlag, 1912); see also Emmanuel Le Roy Ladurie, *The Beggar and the Professor: A Sixteenth-Century Family Saga*, trans. Arthur Goldhammer (Chicago and London: University of Chicago Press, 1997); on social change and the urge to autobiography, see Anette Völker-Rasor, "'Arbeitsam, obgleich etwas verschlafen . . .'—Die Autobiographie des 16. Jahrhunderts als Ego-Dokument," in *Ego-Dokumente: Annäherung an den Menschen in der Geschichte*, ed. Winfried Schulze (Berlin: Akademie Verlag, 1996), 107–120.
3 Valentin Lötscher, "Introduction," in Felix Platter, *Tagebuch (Lebensbeschreibung) 1536–1567*, ed. Valentin Lötscher (Basel and Stuttgart: Schwabe, 1976), 33.
4 Platter, *Tagebuch*, 58–59.
5 Platter, *Tagebuch*, 78–79.
6 Platter, *Tagebuch*, 82.
7 Platter, *Tagebuch*, 93; 166n146.
8 Platter, *Tagebuch*, 239–40.
9 Johann Dietz, *Master Johann Dietz, Surgeon in the Army of the Great Elector and Barber to the Royal Court*, trans. Bernard Miall (London: George Allen & Unwin, 1923), 46.
10 See Paul Griffiths, *Youth and Authority: Formative Experiences in England, 1560–1640.* (Oxford: Clarendon Press, 1996); also see below, Chapters 4 and 6.
11 Platter, *Tagebuch*, 203–4; I have discussed this and some of his other laughing incidents in "Early Modern Embodiments of Laughter: The Journal of Felix Platter," in *Feelings Materialized: Emotions, Bodies, and Things in Germany, 1500–1950*, ed. Derek Hillard, Heikki Lempa, and Russell A. Spinney (New York: Berghahn Books, 2020), 115–26.
12 Platter, *Tagebuch*, 143.
13 Platter, *Tagebuch*, 154.
14 Platter, *Tagebuch*, 312–13.
15 Pamela Epstein, "Advertising for Love: Matrimonial Advertisements and Public Courtship," in *Doing Emotions History*, ed. Susan J. Matt and Peter N. Stearns (Champaign, IL: University of Illinois Press, 2014), 120–40.
16 Platter, *Tagebuch*, 327.
17 Platter, *Tagebuch*, 328.
18 Platter, *Tagebuch*, 363.
19 Platter, *Tagebuch*, 353–354.
20 Mark Taplin, "Switzerland," in *The Reformation World*, ed. Andrew Pettegree (London and New York: Routledge, 2000), 178.
21 Platter, *Tagebuch*, 190.
22 Platter, *Tagebuch*, 373.
23 Diemuth Königs, "Das Olsberger Kloster Hortus Dei—Ein irdisches Paradies?," http://www.koenigs-media.ch/publi05.htm.

24 Louis Dulieu, *La médecine à Montpellier*, 7 vols. (Avignon: Presses Universelles, 1975), 2: 31, 34, 340, 409.

25 Laurent Joubert, *Treatise on Laughter*, trans. Gregory David de Rocher (Alabama: University of Alabama Press, 1980), 94.

26 Joubert, *Treatise on Laughter*, 11.

27 Joubert, *Treatise on Laughter*, 94.

28 Joubert, *Treatise on Laughter*, 126

29 Joubert, *Treatise on Laughter*, 128.

30 Ambroise Paré, *Oeuvres complètes*, ed. J.-F. Malgaigne, 3 vols. (Paris: J.B Baillière, 1840–1841), 1:76.

31 Ambroise Paré, *The Apologie and Treatise of Ambroise Paré*, ed. Geoffrey Keynes (New York: Dover, 1968), 83.

32 Paré, *Apologie*, 27.

33 Dulieu, *La médecine à Montpellier*, 2:49, 79.

34 Platter, *Tagebuch*, 106.

35 Platter, *Tagebuch*, 416–417.

36 St. Thomas Aquinas, *Summa Theologica*, trans. Fathers of the English Dominican Province, 1947, https://www.ccel.org/ccel/aquinas/summa.SS_Q168_A4.html; See also John Morreall, "Philosophy of Humor," in *The Stanford Encyclopedia of Philosophy* (Winter 2016 Edition), ed. Edward N. Zalta, https://plato.stanford.edu/archives/win2016/entries/humor/.

37 Martin Luther, *D. Martin Luthers Werke. Kritische Gesamtausgabe. Tischreden*, 6 vols. (Weimar: Böhlau, 1912–1921), cited hereafter as WA [Weimarer Ausgabe] TR, 5: 6185, p. 527; 5: 5418, p. 131.

38 WA TR 4: 4956, p. 592.

39 For more discussion of Protestant uses of humor, see Barbara C. Bowen, "A Neglected Renaissance Art of Joking," *Rhetorica: A Journal of the History of Rhetoric* 21, no. 3 (Summer 2003): 137–48, 147–48.

40 My thanks to Jeffrey Watt for this reference; *Registres du Consistoire de Genève au temps de Calvin, 1554 (volume 9)*, ed. Isabella M. Watt, M. Wallace McDonald, and Jeffrey R. Watt (Geneva: Droz, 2016), 30.

41 Peter Burke, *Popular Culture in Early Modern Europe,* 3rd ed. (Farnham, UK, and Burlington, VT: Ashgate, 2009), 289–334; see also Ronald Hutton, *The Rise and Fall of Merry England: The Ritual Year 1400–1700* (Oxford: Oxford University Press, 1994).

42 See Johan Verberckmoes, *Laughter, Jestbooks and Society in the Spanish Netherlands* (Houndmills, Basingstoke and New York: St. Martin's Press, 1999), 83–108.

43 Randall Martin, ed. *Women Writers in Renaissance England: An Annotated Anthology* (Harlow: Pearson, 2010), 215; see also Joy Wiltenburg, "Soundings of Laughter in Early Modern England: Women, Men, and Everyday Uses of Humor," *Early Modern Women: An Interdisciplinary Journal* 10, no. 2 (2016): 22–41.

44 Roger Lowe, *The Diary of Roger Lowe, of Ashton-in-Makerfield, Lancashire, 1663–74*, ed. William L. Sachse (New Haven: Yale University Press, 1938).

45 Quoted in M. A. Screech, *Laughter at the Foot of the Cross* (London: Allen Lane/Penguin, 1997), 216.

46 Erasmus, *On Good Manners for Boys* (*De civilitate morum puerilium libellus*, Basel, 1530), quoted in Verberckmoes, *Laughter, Jestbooks and Society*, 76.

47 Quoted in Verberckmoes, *Laughter, Jestbooks and Society*, 46.

48 Quoted in Verberckmoes, *Laughter, Jestbooks and Society*, 47.

49 Quoted in Verberckmoes, *Laughter, Jestbooks and Society*, 46.

50 Robert Burton, *The Anatomy of Melancholy*, ed. Holbrook Jackson (New York: Vintage Books, 1977), part 1, Democritus to the Reader, p. 71. For a recent discussion highlighting Burton's comedy and positive uses of laughter, see Cassie M. Miura, "Therapeutic Laughter in Robert Burton's The Anatomy of Melancholy," in *Positive Emotions in Early Modern Literature and Culture*, ed. Cora Fox, Bradley J. Irish, Cassie M. Miura,

and Michael C. Schoenfeldt (Manchester, England: Manchester University Press, 2021), 44–59.

51 Burton, *Anatomy of Melancholy*, part 2, sec. 2, mem. 6, subsec. 4, pp. 119–20, 123–24.

52 See, for example, Barbara C. Bowen, ed., *One Hundred Renaissance Jokes: An Anthology* (Birmingham, AL: Summa Publications, 1988).

53 Johannes Rütiner, *Diarium 1529–1539*, ed. Ernst Gerhard Rüsch, 5 vols. (St. Gallen: Vadiana, 1996), I(2): 568, item 887a.

54 See Carla Roth, "Obscene Humour, Gender and Sociability in Sixteenth-Century St. Gallen," *Past & Present* 234 (February 2017): 39–70.

55 Rütiner, *Diarium,* I(2): 446, item 765.

56 Sir Nicholas Le Strange, *"Merry Passages and Jeasts": A Manuscript Jestbook*, ed. H. F. Lippincott (Salzburg: Institut für Englische Sprache und Literatur, 1974).

FIGURE 4.1   Dorothy Osborne, after she became Lady Temple, portrait by Caspar Netscher

Source: © ART Collection/Alamy Stock Photo

4

LAUGHTER, GENDER, AND SEX

Dorothy Osborne

Dorothy Osborne is not famous today, except perhaps among scholars of English literary history. Readers of Virginia Woolf's feminist classic *A Room of One's Own* may remember Osborne in the parade of early women writers whose full potential was never realized. Widely admired in modern times for the vivid prose of her letters, Osborne never published a word during her lifetime. It was fear of ridicule—in Woolf's view a "scarcely sane" shrinking at the prospect of hostile laughter—that restrained her from public exposure of her writing. She could serve as a case study in the fear of laughter, but she also used humor and laughter to her own advantage, playfully recasting gender stereotypes. Was laughter friend or foe to women, or both? Relations between the sexes were a central field of laughter at all times—as shown by the merest glance at the often ribald comedy of the early modern age. Osborne's story offers an entry point to the gender dynamics of laughter.

As the daughter of a privileged family, Dorothy Osborne received a private education that enabled her to develop her distinctive writing style. Born in 1627, she lived through the troubled times of the English Civil War and Interregnum. She married her longtime sweetheart and correspondent, Sir William Temple, and was later actively engaged in his political and diplomatic career. Her letters, written during the last two years of their seven-year courtship from 1647 to 1654, owe their drama to more private matters.

Fear of Laughter

When she heard that the Duchess of Newcastle had published a book in 1653, Osborne's response was anything but admiring: "Sure the poor woman is a little distracted [crazy], she could never be so ridiculous else as to venture at writing books and in verse too. If I should not sleep this fortnight I should not come to that."[1] Margaret Cavendish, Duchess of Newcastle, was not deterred by fear of

DOI: 10.4324/9781003247517-5

laughter. She had her own circle of admirers, as well as a supportive husband, and her urge to write and even publish was powerful: "that little wit I have, it delights me to scribble it out, and disperse it about."[2] Her ambitious books in both poetry and prose tackled a wide range of subjects, gaining her praise, fame, and, of course, ridicule. Cavendish knew, and lamented, that she had not received the systematic or scientific education that was available only to men—but she persisted nevertheless. She also knew the risk of ridicule, although her aristocratic status shielded her from much of it.

Osborne's reaction prompted Woolf to declare that Osborne "dreaded with a shrinking that was scarcely sane the ridicule of the world."[3] The criticism of the Duchess's publication was an offhand remark, but a revealing one. In much more important personal affairs, Osborne also took avoidance of ridicule as a decisive guide. It even appeared at one point that the fear of looking foolish would determine the whole course of her life, by preventing her marriage with William Temple. The match was opposed by her family as financially impractical. Although she refused other matches that her family preferred, Dorothy was not prepared to risk an imprudent marriage. She wrote to Temple at a low point in their hopes:

> [I] can be satisfied within as narrow a compass as that of any person living of my rank. But I confess that I have an humor that will not suffer me to expose myself to people's scorn. The name of love is grown so contemptible by the folly of such as have falsely pretended to it, and so many giddy people have married upon that score and repented so shamefully afterwards, that nobody can do anything that tends towards it without being esteemed a ridiculous person.[4]

As she took care to explain, it was not fear of poverty that deterred her, but fear of derision.

The fear of laughter has its own name—gelotophobia, now often classed as a form of social phobia, that is, as a problem of the individual. But this type of fear also varies with social context, heightened in milieus where ridicule is considered especially damaging to reputation. A recent cross-cultural study found that while gelotophobia could be found anywhere, some countries had much higher levels of it than others.[5] Sensitivity to potentially harmful laughter has varied historically as well. The courtly society of France in the seventeenth and eighteenth centuries became famous for dangerous ridicule (more on that in Chapter 5). But this horror of ridicule was a product of historical development. As Sara Beam has shown in her study of French theater, high officials and even the king were not necessarily offended at the earthy humor of sixteenth-century farces. Full of jokes about sex and excrement, the farces skewered the pomposity of authority figures— usually with impunity unless they targeted a specific individual. By the seventeenth century, elites came to see such unbuttoned comedy as dragging them down to the low level of the masses.[6] Again, in the world of Felix Platter and in the jesting of Johannes Rütiner (Chapter 3), the best laughter arose when the butt of the joke was able to share in the laugh. Obviously, not all Renaissance laughter was benign—we have only to recall Cellini and the satirical writing of humanists. But the idea that being laughed at is disastrous, rather than mildly embarrassing or even amusing, is hardly universal.

Among the English gentry of Osborne's time, women appear to have been especially attuned to the harm of being laughed at. Although Osborne's fear appeared pathological to Woolf, she was not alone. Her contemporary Anne Halkett was devastated when jilted by her lover, but "nothing troubled me more than my mother's laughing at me, and perhaps so did others."[7] This laughter had an "I told you so" quality, since Halkett, like Osborne, had fallen in love against the wishes of her family. The daring assertion of a personal choice of mate—far from an accepted right among women of their class—exposed these women to derision if anything went wrong, either before or after marriage. Males, too, were expected to adhere to their families' wishes, but with somewhat more respect for their inclinations. Both sexes had more freedom of choice when there was less property involved—a point on the bright side of being poorer. Perhaps those lower in the social scale were less hampered by laughter at their choices.

Like Osborne, Halkett was troubled by fear of laughter in other areas of her life as well. During a temporary estrangement from her best friend, she was dissuaded from seeking an explanation by a suggestion that she would be laughed at. A troublemaking clergyman, who had caused their quarrel in the first place, convinced her that speaking about it to her friend would be useless and humiliating. As she later told her friend, the man said "that you would but laugh at me, and 'twould expose me to your scorn."[8]

Lucy Hutchinson had a smoother courtship than Osborne and Halkett, but she still had worries about being laughed at. Also a gentlewoman, but with Puritan rather than Royalist loyalties, she was married at eighteen to John Hutchinson, later a prominent figure on the revolutionary side. Lucy, an intellectual and author as well as the mother of nine children, wrote a memoir of her husband after his death. She praised him for many fine qualities, among them his ability to defend her against ridicule. While they were courting, other women made fun of Lucy's clothes and constant studying. In fact, their derision was aimed at thwarting the match, as they "with witty spite represented all her faults to him, which chiefly terminated in the negligence of her dress, and habit, and all womanish ornaments, giving herself wholly up to study and writing." But John stood up for her:

> Mr. Hutchinson, who had a very pleasant and sharp wit, retorted all their malice, with such just reproofs of their idleness and vanity, as made them hate her, who without affecting it, had so engaged such a person in her protection, as they with all their arts could not catch.[9]

This memory remained fresh decades later, his power to defend her against ridicule a heroic feature in a suitor.

As a reminder that women in other social settings did not necessarily share such worries about laughter, one can contrast these English gentry with the seventeenth-century Jewish merchant Glickl of Hamburg. In her memoir laughter was largely harmless, even when directed against herself. She was angry when her husband laughed at her fear of death from seasickness, but she quickly recovered and recounted the episode with good humor. She braved the laughter of her whole family to treat her ailing baby with medlars, based on her craving for the fruit during pregnancy.[10] Gelotophobia had no place in her story.

Turning Laughter to Use

Osborne's correspondence with William Temple, over years of uncertainty about their future together, shows a less angst-filled side of her relationship to laughter as well. Especially with regard to the alternative suitors that her family kept bringing forward, Osborne wrote in a comic vein. Her relationship with Temple, though carried on at a distance, enabled them to joke together. In spite of the serious obstacles to their relationship—embodied in the parade of family-approved suitors— Osborne found her wooers ridiculous, and she invited Temple to join in implied laughter at their absurdities. At the same time, her ridicule, shared with an intimate male partner, punctured a range of pretensions about masculine superiority.

It is hard to say which of the rejected suitors comes off as most laughable in Osborne's portrayals. In terms of social status, they were potentially intimidating figures, full of masculine authority and worldly power. But Osborne laid a double claim to power over them, first by repulsing their offers and then by joking about them in her letters to Temple. She called them "my servants," in line with the conventional pose taken by suitors in proposing marriage to a lady—a very temporary position of mock subordination, usually quickly reversed upon marriage. In 1653 she was courted by the sheriff of a neighboring county.[11] Osborne mocked his pretense of romance as well as his authoritative position:

> What has kept him from marrying all this while, or how the humor comes so furiously upon him now, I know not, but if he may be believed, he is resolved to be a most Romance Squire and go in quest of some enchanted Damsel, whom if he likes, as to her person (for fortune is a thing below him and we do not read in history that any knight, or squire, was ever so discourteous as to inquire what portions [fortunes] their Ladies had) then he comes with the Power of the County to demand her.[12]

Osborne was also courted by a much older admirer, Sir Justinian Isham, whom she playfully dubbed "the Emperor Justinian." A widower with grown daughters, Isham was renewing a suit that had failed earlier: "Would you think it, that I have an Ambassador from the Emperor Justinian, that comes to renew the Treaty in Earnest?" Osborne facetiously offered Temple the hand of one of her four daughters, should she become Isham's wife. As Isham had asked whether she was free to marry, she playfully offered to refer him to Temple for permission, "and when he can bring me a Certificate under your hand, that you think him a fit husband to me, 'tis very likely I may have him."[13] She was especially amused by Justinian's pompous letter-writing style, as she commented in another letter:

> I never had I think but one letter from Sir Justinian but 'twas worth twenty of anybody's else to make me sport, it was the most sublime nonsense that in my life I ever read, and yet I believe he descended as low as he could to come near my weak understanding.[14]

Far from intimidated by Isham's vaunted Latin learning—a largely masculine attainment—she found his writing ridiculous and went on to criticize other stuffed shirts:

> All letters methinks should be free and easy as one's discourse, not studied, as an oration, nor made up of hard words like a charm [a magic spell]. 'Tis an admirable [surprising] thing to see how some people will labor to find out terms that may obscure a plain sense, like a gentleman I knew, who would never say the weather grew cold, but that winter began to salute us. I have no patience for such coxcombs.[15]

And Sir Justinian was perhaps the worst coxcomb (pretentious fool) of the lot, despite his grand estate and reputed wisdom: "the vainest, impertinent, self-conceited, learned coxcomb that ever yet I saw."[16]

Osborne's refusal of Isham's suit caused family conflict, particularly with her brother Henry. An adherent of the old-school view that passionate love would only cause problems in a marriage, he thought the widower a perfectly good prospect. Osborne herself wanted to laugh it all off, but for her brother it was a serious matter:

> I talked merrily on it till I saw my B[rother] put on his sober face and could hardly then believe he was in earnest. It seems he was, for when I had spoke freely my meaning, it wrought so much with him as to fetch up all that lay upon his stomach, all the people that I have ever in my life refused were brought again upon the stage, like Richard the 3rd ghosts to reproach me withall.[17]

This really was serious business; as we know, the fear of ridicule over an imprudent marriage almost scared Osborne away from marrying her chosen partner. Laughter and play offered her a way to cope with a difficult situation, but at the same time she was implicitly skewering her society's assumptions about male superiority and control over women. Her brother's attempt to assert male authority became a comic scene of melodramatic theater. The overbearing suitors, with all their imposing titles, looked like buffoons in her letters. Her insight into the formidable power of ridicule may have come partly from what she could do with it herself.

Of course, the quality of her relationship with Temple created this safe space for jest. She was ready to joke with him too about the conventional expectations of wifely subordination, and about her own fitness for the role. Her long resistance to family pressure over her marriage, though in Temple's favor, was also an assertion of her own will. Several months before their marriage, she wrote:

> I make it a case of conscience to discover my faults to you as fast as I know them that you may consider what you have to do. My aunt told me no longer ago than yesterday that I was the most willful woman that ever she knew and had an obstinacy of spirit nothing could overcome. Take heed, you see I give you fair warning.[18]

Obviously, she knew Temple would not be intimidated by the prospect of a willful wife.

Negotiating Gender

Dorothy Osborne's story takes us only a short way into the vast territory of gender and laughter, but it touches on a range of points for further exploration, both in her own setting of seventeenth-century England and more broadly. Her laughter took place in the intimate context of her loving relation to a sympathetic male partner; her fear of ridicule occurred in the context of a public concept of female decorum. Prevailing concepts of binary gender difference sought to constrain roles and behavior according to gender-defined categories. The setting of intimate relationships, particularly in courtship and marriage, offers evidence of how laughter and humor could serve to renegotiate the terms of broader gender rules. Conversely, the use of ridicule to enforce gender norms—evident in public culture and applied to both men and women in different ways—can be followed into everyday encounters that shed more light on its workings. Both public and private converged in positioning gender and sexual relations as the focus of laughter. But the laughter dynamics worked very differently in different settings, as public comedy could become private injury, or somber public directives turn to fodder for intimate ridicule. Laughter was linked with sex in a range of ways, both intimate and public. This association took many forms, from the prevalence of sex in popular humor, to the physical parallels between the involuntary spasms of laughter and those of sex, to the actual laughter of sexual prelude or climax, and back to the strictures on laughter, especially for women, as a cause of potential sexual suspicion.

To explore these issues we look first at uses of laughter in some other intimate contexts. Then we turn to comic views of marital relations and their reflection in real-life shaming rituals directed at people who failed to conform. This broad ground of gender-based mockery, which could be seriously hurtful, leads into the complex interplay between the public culture of sex/gender laughter and the everyday encounters of men and women. Matters that were culturally comic— particularly illicit sex—were also dangerous ground. For women, laughter itself could come to seem sexually risky, at least to moralists.

Like Osborne, Maria Audley (Thynne) entered a daring marriage, show- ing herself to be another willful young woman. Her wedding with Thomas Thynne was approved by her family but strongly opposed by his. The Thynnes' opposition went so far as litigation in an attempt to force an annulment, with lasting bad feeling on all sides. Between Thomas and Maria, however, there were jesting relations that come through strongly in Maria Thynne's letters. She hinted playfully at their sexual relations, while also poking fun at conventional gender stereotypes. While her husband was in London as a Member of Parlia- ment, Maria took on substantial management responsibilities at their country estate in Wiltshire. Early in their correspondence she complained of lacking such authority—being left "like an innocent fool"—probably partly because of the ongoing litigation over their marriage. Later on she could playfully push for more latitude.

Thomas's "kind wanton letters" to his wife have not survived, but Maria responded in the same vein:

> My best beloved Thomken, and my best little Sirrah, know that I have not, nor will not forget how you made my modest blood flush up into my bash- ful cheek at your first letter, thou threatened sound payment, and I sound repayment, so as when we meet, there will be pay, and repay, which will pass and repass, allgiges vltes fregnan tolles, thou knowest my mind, though thou dost not understand me.[19]

The fractured imitation of Latin here implies a sexual pun with hints about ris- ing up—so Thomas would "know her mind" even though the language is not comprehensible.

In addition to sexual joking, there were jests that played with conventional ideas about women. About 1610 she wrote:

> My best Thomken I know thou wilt say (receiving two letters in a day from me) that I have tried the virtue of aspen leaves under my tongue, which makes me prattle so much, but consider that all is business, for of my own natural disposition I assure thee there is not a more silent woman living than myself.[20]

Aspen leaves, with their continual murmuring in the breeze, were constantly com- pared with the tongues of women in popular jokes, stories, and sayings. An aspen leaf placed beneath the tongue of a dumb woman would make her speak—but nothing could shut her up. Maria joked about this proverbial female failing, and also about the supposed virtue of silence, which was so often recommended to women. The notion of her being naturally silent is ridiculous, given the frank assertiveness of her letters. Aware of the stereotypes, she could turn them into something laughable.

She made fun, too, of conventions about the relations of husband and wife. In an earlier letter, she joked about Thomas's possible resistance to her requests, suggesting that he "ask all the husbands in London, or ask the question in the Lower House, what requests they grant their wives, and then good husband think upon your fool at home as there is cause."[21] She facetiously called herself a fool, but she clearly thought herself anything but.[22] As in her demands for respect and responsibility, she relied on both her wit and her relationship with Thomas. The letters highlight her ability to make Thomas smile or laugh in the reading. The humor both depended on and furthered their intimacy, even as she used it to negotiate fuller scope for her own action.

These women were using laughter in their relationships of courtship or marriage to renegotiate the terms of gender norms. Not directly attacking subordination, they played with it and created room to assert themselves. One can also find cases in close relationships where, even in seemingly sexist joking, the playfulness acknowledged some real areas of female power. Going back to the sixteenth century, the case of Martin Luther and his wife is an instructive one. The famous reformer, in addition to all his voluminous writings, loved to talk and joke. His followers recorded a lot of his "Table Talk" conversation at home, in the company of students as well as boarders, visitors, and family. He and his wife, the former nun Katherina von Bora, enjoyed a long and loving relationship, full of teasing and jest on his part. Luther believed deeply in male superiority as God's plan, and of course this view was reinforced by the surrounding culture. He drew plenty of negative stereotypes about women into his conversation. But reading these completely at face value can create a misleading impression.[23]

To take one well-known example, there is Luther's widely quoted comment linking women's broad buttocks with a lack of intellect:

> Men have broad chests and narrow hips; therefore they have wisdom. Women have narrow chests and broad hips. Women ought to be domestic; the creation reveals it, for they have broad backsides and hips, so that they should sit still.[24]

He was serious about the idea that women's place is in the home, yet he was also teasing his wife. A fuller account of this same anecdote comes from a different recorder of Luther's "Table Talk." This version restores the jesting scenario, as well as the characteristic bit of bathroom humor that gives the joke more bite:

> Doctor Martin Luther laughed at his Ketha, who wanted to be clever, and said, "God created man with a broad chest, not broad hips, so that in that

part of him he can be wise; but that part out of which filth comes is small. In a woman, this is reversed. That is why she has much filth and little wisdom."

Again, he laughed at his Ketha on account of her chattering and talkativeness. He asked whether she had prayed the Our Father before she preached so many words. "But women," he said, "don't pray before they start to preach, for otherwise they would stop preaching and leave it alone; or, if God overheard them, He would forbid them to preach."[25]

Of course, there is some serious misogyny in these jests. Luther really did think women should not take part in intellectual discussions, as Käthe did when she "wanted to be clever." It was a matter for laughter and for reference to women's talkativeness, as in the legend of the aspen leaves. But the part about the broad bottoms was a bit of scatological silliness. And Käthe was still talking, even though she knew his opinion; she was not intimidated by his teasing. She even tossed in the occasional jest herself, such as when she joked that he ought to charge those at the table for all the words of wisdom he was giving away for free.[26] (Perhaps she thought it was Martin who was talking too much!)

Luther's joking with his wife appears in his letters as well as the snippets of conversation recorded by his followers. Letters to her are spiced with drollery, heaping Käthe with titles like lord, mistress, and empress. The Luthers hosted a substantial household, full of student boarders and visiting clergy, as well as their own children. Luther himself, of course, was occupied with theology; it was Käthe Luther who ran the place. When Luther joked about how she was the boss, jest enabled him to play with an element of truth—because his wife kept their operation running with business activities from provisioning the boarders to brewing beer. Certainly he believed male dominance was the order of nature, but the space of play could provide means of averting conflict, negotiating personal boundaries and distribution of power. At the same time, as Susan Karant-Nunn has argued, the jests helped bolster Martin's masculine identity as husband and master while acknowledging Katharina's responsible role and initiative.[27]

Among the family and friends of the seventeenth-century English gentleman Sir Nicholas Le Strange, misogynistic stereotypes abounded, yet women were active participants in jesting along with men. They were not shy about telling bawdy jokes, either. In fact, Nicholas's mother, Dame Alice, was the funniest source in his manuscript jest collection, credited with 43 jests; her husband was runner-up, with 38.[28] Le Strange does not usually describe the setting in which each joke was told, but some of them give a clue, as in this quip:

> The Lady Hobart every one being set at the table, and no body Blessing it, but gazing one upon another, in expectation who should be Chaplain: well, says my Lady, I think I must say as one did in the like Case, God be thanked, Nobody will say Grace.[29]

Le Strange drew heavily on family for his collection, but we should not imagine a modern family table here. Early modern households, especially those of the upper classes, housed non-relatives from servants to boarders, while households more broadly were typically business enterprises where both family members and employees worked. Lady Hobart was likely talking (and joking) not just to her intimate relatives, but to a larger group.

To a modern reader, many of the women's jests, like the men's, seem to reinforce gender stereotypes, especially those about the loose sexual behavior of lower-class women. For instance, Dame Alice told a joke about an illiterate servant: when asked by her new mistress (Dame Alice's grandmother) for a written reference from her last place,

> O Mistress says she, I have one of those above in my Box; and up she runs, and for her Testimonial, brings down a very fair and formal warrant, signifying that she had lately had a Bastard, and was to be passed from Constable to Constable, to such a place.[30]

As Pamela Brown has remarked, the fate of the servant goes unmentioned, but her illiteracy and sexual transgression together made her laughable to the gentry for years (if she was not invented for her comic value).[31] Other standard failings of women appeared also. Lady Spring told the old chestnut about a doctor who cured a mute woman but then had no remedy for her constant chattering: "A woman that hath lost her speech, thou see'st may be recovered; but if once her tongue sets a running, all the Devils in Hell cannot make it lie still."[32] Like Maria Thynne, Lady Spring was not cowed by the idea that women talk too much. The jesting women here were not defying gender stereotypes, but rather shared in a culture of sociability that recognized what Brown has called their "jesting rights."

Battle for the Pants

Some intimate relationships, between men and women who loved each other, were a protected space for laughter. Obviously, many couples were not so fortunate. Marital discord was a recognized social problem, sometimes adjudicated by courts in extreme cases of abuse or unauthorized separation. In some areas courts intervened to discipline "wastrel" husbands or rebellious wives. Adultery was increasingly criminalized in the sixteenth and seventeenth centuries, particularly in Protestant areas.[33] In public culture, however, and in the world of laughter commodities, both marital discord and adultery were comic.

Relations between the sexes were a perennial subject of jest. Marital quarreling was especially funny—a convention that has persisted into modern times in the stock images of women chasing their husbands with the housewifely weapons of frying pan or rolling pin. This modern stereotype is always comic, slapstick violence, like the falling pianos of cartoons—even though real kitchen implements would be nothing to laugh at, especially a cast-iron pan! The humor here depends on reversal of the expected gender hierarchy, and also on the idea that angry women are not really dangerous (unlike angry men). Domineering wives were comic material in the early modern period, but the opposite scenario of a husband beating his wife also received comic treatment, in jokes, songs, and images that are more foreign to modern senses of humor. It was in the seventeenth century that humor shifted toward seeing husband-beating rather than wife-beating as funny, at least in England. Enjoyment of an unruly wife's comeuppance is familiar to audiences of Shakespeare's *Taming of the Shrew*. That taming is tame compared with the "merry jest" of the Wife Lapped in Morel's Skin, in which the husband beats his rebellious wife and then wraps her in a salted horse's skin to increase the pain.[34] Violent shrew-tamings appeared in popular literature elsewhere, notably in Germany, especially in the sixteenth century.

Comic scenes of shrew-taming had their real-life counterparts. Husbands' actual beating of their wives was (usually) not considered funny. But popular shaming rituals aimed ridicule at women who could be publicly identified as "shrews" and at the husbands who failed to keep them in line. In England, the "skimmington" or "riding" targeted couples in which the wife was accused of dominating her husband or committing adultery. Either form of wifely misbehavior denoted a misgoverned household. The husband (or a surrogate) might be made to ride backwards on an ass, or the wife subjected to anti-shrew measures like ducking in water. Contemporaries saw these as occasions of communal fun,

> an old country ceremony used in merriment . . . whereby not only the woman which had offended might be shunned for her misdemeanor towards her husband, but other women also . . . might be admonished.[35]

The crowd that came to ridicule John Day of Ditcheat, Somerset in 1653 was there to "make merry with Skimmington" as they called him cuckold and threatened to duck his wife.[36] As Susan Amussen and David Underdown have pointed out, those targeted did not find these events funny; some even moved to get away from the community where they had been ridiculed.

Laughter over marital discord could intrude into the usually serious realms of real-life violence and litigation. Johann Dietz, a Prussian barber-surgeon, wrote his memoir in the early eighteenth century. In the course of his struggles to set up as a barber in Halle, he married Elizabeth Schober, a barber's widow, but regretted it ever after. Their conflict began over money and became a matter of constant quarrels. He recounts at length an incident that began with jest and ended in violent "shrew-taming" accompanied by laughter. He had brought a fox pelt back from the Leipzig fair:

> I wanted to beat the moth out of it in the house. The students amused themselves for a while, and laid hold of the skin; and so did my wife. I had a

thin switch for beating it, and said, jestingly: "I shall go fishing in my lord's fishpond," and gave each of them a little tap on the hand, and I did the same to my wife. This annoyed her, and she flew into a rage with me, and seized the stick, which she broke in pieces, and beat me around the head with the broken pieces. I asked her: "Are you beating me in earnest?" "Yes, I am, I am," said she; "Godless creature that you are, why did you beat me?" As she would not cease beating me I took the skin and threw it over her, and took another stick in my hand and gave the skin a thorough beating on her.—This caused a great deal of laughter, which infuriated her even more. She at once ran off to see her friends, and engaged an advocate and laid an accusation against me before the Consistorium, and was going to get a divorce and an extremely handsome alimony. But nothing came of it all.[37]

The "little tap," he tells us, was done in jest, the wife's anger both unreasonable and godless. Her actions against him were a sin and, he carefully confirms, not a joke (although evidently he could not tell this from the blows themselves). The beating through the fox skin, by contrast, was thorough. The scene closely parallels the "Morels skin" comedy, and also, closer to home, the German "Nine Skins of a Shrew" popularized by Hans Sachs in the sixteenth century. Here the husband beats through eight different animal skins, each representing a different bad quality of the wife, before he reaches the human skin and gains a docile spouse. The laughter among the onlookers at the Dietz house was certainly heightened, if not inspired, by the comic treatments of wife-beating in the laughter market.[38]

The discord between the Dietzes was not over, however, and neither was the accompanying laughter. Annoyed at his wife for staying with her relatives until late at night, he beat her in the dark and tried to pretend he hadn't done it. She brought charges against him in court, with this result: "Both of us looked fools. For as the *species facti* was read out there was an outburst of laughter as though the court were fit to split its sides." Their advocates contested the case vigorously, "But when we had to leave the court the two lawyers were the best friends in the world, and were laughing over the whole affair, and at their excellent acting."[39] The court ordered the wife to stay obediently at home, while admonishing the husband to refrain from hasty chastisement.[40]

At length Elizabeth Dietz succeeded in getting a legal separation with alimony. But it only lasted 18 weeks before they got back together. Johann could not rest and would go by her lodgings daily, "Or I used to see her, and go into the house and ask after her; so that I believe it became the subject of jest. And it was the same with her, as she told me later!"[41] Both their discord and their reconciliation became fodder for the laughter of others.

Laughing at Cuckolds

The laughable female figure of the shrew was paralleled by the cuckold, so dear to comic writers of the seventeenth century. Calling a man a cuckold was really about the sexual behavior of his wife, but it was he who became the butt of ridicule. Like the shrew, the adulterous wife dramatized her husband's failure in his masculine responsibility to govern his household. Tales of adultery had been comic since the Middle Ages, with stories full of lecherous clergy and wives who pulled the wool over their husbands' eyes, from the French *fabliaux* to Boccaccio and Chaucer. These same themes, and sometimes the same stories, were repeated in popular printed jestbooks in the sixteenth and seventeenth centuries. The hapless figure of the deceived husband was a staple in street ballads, drama, and comic literature.

Both sexes used the charge of cuckoldry to ridicule their neighbors, in cases that resulted in lawsuits for defamation, as the injured parties, or sometimes their wives, sought to defend their reputations. In Oxfordshire in 1617, William Combe publicly taunted John Langley by dancing before him on Greenham Common and saying "with a tuning voice, Cuckold, Cuckold."[42] Even without explicit mention of the word, the implication was often clear, especially when people referred to the cuckold's proverbial affliction of horns on the head. Jokes about the great size of a man's head held the same innuendo. In a London case from 1639, for instance, Mary Okeham jeered at a man of higher status—labeled with the honorific "Mr." Bushwell—as she "bid him make his door bigger or wider for his horns to come in at and asked him how he could turn him self in his bed for his horns."[43]

The makers of libels—typically verses or songs that lampooned the sexual behavior of particular people—usually hoped for "merriment," but they were clearly aware of the aggressive character of their targeting of sexual failings (see Chapter 1). Other cases of defamation reveal a broader field of sexual jesting, in which defendants might feel they were participating in lighthearted sociability. After all, cuckoldry and illicit sex were widely laughed about. But of course, while sexual behavior was a perennial theme of jokes and comedy, it was also the prime territory of insult. Sexual jesting was pervasive but could also be dangerous. While the intention of jest was sometimes put forward in excuse, the claim that all was in fun did not necessarily settle the matter. Laughter was too close to mockery and could itself be cited as evidence of harm, as in the case of John Nicholas's wife and daughters in 1602. Witness testimony asserted that sexual slander had so affected their reputations that "neither she nor her daughters [could] come in any company but they [were] laughed and jested at."[44]

The case of Jane Jollie of Wigan in 1613 is an ambiguous one: did she knowingly slander her neighbors, or was it all in fun? She told a funny story, echoing the plot of medieval comic tales of adultery. Two boon companions went regularly at night "to game and make merry." John told Richard where he left the key to his house so that he could slip back late at night without disturbing anyone. One night, while John was out carousing, Richard let himself into the house and had sex with John's wife. She "did not know or would not know him from her own husband but said I pray god it be our John."[45] This punch line might have been funny in an anonymous joke, but the men were her neighbors John Leigh and Richard Ashton. Ashton, the supposed adulterer, and John's wife, Katherine Leigh, filed suit.

Grace Belcher was joking when the talk turned to illicit sex among a group of women at a christening party in 1633. They were "discoursing merrily together of new married women and of singlewomen . . . unlawfully begotten with child" in

Chipping Norton. When someone mentioned a maid in town with an illegitimate child without naming her, Belcher said to Joan Peesley, "so it was said of you, Joan." Witnesses testified that the words were not seriously intended to harm Peesley's reputation, but Peesley filed suit to clear herself after the merry remark.[46] Similarly, Robert Strudwicke of Suffolk sued a woman in 1636 for "jesting and laughing" that he had gotten his servant maid pregnant.[47]

Edward Peckett, a butcher of North Yorkshire, felt so innocent about his joke that, after being named in a formal complaint in 1687, he repeated it to others to prove its harmlessness, as in, "All I said was. . . ." But the repetition became yet another count against him, a renewal of the offense. The trouble started in a scene of male sociability and jest over drink, a common space for both mirth and conflict. The men, including Edward and his cousin Thomas Peckett, began to joke about exchanging wives. One quipped that Thomas Peckett's wife, Dorothy, was worth extra, "near profit," because of pregnancy. "What! has Billy Elwood gotten her with child?" cried Edward. These were the words that sparked a long-running defamation case. It was Dorothy Peckett, Thomas's wife, who brought suit to clear her reputation, alleging that Edward's words had led to abuse and discord in her marriage. By Edward's account, Thomas had earlier claimed Elwood was sleeping with his wife, and the joke merely twitted Thomas for his unreasonable jealousy, since everyone else considered Dorothy to be chastely respectable. The words were said "merrily and jestingly & not otherwise," and witnesses testified that Edward was known to be "a very merry and a jesting man." Nevertheless, Peckett v. Peckett went on for months, with charges, rebuttals, and failed mediation. Several witnesses testified that they took Peckett's words as a jest and no one in the community (except Thomas) seriously suspected Dorothy of adultery. Edward strongly denied any harmful intent, complaining of "his trouble that there should be so much ado about words that were neither meant ill nor spoke ill." By most accounts it was Thomas's bad humor that spoiled the joke. But Dorothy's legal recourse was against the jester and not her husband.[48]

Male sociability over drink was a common scene where jests went awry (although, as we have seen, it could also happen among women gathered at a christening). In an Oxfordshire case in 1589, Thomas Collins, among a convivial group that included James Warcopp, was offered six pots of ale if he could get to Warcopp's house and have sex with his wife while they waited. On returning he said he had done it, but the words were spoken "merrily and in jest sort." Witnesses thought no serious discredit was meant to Warcopp's wife, and the parties had been reconciled, but the case came to court nevertheless.[49]

Bernard Capp cites a number of other sex jokes that crossed the line into litigation in early modern England. In 1636 in Leicestershire, Edmund Petty put his hand on Elizabeth Lee's stomach and announced that she was pregnant. He had witnesses who agreed with his claim that it was all a joke, but the unmarried Lee took the case to court.[50] In 1615 Dorothy Hemmynge was "merrily disposed" and listed eighteen local cuckolds while in company at an inn. This too was treated seriously in court.[51] The comic aura surrounding sex drew both men and women into risky jesting.

Unfunny Laughter?

Another frequent theme of comic sexual territory in public culture was rape— although early modern laughers would likely not have called it that, because the usual premise of such jokes was that women really wanted sex and their resistance was false. Like the comedy of the skillet-wielding wife, this theme has persisted in humor, so perhaps will not be foreign to current readers, though it may be repugnant. The manuscript jestbook of Le Strange gives a representative example, told by his relative Ned Gurney. A wench complained of rape, but the man insisted she had consented and "took up her Smock [undergarment] very willingly; O Lord Sir, says she, If I had not done so, he kept such a Wimbling, as he had bored a great hole in my smock presently."[52] Printed ballads and jestbooks had many such jokes, and one can find a similar view in records of actual encounters. Bernard Capp cites the case of Mary Salisbury in Leicestershire, who told the church court that she had escaped a would-be rapist by hitting him and running away; "her male auditors treated the incident as a jest."[53] Simon Dickie has noted that comic views of rape continued to appear in both popular print and Old Bailey court cases into the eighteenth century.[54]

The line between sexual play and jest was a contested one. In the case of Joan Tull and John Baylie in Oxfordshire in 1610, Baylie approached Tull in a "merry and sporting" manner, with sexual aspersions on her husband and an offer to do better:

> he said unto her I can beget a boy but Tull can beget nothing but squirt tailed wenches, and then laying his hand over his breeches he said, here it is that will do it in less space than an hour.

He was rebuffed, but continued taunting her. By the time the case came to trial more than a year later, common report had Baylie offering "violence" to Joan Tull and attempting to "abuse [her] in unseemly manner." Clearly it was no longer a matter for laughter—but we do not know whether anyone other than Baylie found it funny in the first place.[55]

In another case in Huntingdonshire in 1575, a man accused of attempted rape used laughter to discredit the claim, rather differently from the standard joke. Here the girl supposedly laughed, not in sexual enjoyment but when discovered in an attempted theft. William Snasedale was accused of defamation for saying that John Hyde had attempted to rape his servant maid. According to Snasedale's testimony, reporting what his maid had told him, Hyde had seized the girl and tried to rape her, but let her go when she screamed, then accused her of robbing his traps. Snasedale added that Hyde had made similar rape attempts against two other local maids. Hyde had a different version of the events, however: according to him, he had seen the girl stooping over one of his traps and accused her of theft, whereupon she ran off laughing. "It is no laughing matter," he told her, and threatened to deliver her to the constable, whereupon she cried out. Snasedale was ordered to confess himself in the wrong, since the bishop's court found him unable to prove his case. To modern eyes, Snasedale's may seem the more likely story. Why would the maid, sent out to milk the cows, have been tampering with Hyde's traps? Even if she had invented the attempted rape to counter accusations of theft, it seems unlikely that her master would concoct a tale of two other victims. In any case, the report of laughter served to undermine the girl's story, not only by denying her version, but also by portraying her as light and frivolous.[56] The higher status of Hyde (a prominent family name among the gentry) likely played a role as well.

All the hilarity over sex and gender suggests the complex relationship between laughter and sex. Failures to meet societal expectations of sex and gender were the bread-and-butter of comedy: cuckoldry, illicit sex, impotence, marital strife, rape—all could be deeply shaming in real life yet were readily and persistently turned into joke. This means, of course, that people laughed about things that were actually serious, and that the boundaries between jest and earnest could be tricky to discern and police. At the same time, the physicality of laughter, as a potentially uncontrolled eruption, linked it to concerns about bodies and their disorderly drives.

Gender norms about laughter, especially rules restricting female laughter, sometimes linked laughter with sex by assuming that laughing women were likely to be sexually loose. The cover image of this book, for example, depicts a painting by the Flemish artist Jan Massys of a "merry company" in which one woman appears laughing with an open mouth. The other figures in the picture show that the scene is set in a high-class brothel. The attractive women in the foreground entertain men, while behind them appears the laugher, along with a crone-like procuress. In contrast to modern stereotypes, the old woman was a proverbial source of illicit sexual knowledge and promoter of sexual sin. Here her devilish grin serves as a well-recognized sign of her immorality. In the distance, in the doorway, another loose woman encounters another customer.[57]

There was also an association between laughter and the sexual act itself. The physical effects of laughter, with its rhythmic vocalizations, suffusion of blood to the face, and seeming loss of rational control—as described, for instance, in Laurent Joubert's sixteenth-century treatise on laughter—were reminiscent of the effects of orgasm. The association was reflected in double meanings like that of the German *scherzen*, which could mean either joke or sex.[58] John Bulwer drew a parallel between laughter and sexual arousal in his 1649 work on the body and mind: laughter affected the whole body,

> So that the Muscles of the Face are filled with Spirits after the same manner as a certain member directly opposite unto it which importunately

sometimes looks us in the Face, which being filled with Spirits grows stiff and is extended.[59]

Laughter overheard between women and men might suggest a sexual relationship between them. Conversely, intimate relations were assumed to come with a freedom to laugh together. In some settings laughter could suggest sexual intercourse itself. The laugh was a frequent euphemism for sex in German songs: when "the maiden began to laugh," everyone knew what it meant. The woman's laugh here suggested her enjoyment of orgasm. A reported laugh sparked a defamation suit against Joane Gregory in London in 1628, when she claimed that Isabell Smalridge "did suffer one Henry Hackell to dip in her Tail up to the elbow in Whitefriars Lane whilst she did consent thereunto and did laugh or cry aloud hah hah hah."[60] Similarly, in a defamation case from Chester in which Rebecca Davies was said to have had sex in the fields with Mr. Lewis, they were described as laughing together.[61] The court declared this a malicious slander, and Mary Jones had to make a formal apology. Laughter was reported in adultery cases too—particularly the laughter of women, either at their husbands or with men other than their husbands. Even if not during the actual act, the laughter made them sexually suspect and could strengthen a case against them.[62]

A remarkable court case from the fifteenth century links jest with sexual arousal, and also shows a level of frankness that was increasingly curtailed in the following centuries by movements toward religious and moral reform. In the church court of York in 1432, the question at issue was whether John Skathelok was impotent and therefore cheating his young wife of her due. The witnesses, women ranging in age from 26 to 50, testified that a group of seven of them had examined John in a warm room, exposing his penis and trying to arouse him. They bared their breasts, fondled his genitals, embraced him, "kissed him and spoke various jestful words to the same John telling him that he should for shame show these women his manhood if he were a man." The prettier ones even lay in bed with him and had him feel their private parts. But his member remained limp. The women readily attested to all this in court, and in fact it was their good standing in the community that made their word reliable. The court accepted their testimony and dissolved the marriage on account of impotence.[63]

Laughter and the "Virtue" of Silence

Of course, there was plenty of laughter that was not about sex. Yet associations with looseness colored some moralists' views of laughter, particularly in relation to women, who were seen as needing distinctive discipline to curb their impulses. Women were continually lectured about the virtue of silence. Their speech should be quiet, private, and scarce, to preserve feminine modesty and decorum. Their laughter, too, was in need of curbing. As Maria Thynne's joke about aspen leaves and female silence suggests, however, the stereotypes and proverbs about women's talkativeness show that many did not follow the advice. Women talked too much, and they laughed too much, and many moralists could not resist telling them so.

In sixteenth-century Italy, the ideal woman's laugh would not be audible. Instead, subtleties of eye and smile would communicate her amusement. A married woman should not laugh in the absence of her husband, wrote Orazio Lombardelli in 1583.[64] Laughter that was controlled, never too loud or too frequent, was an adequate expression of one's delight. Of course, upper-class men were sometimes warned against excessive laughter too, lest they be seen as buffoons; but for women everything had to do with their sexual reputation. Immoderate female laughter could indicate, not just foolishness or faulty manners, but sexual looseness. A dialog of the satirist Pietro Aretino paints open-mouthed laughter as the laughter of prostitutes.[65] Conversely, the courtesans of Rome reportedly mocked respectable women for their failures at jest; instead of engaging in witty repartee, the chaste ladies were "as silent as stones."[66]

The prominent humanist Juan Luis Vives, in his "Instruction of a Christian Woman," warned that laughter was a sign of "a very light and dissolute mind" and women should keep it under control. He criticized the vanity of women who laugh together in groups, but laughter of an individual woman was even more suspect: "For this I need not to bid her, that she shall not laugh again unto young men, that laugh toward her, which none will do, but she that is nought [unchaste], or else a fool."[67] He assumes young women ought to know that laughter in response to a young man would be read as a sexual invitation. While men might seem to approve vivacious women, in fact their manners made them sexual prey, even if men might flatter them with words of praise for their merry laughter and pleasing talk; the men really see them as light-minded and wanton, hardly as suitable wives.[68] There were dissenting voices in defense of women's laughter. Shakespeare memorably assured audiences that "wives may be merry, and yet honest too."[69] But as his phrasing shows, the combination of laughter with honesty—that is, with sexual chastity—was contested.

Most authorities agreed that it was okay for women to laugh at home with their husbands. Vives even advised wives to cultivate a stock of funny stories that they could use to lift their husbands' spirits when they were sad.[70] But even at home and within the sanctioned intimate relations of marriage, laughter should be kept within bounds. Lombardelli advised a calm demeanor for wives when with their husbands, "for a laughing, lascivious, or changing and disturbed face is sign of an evil mind, particularly if she laughs when he is sad."[71] Boisterous laughter was to be avoided by the virtuous woman, whether married or not.

Despite the strictures of moralists, women persisted in laughing to excess. Vives thought that everyone's laughter should be "controlled by habit and reason to prevent excessive outbursts that shake the entire body." But while civilized men might succeed at this self-discipline, "the ignorant, the peasants, children, and women" would "lose their self-control as they are overcome by laughter."[72] The giggle, connoting silly laughter, was already linked with women, as Alexander Barclay asserted in the *Mirror of Good Manners* in 1510: "Loud giggling and laughing is but a foolish sign And evident token of manners feminine."[73] The idea of women's excessive laughter persisted into the seventeenth and eighteenth centuries, along with suspicions about its sexual implications. An advice book warned in 1683 that "to laugh as women do sometimes, with their hands on both sides, and with a lascivious agitation of their whole body, is the height of indecency and immodesty."[74]

The post-Reformation period saw increasing attempts to contain unruly laughter, and women's laughter was often especially suspect to ministers and moralists. One of the criticisms of the custom of "churching" women—celebrating their return to the church community after childbirth—was the "effeminate speeches, wanton behaviour, and unseasonable mirth, which often doth accompany such meetings." Thus the seventeenth-century cleric Robert Hill.[75] Thomas Cartwright, bishop of Chester in the 1680s, admonished several women for laughing in church; they countered by pointing out that he had not chided a man who was doing the same: "I rebuked as they deserved Mrs. Brown, Mrs. Crutchley, Mrs. Eaton and her sister for talking and laughing in the Church; and they accused Mr. Hudleston for being as guilty as themselves."[76] He does not tell us whether he ever did reprimand Mr. Hudleston.

★★★

We will never know whether women really were laughing more than men. But we know that they did laugh, and that their laughter was often read by male observers as flouting the prescribed rules for female behavior. This was true even when they were not in fact making fun of men or mocking those very rules, as we know they sometimes did. Pamela Brown has traced literary evidence of female jest, arguing that these comic scenes both drew on surrounding social practices and gave women an arsenal of funny ways to exert power.[77] While most actual deployments of such comic weapons are lost to us, we have evidence that they were used and that there was active exchange between printed literature and oral culture. People borrowed language and strategies from what was printed and read, and conversely, things they said made their way into writing and print.[78]

Obviously, the gender dynamics of laughter cannot be reduced to a simple formula. The many modes in which laughter intersected with gender and sex show, on the one hand, the ways in which public culture and the laughter market promoted widely held assumptions about what was laughable and, on the other, the multiple ways in which men and women could tweak these to their own purposes within the context of social relations. Intimate relations offered a scene for subtle renegotiation of gender norms, as in the cases of Osborne, Thynne, and even the Luthers; or, potentially, for re-enactment of misogynistic comedy, as in the case of Dietz. The laughers and libelers of everyday social relationships might seize on sexual barbs to laugh at their enemies, or might accidentally overstep the bounds of companionable jollity. In using sexual jest, they of course reinforced the rules of sexual honor that bound both women and men to demands for sexual restraint and maintenance of household order. The perception of laughter as dangerous for women, put forward by the sterner moralists, hardly seems to have put a dent in actual merriment, any more than the constant recommendations of silence put an end to their proverbial chattering. But the power of ridicule may have seemed especially formidable to those, like Osborne and other gentlewomen, with a respected status to lose.

Notes

1 Dorothy Osborne, *Dorothy Osborne: Letters to Sir William Temple,* ed. Kenneth Parker (Aldershot, UK: Ashgate, 2002), 89. Some spellings and punctuation modernized. See also *Letters from Dorothy Osborne to Sir William Temple (1653–1654),* ed. Edward Abbott Parry (London and New York, c1914), http://digital.library.upenn.edu/women/osborne/letters/letters.html.

2 Quoted in David Booy, *Personal Disclosures: An Anthology of Self-writings from the Seventeenth Century* (Aldershot: Ashgate, 2002), 253.

3 Virginia Woolf, *The Common Reader: Second Series* (London: Hogarth Press, 1965), 64, https://archive.org/details/woolf_commonA/mode/2up.

4 Osborne, *Dorothy Osborne,* 170.

5 René T. Proyer et al., "Breaking Ground in Cross-Cultural Research on the Fear of Being Laughed at (Gelotophobia): A Multi-National Study Involving 73 Countries," *Humor* 22, no. 1/2 (2009): 253–79.

6 Sara Beam, *Laughing Matters: Farce and the Making of Absolutism in France* (Ithaca: Cornell University Press, 2007).

7 Anne Halkett, *The Autobiography of Lady Anne Halkett* (Camden Society, 1875), 18, https://archive.org/stream/autobiographyofa00halkrich#page/n5/mode/2up.

8 Halkett, *Autobiography,* 46.

9 Helen Ostovich and Elizabeth Sauer, eds., *Reading Early Modern Women: An Anthology of Texts in Manuscript and Print, 1550–1700* (New York and London: Routledge, 2004), 285.

10 *Glikl: Memoirs 1691–1719,* ed. Chava Turniansky, trans. Sara Friedman (Brandeis University Press, 2019), 161, 191, https://doi-org.proxy.library.upenn.edu/10.2307/j.ctv102bd6s.

11 Levinus Bennet (b. 1631), sheriff of Cambridgeshire; Osborne, *Dorothy Osborne,* 242.

12 Osborne, *Dorothy Osborne,* 96.

13 Osborne, *Dorothy Osborne,* 106.

14 Osborne, *Dorothy Osborne,* 138.

15 Osborne, *Dorothy Osborne,* 139.

16 Osborne, *Dorothy Osborne,* 61.

17 Osborne, *Dorothy Osborne,* 107

18 Osborne, *Dorothy Osborne,* 202.

19 Alison D. Wall, ed., *Two Elizabethan Women: Correspondence of Joan and Maria Thynne 1575–1611,* Wiltshire Record Society, vol. 38 (Devizes: Wiltshire Record Society, 1983), 37; on the litigation over the marriage, see Alison D. Wall, "For Love, Money, or Politics? A Clandestine Marriage and the Elizabethan Court of Arches," *The Historical Journal* 38, no. 3 (September 1995): 511–33.

20 Wall, *Two Elizabethan Women,* 48.

21 Wall, *Two Elizabethan Women,* 33.

22 Cf. Anthony Fletcher, *Gender, Sex and Subordination in England 1500–1800* (New Haven and London: Yale University Press, 1995), 156–7. In another letter, I think Fletcher takes her professions of submission a bit too literally, when she refers to being left like an "innocent fool"; in fact, Maria was quite acerbic, not at all amused at being denied what she considered proper wifely authority to manage affairs. Underlining her annoyance, she pointedly signs herself, "your loving wife, howsoever"; Wall, *Two Elizabethan Women,* 32.

23 On the importance of jest in their relationship, see Susan C. Karant-Nunn, "The Masculinity of Martin Luther: Theory, Practicality, and Humor," in *Masculinity in the Reformation Era*, ed. Scott H. Hendrix and Susan C. Karant-Nunn (Kirksville, MO: Truman
   State University Press, 2008), 167–89.
24 Susan C. Karant-Nunn and Merry Wiesner-Hanks, eds., *Luther on Women: A Sourcebook*
   (Cambridge: Cambridge University Press, 2003), 28; Martin Luther, *D. Martin Luthers
   Werke. Kritische Gesamtausgabe. Tischreden,* 6 vols. (Weimar: Böhlau, 1912–1921), cited
   hereafter as WA [Weimarer Ausgabe] TR; 1:19, no. 55; 2:285, no. 1975.
25 The fuller version comes from Konrad Cordatus; see WA TR II: xxviii.
26 Martin Luther, "Works," vol. 54 in *Table Talk*, ed. and trans. Theodore G. Tappert
   (Philadelphia: Fortress Press, 1967), 396, no. 5187; for another of Luther's jokes about
   Käthe's volubility, see 317, no. 4081.
27 Karant-Nunn, "The Masculinity of Martin Luther."
28 See Pamela Allen Brown, "Jesting Rights: Women Players in the Manuscript Jestbook of
   Sir Nicholas Le Strange," in *Women Players in England, 1500–1600: Beyond the All-Male
   Stage*, ed. Pamela Allen Brown and Peter Parolin (Aldershot, England, and Burlington,
   VT: Ashgate, 2005), 305–14, 307; Sir Nicholas Le Strange, *"Merry Passages and Jeasts":
   A Manuscript Jestbook*, ed. H. F. Lippincott (Salzburg: Institut für Englische Sprache und
   Literatur, 1974).
29 Le Strange, *Merry Passages*, 18 (spelling modernized).
30 Le Strange, *Merry Passages*, 104.
31 Brown, "Jesting Rights," 310.
32 Le Strange, *Merry Passages*, 120.
33 See, for example, Heide Wunder, *He Is the Sun, She Is the Moon: Women in Early Modern
   Germany*, trans. Thomas Dunlap (Cambridge, MA and London, England: Harvard University Press, 1998), 189; Cissie Fairchilds, *Women in Early Modern Europe 1500–1700*
   (Harlow, England: Pearson Longman, 2007), 71, 203.
34 See Joy Wiltenburg, *Disorderly Women and Female Power in the Street Literature of Early
   Modern England and Germany* (Charlottesville and London: University Press of Virginia,
   1992), 126–28.
35 Quoted in Susan D. Amussen and David E. Underdown, *Gender, Culture and Politics in
   England, 1560–1640: Turning the World Upside Down* (London and New York: Bloomsbury Academic, 2017), 30.
36 Amussen and Underdown, *Gender, Culture and Politics*, 70; see also Martin Ingram,
   "Ridings, Rough Music and the Reform of Popular Culture in Early Modern England,"
   Past & Present 105 (November 1984): 79–113.
37 Johann Dietz, *Master Johann Dietz, Surgeon in the Army of the Great Elector and Barber to
   the Royal Court*, trans. Bernard Miall (London: George Allen & Unwin, 1923), 227.
38 See Wiltenburg, *Disorderly Women*, 110–16.
39 Dietz, *Master Johann Dietz*, 232.
40 Dietz, *Master Johann Dietz*, 233.
41 Dietz, *Master Johann Dietz*, 252.
42 Langley v. Combe, 1618, Ms Arch Papers Oxon c118, 129v, Oxfordshire History
   Centre.
43 Laura Gowing, *Domestic Dangers: Women, Words and Sex in Early Modern London* (Oxford:
   Clarendon Press, 1996), 96; see also Pamela Allen Brown, *Better a Shrew than a Sheep:
   Women, Drama, and the Culture of Jest in Early Modern England* (Ithaca and London: Cornell University Press, 2003), 83–117, on such taunts and jests by women in literature.
44 Martin Ingram, *Church Courts, Sex & Marriage In England, 1570–1640* (Cambridge:
   Cambridge University Press, 1987), 312.
45 EDC5/1613/31, Wigan 1613, Cheshire Record Office.
46 Jack Howard-Drake, *Oxford Church Courts: Depositions 1629–1634* (Oxford: Oxfordshire County Council, 2007), 63; Ms. Oxf. dioc. papers C.26, ff 342v–344, Oxfordshire
   History Centre.

47 Bernard Capp, *When Gossips Meet: Women, Family, and Neighborhood in Early Modern England* (Oxford: Oxford University Press, 2003), 254.

48 Peckett v. Peckett, 1687–1688, GB 193, Cause Papers, C.P.H.3718, Borthwick Institute, University of York.

49 Warcopp v. Collins, 1589, Ms Oxfd Dioc Papers d16, fol. 56, Oxfordshire History Centre.

50 Capp, *When Gossips Meet*, 251.

51 Capp, *When Gossips Meet*, 274.

52 Le Strange, *"Merry Passages and Jeasts"*, 38.

53 Capp, *When Gossips Meet*, 239.

54 Simon Dickie, *Cruelty and Laughter: Forgotten Comic Literature and the Unsentimental Eighteenth Century* (Chicago and London: University of Chicago Press, 2011), 235–46.

55 Ms Oxford Dioc Papers c25, f62, 62v, 64v, Oxfordshire History Centre; Howard–Drake, *Oxford Church Courts: Depositions 1609–1616* (Oxfordshire County Council, 2003), 16.

56 Paul Hair, ed., *Before the Bawdy Court: Selections from Church Court and Other Records Relating to the Correction of Moral Offences in England, Scotland and New England, 1300–1800* (New York: Harper & Row, 1972), 82.

57 Jan Massys, *A Merry Company*, sixteenth century, held at Nationalmuseum Stockholm. For a study of medieval treatments of female laughter as suspect, and clerical suspicion of laughter's erotic overtones, see Olga V. Trokhimenko, *Constructing Virtue and Vice: Femininity and Laughter in Courtly Society (ca. 1150–1300)* (Göttingen: V&R Unipress, 2014).

58 See *Deutsches Wörterbuch von Jacob Grimm und Wilhelm Grimm*, s.v. scherzen; https://woerterbuchnetz.de/?sigle=DWB#0.

59 John Bulwer, *Pathomyotornia* (1649), 110, quoted in Stephen Greenblatt, "Mutilation and Meaning," in *The Body in Parts: Fantasies of Corporeality in Early Modern Europe*, ed. David Hillman and Carla Mazzio (New York and London: Routledge, 1997), 221-41, 234.

60 Gowing, *Domestic Dangers*, 81; DL/C 231, f297v, 1628, Greater London Record Office.

61 EDC5/1697/13, Chester (St. Mary), Cheshire Record Office.

62 For example, see Gowing, *Domestic Dangers*, 203.

63 P. J. P. Goldberg, ed. and trans., *Women in England c. 1275–1525: Documentary Sources* (Manchester and New York: Manchester University Press, 1995), 219–21.

64 Helena L. Sanson, "Donne Che (non) Ridono: Parola E Riso Nella Precettistica Femminile Del XVI Secolo in Italia," *Italian Studies* 60, no. 1 (2005): 6–21, 15.

65 Sanson, "Donne Che (non) Ridono," 16–17.

66 P. de Brantome, *Les Dames Galantes* (pre-1614), quoted in Peter Burke, *The Historical Anthropology of Early Modern Italy: Essays on Perception and Communication* (Cambridge: Cambridge University Press, 1987), 83.

67 Juan Luis Vives, "Instruction of a Christian Woman (1541)," in *Conduct Literature for Women*, ed. William St Clair and Irmgard Maassen, 6 vols. (London: Pickering & Chatto, 2000), 1:118.

68 See Ruth Kelso, *Doctrine for the Lady of the Renaissance* (Urbana: University of Illinois Press, 1956), 55.

69 William Shakespeare, *The Merry Wives of Windsor*, Act IV, Scene ii, l. 99, in *The Arden Shakespeare Complete Works*, ed. Richard Proudfoot, Ann Thompson, and David Scott Kastan (Walton-on-Thames, Surrey: Thomas Nelson, 1998).

70 Vives, *Instruction*, 1:215.

71 Kelso, *Doctrine for the Lady of the Renaissance*, 106.

72 From Juan Luis Vives, *De Anima et Vita* (1538), quoted in Chris Holcomb, *Mirth Making: The Rhetorical Discourse on Jesting in Early Modern England* (Columbia, SC: University of South Carolina Press, 2001), 177.

73 *Oxford English Dictionary*, s.v. giggle, giggling.

74 Cited in Capp, *When Gossips Meet*, 4.

75 David Cressy, "Purification, Thanksgiving and the Churching of Women in Post-Reformation England," *Past & Present* 141 (November 1993): 106–46, 114.
76 Arthur Ponsonby, *English Diaries* (London: Methuen & Co., 1923), 146.
77 Brown, *Better a Shrew than a Sheep*.
78 Brown, *Better a Shrew than a Sheep*; Adam Fox, *Oral and Literate Culture in England 1500–1700* (Oxford: Clarendon Press, 2000).

FIGURE 5.1   Madame de Sévigné, portrait by Claude Lefebvre

Source: © Art Collection 3/Alamy Stock Photo

5

COURTLY LAUGHTER

Madame de Sévigné

In a 1996 French film called *Ridicule*, the hero makes his way to the French court with high ideals, only to face a heartless ridicule that corrupts all other values. Set in the eighteenth-century court of Louis XVI, the film depicts this irresponsible laughter as a sign of the decadence that will soon lead to revolution. The story is fiction, but it could claim a grounding in some actual historical occasions of ridicule—in particular, a fall during a dance that one poor courtier could never live down.[1] Such merciless derision could be seen as a nightmare scenario for the critics of aggressive laughter, not only causing harm to worthy individuals, but even undermining the stability of a nation. Yet, courtly laughter looked much more benign in its beginnings. Courtesy books of the sixteenth century, largely aimed at the courtly elite, were among the first to prescribe curbs to rude laughter, schooling their readers in the etiquette of jest. So, was courtly laughter nasty or nice? And if it started out nice, how did it get so nasty?

Our central figure here, Madame de Sévigné, takes us into the social world of the high aristocracy in France, in the age of the Sun King, Louis XIV. This was the apex of courtly society, with the most elaborate development of its norms, providing a model that was imitated, though never equaled, across Europe. It was the court of France, and that of Louis XIV in particular, that inspired Norbert Elias's powerful analyses of courtly society and the "civilizing process." From the Renaissance through the eighteenth century, he traced changes in manners that increasingly demanded strict controls over bodily comportment. Some of the new rules were aimed at hiding body functions that came to be viewed as unseemly, such as spitting, nose-blowing, and elimination of other wastes. The growing concepts of decorum cast suspicion on uncontrolled movements like boisterous laughter. The rules of manners also aimed at avoiding offense to others, which in theory should have discouraged harsh derision or the insolent laughter of someone like Cellini. In Elias's view, by the age of Louis XIV in the later seventeenth century,

DOI: 10.4324/9781003247517-6

courtiers needed firm control over their emotions in order to craft an effective self-presentation at court: one that would show no weakness that might be exploited by their rivals for precedence and favor.[2] The historian Colin Jones has even posited a "facial immobility" cultivated by the courtiers of Louis XIV, in contrast to the freer smiles of the later eighteenth century.[3] The evidence on laughter suggests that the idea of emotional suppression can be overdrawn; but the larger trend toward stricter etiquette in the highest society was certainly there.

A Courtly Flashback

The roots of courtly laughter go back centuries before, to the Middle Ages, and especially to the Renaissance with its trend toward more refined courtly etiquette. Right from its start, courtliness was infused with laughter. Among the Renaissance books of manners that promoted more "civilized" behavior, one of the most influential was Baldassare Castiglione's *The Courtier*. Written in 1528, it was roughly contemporary with our opening exemplars of "good" and "bad" laughter; Benvenuto Cellini was a young man and Felix Platter would be born a few years later. The standards for courtly society sought to tame the potential aggression of laughter, but laughter was also presented as an essential tool for the successful courtier.

Widely read and translated across Europe, *The Courtier* became an instant classic.[4] Its advice on moderation in jest is often quoted as part of the received wisdom about courtly politeness in the sixteenth and seventeenth centuries. But there was far more than advice about laughter here, to lay alongside the advice about manly exercise, gracious carriage, and other qualities of the ideal gentleman. *The Courtier* deserves special attention as a milestone in the history of laughter: laughter was not just one subject of discussion, but a constitutive element of the whole book and the courtly society it painted.

Castiglione set his book in the palace of Urbino in 1507, seat of the virtuous Duke Guidobaldo da Montefeltro and his peerless Duchess, Elizabetta Gonzaga. The author had actually been at this Urbino court, but the book's dialogues are his invention. It was the Duchess who presided over the scenes of sociability in *The Courtier*, as the character of courtliness is dissected from various angles. What was it, in Castiglione's telling, that made the Duchess's circle such a model of courtly excellence? It was a place where "gentle discussions and innocent pleasantries were heard, and on the face of everyone a jocund gaiety was seen depicted, so that the house could truly be called the very abode of mirth."[5] The laughing atmosphere was a signal and promoter of warm emotional ties: "Nor do I believe that the sweetness that is had from a beloved company was ever savored in any other place as it once was there." In fact, the collective emotion went beyond companionship to love, a relation that bound the courtiers together like brothers:

> we all felt a supreme happiness arise within us whenever we came into the presence of the Duchess. And it seemed that this was a chain that bound us all

together in love, in such wise that never was there concord of will or cordial love between brothers greater than that which was there among us all.

If the men felt like brothers, Castiglione tells us, the same warm feelings extended to the ladies,

> with whom one had very free and most honorable association, for to each it was permitted to speak, sit, jest, and laugh with whom he pleased; but the reverence that was paid to the wishes of the Duchess was such that this same liberty was a very great check.[6]

The license to laugh with anyone, across gender, was not to be taken for granted, but was enabled by this special spell of the Duchess's influence, fostering love, curbing lust, and freeing everyone to laugh.

Of course, Castiglione was not completely serious about this idealized picture of perfect loving companionship. In describing old men's nostalgia for the idealized courts of yore, he noted that all courts, past and present, have a mixture of good and bad elements, good and bad men (and women). The rosy view of the past comes of a wistful longing for one's own days of youthful vigor. And, somewhat similarly, the idyllic society at the Urbino court is a fleeting one, fostered by the Duchess's presence in the evening enjoyment of conversation. Did they all feel like such brothers during the day when serious business was afoot, one wonders? As the dialogues progress, the veiled but sharp contests among the participants demonstrate how firmly the author's tongue was in his cheek.[7] Still, in theory the best court—the pinnacle of courtliness—was the scene of good laughter that bound together the hearts of all.[8]

The art of conversation was one that Castiglione took somewhat seriously, given that without it the courtier would cut a poor figure indeed. The imagined discussions deal at length with questions of how the courtier should converse—with princes, but more especially among relative equals, fellow gentlemen and also the ladies, whose presence was seen by most of the men as defining the "courtliness" of court life. Of course, given the dialogue form, the speeches are not direct prescriptions from the author, but the book was read for models of courtly excellence. Here, the courtier should be adept in arms and many practical arts, knowledgeable, and educated in classic literature. In discussion of the art of conversation, knowing how to raise laughter actually receives equal billing with knowing what you are talking about. The most general rule for the courtier's conversation is that

> he should be one who is never at a loss for things to say that are good and well suited to those with whom he is speaking, that he should know how to sweeten and refresh the minds of his hearers, and move them discreetly to gaiety and laughter with amusing witticisms and pleasantries, so that, without ever producing tedium or satiety, he may continually give pleasure.[9]

The courtiers talk about various subjects, engaging in lengthy debates about the virtues (or lack thereof) of women and the proper conduct of love affairs. Some of the company ultimately declare that these are trivial matters, and that the courtier's real calling is to advise his prince, leading the ruler toward the path of virtue. Even here, although "dancing, merrymaking, singing and playing" may be "frivolities and vanities," the courtier still needs skill in affairs of laughter.[10] He must not be a flatterer; he must aim always to speak the truth and move the prince toward virtuous and beneficial rule. But in order to speak the truth safely, he must know how to please, sweetening the sometimes unpalatable truths with humor. Thus, he will need his wit and charm along with his "knowledge of letters and many other things" in order to succeed.[11]

The ladies are remarkably silent through these exchanges, despite their privilege of presiding over the occasion and appointing the main speakers. The company has the right to interrupt and contradict, but only the men make real use of it. I would love to believe that such witty ladies as the Duchess and Emilia Pia would hardly have put up with such a mansplaining marathon in real life—about subjects like love and the merits/demerits of women, no less! But is this just wishful thinking on my part? Or was the wishful thinking on the part of Castiglione and his fellows, as he creates a scenario in which women belie all their proverbial propensity to talk too much? And this in a setting where, by the men's own showing, conversation was the court lady's chief occupation? We know that advice books constantly offered women silence as their chief ornament, but men seldom seem to have thought they actually conformed to this ideal.

Despite their relative silence in Castiglione's dialogues, it is taken for granted that the court lady as well as the court gentleman will jest and laugh in company. The Duchess, Emilia, and the other ladies laugh at many points in the conversation, including at anti-female sallies uttered by the resident misogynist, Gasparo. Emilia interjects the occasional witticism. In the discussion of love, even a woman of "grave beauty," who would intimidate many potential lovers with her dignity, was someone who when "joking or jesting" could preserve her respected decorum. The ideal court lady would not "mingle serious matters with playful or humorous discourse, or mix jests and jokes with serious talk."[12]

Arguably, there are parallel rules of discretion for the male courtier to keep his jesting within bounds. But the excesses of male humor run to dirty jokes and crude physical pranks, or to constant frivolity: "it is not seemly for the Courtier to be always making men laugh, nor yet by those means that are made use of by fools or drunken men, by the silly, the nonsensical, and likewise by buffoons."[13] It appears that as long as he maintained gravity when appropriate, the courtier indeed might mix humor with serious matters—as advised for his benevolent manipulation of his prince's inclinations. In addition, people's willingness to laugh at his jokes was a serious indicator of his status at court: a man disfavored by the prince, even for no fault of his own, would find that

> everyone will find the man to be of little worth, nor will there be any who prize or esteem him, or laugh at his witticisms, or hold him in any respect; nay, all will begin to make fun of him and persecute him.

Even his wit will not help him. Conversely, with the prince's favor even a dolt will be esteemed and praised, "and everyone will appear to laugh at his jests and at certain rustic and stupid jokes that ought to excite rather disgust than laughter."[14] The ideal aim of laughter was to please others and spread goodwill, and the courtier "must take care not to appear malicious and spiteful"; yet the sallies of wit might need to "sting a little."[15] Management of laughter was an essential skill, but laughter was also dangerous ground.

In the modeling of courtly manners, many besides Castiglione echoed the disdain for low buffoonery. Chris Holcomb has examined the trend at the English court of the sixteenth century. In place of more boisterous practices of physical humor, admiration was increasingly accorded to a more sophisticated style of laughter and jest. Professional jesters still had license for more slapstick humor, but the civilized gentry were urged never to be mistaken for them. They should avoid, in the advice of Thomas Wilson, "gross bourding and alehouse jesting . . . [and] foolish talk and ruffian manners, such as no honest ears can once abide, nor yet any witty man can like well or allow."[16] The cultivation of wit was an appropriate elite goal, but not crude or excessive jesting and laughter. By the seventeenth century in England, the word "wit" had shifted from its earlier meaning of intellect to its dual meaning of both intelligence and a special skill at inventing cleverly laughable material.[17] A number of authorities, in line with Castiglione, stressed the bodily control that would curb "ill-favored gestures," physical contortions, and overly loud laughter.[18] Bodily contortion was for the vulgar—a class distinction made especially palpable by the eighteenth-century German courtiers who amused themselves with physical abuse of the traveling jester Peter Prosch.[19]

In France, the shifting meanings of the terms for laughter, *ris* and *rire*, offer much food for thought. In the sixteenth century, when Laurent Joubert published his *Traité du Ris*,[20] he clearly was talking about real laughter—the kind that involved the diaphragm as well as the face, the kind that raised such physiological questions as whether one could actually die laughing. And yet, in the following century, when educated Frenchmen began compiling dictionaries of the language, the definitions of *rire* (laugh) began to strip it of sound and confine it to the muscles of the face. The 1694 *Dictionnaire de l'Académie française* defined it as a movement of the mouth in response to amusement—providing a model that persisted into the eighteenth century and, as Colin Jones has pointed out, sounds more like a smile than a laugh.[21] And yet, the same dictionary went on to list common expressions that tell a different story. We have, among many others, *esclater de rire* (break out laughing), *rire à gorge desployée* (full-throated laugh), *crever de rire* or *mourir de rire* (die laughing), *pasmer de rire* (swoon with laughter), *rire aux larmes* (laugh till one cries), *rire comme un fou* (laugh like a madman).[22] These are not mere smiles, or any other movements of the mouth alone. How do we explain the discrepancy? The illustrious members of the French Academy, that most exclusive of intellectual bodies, appear to have been prescribing what they thought the word ought to mean, in its purest and most civilized sense: a sophisticated and restrained acknowledgment of wit. But they could not fully suppress what people often were really doing, even among the elite: laughing out loud. Unfortunately, the ambiguity of the language sometimes creates doubt about exactly how people were expressing their amusement.

"Laugh, Laugh!"

Marie de Rabutin-Chantal, Marquise de Sévigné (1626–1696), was a champion of laughter, in an age and in an aristocratic milieu where decorum might call for its suppression. "Laugh, laugh!" she wrote to her daughter, in one of the famous series of letters that have made her a luminary of French literature. Meanwhile, her good friend the Duke de La Rochefoucauld (another literary giant) was claiming that he almost never laughed.[23] The cultivated ideal of the blasé aristocrat, too dignified to go beyond a superior smirk, was very much in the air. Yet Sévigné persisted in laughing, and she pulled it off with aplomb. Sévigné's aristocratic status, particularly after her marriage to the Marquis de Sévigné, gave her access to all the venues of elite sociability—the court, the salons of Paris, and rural estates in Brittany. Even as severe a judge as the Duke de Saint-Simon (of whom more later) thought her a model of manners—another sign that laughter was more prevalent in high circles than is sometimes thought. Many of the heightened laughter terms that appear in the dictionary recur in her correspondence. She and her friends swooned with laughter, died laughing, laughed till they cried, burst out laughing—and while some of these expressions were metaphorical, there was clearly some audible laughter.

In contrast to the idea of aristocratic restraint, Sévigné's letters suggest that it is the elite—not just the nobility but those who also have wit—who truly know how to laugh. Eckhard Schörle, in his otherwise excellent book on laughter, is mistaken in seeing Sévigné as evidence that women needed to apologize for laughing. The passage he cites—where she says she would be ashamed of laughing if she had not been crying for a week before—has a very different meaning in context: it was one of the first of her letters to her daughter, written just a week after the separation that threw her into a frenzy of grief.[24] At other times, she was happy to vaunt her laughter and encourage her daughter to do the same.

The freedom of all this laughter, however, can actually be read as a sign of how thoroughly courtly manners had become ingrained among her partners in sociability. They laughed freely, but they laughed well: that is, in response to clever witticisms, in response to farcical scenes reminiscent of the courtly comedies of Molière, or in response to gaffes by others that showed their lack of courtly polish. Clumsy movements or speech, provincialisms, ignorance of correct protocol, all were fair game for laughter, especially if committed by people with pretensions to gentility. They were able to laugh at themselves as well—this too in a spirit of urbane self-observation spiced with irony and detachment. Even self-deprecating laughter could serve as a sign of their superior wit and self-confidence. The laughter, like Felix Platter's benign laughter, helped define lines of community and intimacy; in contrast to the harsher laughter of Saint-Simon, Sévigné managed to maintain cordial relations with those she laughed at. Still, Thomas Hobbes would have seen confirmation of his idea that laughter was a "sudden glory" in one's own superiority.

The spread of laughter, or at least amusement, was one of her key goals in composing the voluminous letters, written across a span of fifty years, that have survived. They were mostly written to her daughter, the Marquise de Grignan, with the goal of maintaining a close relationship despite the separation of distance after her daughter's marriage. For much of the correspondence, Sévigné was at her country home in Brittany, the far northwest of France, while Grignan lived far south in Provence. Even when Sévigné was in Paris, Provence was a long way away. The provincial yokels in these remote districts provided one reliable source of amusement; but Sévigné was seldom at a loss for others. Of course, familial affairs and non-laughable events had their share of attention. But a proper letter should be amusing if at all possible.

Given the renown of Sévigné's wit, it is perhaps not surprising to find a lot of laughter talk in her letters. Her correspondence is exceptionally full of vivid experiences and emotions, described in a highly engaging style. On first being separated from her daughter in 1671, Sévigné wrote at length of her love and of the tangible signs of that affection. She sighed and sobbed at her daughter's absence, she yearned to embrace her, she kissed the baby granddaughter who had been left in her care, as a proxy for the absent child of her own. The descriptions evoke an intensely lived life. And yet everything is done on purpose, as it were. There can be no doubt that Madame de Sévigné was sincere in her constant expressions of maternal love, and in her comments about how much pleasure she took in writing to her daughter, so much dearer than the daily company left to her. But the letters were also works of art, composed to give pleasure and display a distinctive style of wit.

While the letters relied on her relationship with the recipient, Sévigné also wrote with an eye to a larger audience. Letters were often read to others, copied, or passed from hand to hand, especially if they were witty or informative. Already in the 1660s, when writing to a friend about the trial of Fouquet (finance minister and friend of Sévigné, now fallen out of the king's favor), she was expecting her letters to be shared.[25] In 1671, Grignan was spreading her mother's letters around "like the Holland Gazette."[26] Meanwhile, Sévigné found her daughter's letters so amusing and charming that they were worthy of the press. She warned playfully, "one of these days you will find a treacherous friend has printed them."[27]

Sévigné was pleased to hear that her letters were in demand for their entertainment value, though she professed disbelief. "Is it possible, that my letters should be so entertaining as you say they are?" she asked her daughter. This was not all modesty, however false. The ability to appreciate her letters was a mark of high intelligence, an opinion in which she joined with her friends:

> M. De Coulanges wants sadly to know which of your ladies it is that has a taste for them; we reckon it a favourable sign for her, for my style is so loose, that it requires a good share of natural understanding and knowledge of the world, to be able to bear with it.[28]

All those who heard her letters read were likely of high social rank—but not all were smart enough to relish them.

How could one tell what was the right kind of laughter or a sign of true wit? Well, if you had to ask, you could be pretty sure that you didn't have it! But an influential measure was derived from professional comedy, particularly the plays of Molière. His plays were applauded at court by the king himself, and also made their way into the provinces, enacted by traveling troupes. Sévigné was not in the laughter market herself, of course—and yet her letters were a performance, circulated among select readers. Her experience of theater performance provided a shared standard for the laughable that she used in painting scenes from her own life. In 1671, for example, she was delighted that her son had been dropped by the famous courtesan Ninon de l'Enclos. The break was precipitated by an embarrassing occasion of impotence which her son recounted to her in amusing style, and she, in turn, to her daughter:

> he was dying to tell me of his disaster. We laughed very heartily; I told him I was overjoyed to find him punished where he had sinned. He said it was my fault, that I had passed on to him some of my icy character, which he could well have done without, and that I should better have given it to my daughter. . . . He said the silliest things in the world, and so did I. It was a scene worthy of Molière.[29]

She was reminded of Molière again when Mademoiselle Du Plessis, a young neighbor in Brittany, told a lie at the table. When charged with it,

> she lowered her eyes and answered, "Yes, indeed, Madame," said she, "I am the greatest liar in the world; I am very much obliged to you for telling me of it." We all burst out laughing, for it was exactly the tone of "Tartuffe."[30]

The style of Molière provided a lens through which Sévigné viewed her own experiences and their laughability.

One sign of the importance of wit in Sévigné's worldview was the delight she took in praising it in her children. Her son, in the episode above, was spouting quips worthy of stage comedy. She considered her daughter a paragon of wit as well, not only in her letters but in conversation that left lasting impressions on her hearers. In one letter to Grignan, Sévigné recounted how thrilled she was at a convivial dinner, when someone remembered

> a witticism of yours full six years ago, upon Count Dietrichstein, who, you said, was very like Monsieur de Beaufort, only that he spoke better French: we thought it singular that he should remember it so long; this gave us an opportunity to talk of your wit.[31]

The quality of wit was one that distinguished intimates in her social circle from others. The people you could laugh with were ones who were perceptive enough to recognize the ridiculous, as well as trusted to engage together with goodwill and not malice. Knowing how to laugh was a valuable characteristic, even in those of slightly lower social station. Praising one of her daughter's lady companions, Sévigné wrote, "Montgobert knows how to laugh; she understands your language. How lucky she is to have wit, and to be with you! To have wits without remedy makes the blood boil."[32] Montgobert had the benefit of congenial company in Grignan, their shared laughter a marker of intellectual compatibility. The last sentence complains of the opposite: maddening to be a person of wit, craving the relief of understanding laughter, but finding oneself among fools. In another letter she complained that, amused at the absurdity of Mademoiselle du Plessis, "I am in despair when I have nobody to laugh at it with me."[33]

Who were Sévigné's companions in laughter? Family foremost, of course: one of the cherished aspects of writing to her daughter was the freedom to share laughter on paper with an understanding ear. Sévigné did not have the same kind of intense relationship with her son, but with him too, a common culture of laughter was a repeated thread. He read Rabelais to make her laugh, imitated farces, and turned his own amorous misadventures into family comedy. Other family members like her uncles were also reliable partners. Her friend La Rochefoucauld, author of a collection of maxims prized by elites across Europe, was in on many jokes. She was especially delighted when La Rochefoucauld laughed at witty passages in Grignan's letters—which he evidently did, despite his own claim that his melancholy character kept him from laughing more than once or twice a year.[34] There were other nobles at court and in Paris with whom she laughed. A step down in the social scale were companions like Montgobert, with whom one could also laugh, as long as they kept proper bounds. On one occasion Sévigné's maids went so far as to play a joke on her, writing a fake letter and then becoming slightly alarmed when it was taken as real: "They saw me sending you this letter, torn between dying of laughter and dying of fear. 'What,' said Helene, 'make fun of one's mistress!' 'But,' said Marie, 'it is a joke, that will delight the countess.'"[35] Finally they confessed and asked for forgiveness. It was slightly daring to venture so far for a laugh—but Sévigné does not appear to have been disturbed. After all, it gave her good material for an amusing letter.

The cultivation of laughter was not only good for one's own amusement and for enjoying the company of like-minded friends. It could even be important to be laughed at oneself, as a corrective to excess—a curb on behavior that might veer toward the ridiculous, but also a hedge against negative emotion. Sévigné sometimes wrote of laughable qualities in her own behavior or writings, a bit of self-deprecation that also could disarm criticism. Having one's absurdity recognized would be good for her daughter too:

> When you wish you could break some iron, finding porcelain unworthy of your anger, it seems you are really upset. When I consider that there is no one there to laugh about it and make fun of you, I worry about you, because I think such repressed feeling is even more dangerous than the smallpox.[36]

It was a special quality of aristocratic aplomb to know how to be laughed at while maintaining one's status and dignity. Sévigné was happy to laugh at herself or to be laughed at by her intimates, especially her children, over minor foibles. She was also delighted by the self-referential comedy of her son, as he exposed to family and friends some of the follies he committed while sowing his wild oats. At the conclusion of an affair with an actress, he recovered from her the love letters he had written. Evidently finding them amusing in retrospect, he showed them to his mother. And, of course, Sévigné wrote all about it to her daughter:

> He showed me some letters which he had recovered from this actress. I never saw any so warm, so passionate: he was in tears, he was dying. He believed it all while he was writing it, and laughed at it the moment afterwards. I tell you, he is worth his weight in gold.[37]

She said to La Rochefoucauld that her son

> was not a fool in head, but a fool in heart; his sentiments are all just, and all false; all cold, and all warm; All deceitful, and all sincere; in short, it is his heart that should wear the cap. This remark occasioned a general laugh, and my son joined in it, for he is very good company.[38]

Targeted Laughter

Within the circle of intimates, laughter could be shared with its target. At the same time, the confident could laugh about their own follies without loss of face. Laughter had a somewhat different ring when inspired by outsiders. Among the courtly nobility conversant with Paris and Versailles, the nobles who remained in the provinces were increasingly viewed as unsophisticated, and therefore laughable. The lower classes of the provinces were funny too, particularly because of their accents. Sévigné was familiar with the court and the salons of Paris, but she spent a lot of time at her country home in Brittany. Her daughter Grignan, living with her husband in Provence, was also out in the provinces. They were both amused by the manners, dress, and speech of local inhabitants, including the nobility. Sévigné could not help laughing about an incident at a dinner in Brittany: finding the meal delayed, she approached a man she thought was a servant, asking to have it hastened. But it turned out he was a local nobleman. Sévigné first told the story at length and then, in a later letter, reminded Grignan of the story and invited her to laugh once more. Though she called it a "droll mistake," the laughter suggests she thought there was some excuse for not recognizing this provincial gent as a social equal.[39] Another time, at a ball, "We saw a girl of Lower Brittany, who, they said, bore away the palm [took the prize]. She was most ridiculous, and threw herself into attitudes that made us burst out laughing."[40] Even a seemingly minor error could evoke intense laughter. When one Breton gentleman, in compliment to

Sévigné, wanted to toast her daughter, he called her Carignan rather than Grignan: "this ridiculous mistake made M. De Chaulnes laugh till he cried."[41]

One particular provincial, Mademoiselle du Plessis, was a frequent target for laughter among Sévigné's friends, even though she was a close acquaintance. In fact, the whole Du Plessis family—neighbors of Sévigné's home in Brittany at Les Rochers—was a source of amusement. Sévigné mocked their provincial pronunciation and manners—although they were of noble status and were always named by their honorific titles. Du Plessis was an agemate of Sévigné's daughter and the two spent time together as children, though not happily. On one occasion the young Françoise de Sévigné struck the other in annoyance; Sévigné persuaded the other girl's mother that the whole thing was laughable. Sévigné celebrated her own ability to use laughter to advantage by turning her child's potentially embarrassing misbehavior—hitting the other child—into a joke. She was able to enjoy it again, years later, with friends who laughed from a very different perspective—in amusement at the very idea of a friendship between Françoise de Sévigne and the ridiculous Du Plessis: "This camaraderie between you and Mademoiselle du Plessis, which I invented . . . made them nearly die with laughing."[42]

Du Plessis was a regular butt of laughter in the Sévigné household—recall the "Tartuffe" incident at the table. She was usually not a party to the hilarity at her expense. Yet she remained in intimate association with Sévigné and her circle. In 1676, Sévigné was amused by Du Plessis's jealousy about her own attentions, telling how others teased her with tales of their supposed greater intimacy:

> Dying from jealousy, she asks all our people how I treat them; they all amuse themselves by digs at her. One says that I love her as much as I do you [her daughter]; another, that I have her sleep with me, which assuredly would be the greatest mark of my affection; another, that I take her to Paris with me, that I kiss her, that I'm crazy about her, that my uncle the abbé gave her ten thousand francs, that if she only had twenty thousand écus, I would have her marry my son. In short, they are such follies, and so well spread in the little household, that we have to laugh often at the stories they make up.[43]

Evidently, Du Plessis did feel the slights—or why worry about how Sévigné treated others? Yet she remained on the invitation list and in regular interaction with the whole household.

At lower social levels, peasant gestures and speech were perceived as absurd. A peasant dance in 1671 was highly amusing:

> There was a man and a woman amongst them, that would not have been suffered to dance in any well-governed nation, for their postures were enough to kill one with laughing. Pomenars roared, for he had lost all power of speech.[44]

That same year, on the departure of her son from her home in Brittany, the ridiculous weeping of the Breton servants turned her own grief into laughter:

> I wish I could describe the tears and cries and Breton language of Jacquine and la turquesine, when they saw your brother mount his horse: it was a scene. For myself, I could have cried, but seeing them like that, I had to laugh, and everyone else laughed too.[45]

In 1680, traveling in Brittany, she and her companions lost their way in the dark and received help including "a dozen stout country-fellows, some of whom held the carriage, while others went before with wisps of lighted straw; and all spoke such extreme Breton that we were ready to die with laughing."[46]

Sévigné's stories of laughter at court and among the Parisian elite have a slightly different ring. There were no Bretons with ridiculous accents, but there were people who fell short of the best standards of behavior. Their gaffes could arouse laughter, although in Sévigné's account it does not rise to the level of cruelty. Sometimes the laughter was suppressed to avoid giving offense. At a meal in 1671, one Courcelles made a foolish remark—about having bumps on his head that prevented him from getting his wig on: "this silly speech made us all leave the table before we had done with the fruit, for fear of laughing in his face."[47] Talking about his own head and his wig, besides being trivialities of no interest to others, evoked details of personal hygiene that were no longer considered appropriate for polite conversation. But no one wanted to shame him with open laughter.

Violations of the rules of precedence could also be laughable faux pas, when they stemmed from clumsiness or ignorance and not insulting intent. Seemingly trivial concerns, such as who went into dinner first, or who sat where, were serious business. As Elias pointed out in his analysis of court society, these niceties of behavior had a rationality of their own. In this closed world where everything depended on reputation and respect, no one could afford to be casual about protocol. It was crucial to know the rules and one's own proper place within them.[48] Sévigné tells how one lady, entering the queen's apartment at Versailles during the performance of a play, made an "egregious blunder, by taking the upper-hand of Madame Dufresnoi, which made her laughed at, as a foolish and ill-bred creature."[49]

This lady had made herself ridiculous by stepping out of her proper place in the social hierarchy. Importantly, however, Sévigné could laugh at her—not "in her face"—without breaking off relations, even quite friendly ones. Just a few years later, the same woman renounced worldliness and took up religious devotion. This was a somewhat fashionable trend among the elite of the time; Sévigné at times seems to have been a bit tempted by it herself. At any rate, she visited the lady in her new humble surroundings, and "we embraced each other tenderly." They talked of her religious vocation and laughed together about her former life: "We laughed a good deal at her former manners, and turned them into ridicule."[50] As with Du Plessis back in Brittany, Sévigné could maintain cordial relations even while laughing (to herself and with her more intimate friends) at the other's foibles.

Gossip and Ridicule at Court

This relatively gentle court laughter, which avoids giving offense and preserves relationships, contrasts with the often more caustic laughter reported by her much younger contemporary, the Duke of Saint-Simon. He was not as enthusiastic a recorder of his own laughter as Sévigné, but his memoir provides insights into the laughter of others. Saint-Simon thought well of Sévigné, memorializing her upon her death as someone who was beloved by practically everyone:

> This woman, by her natural graces, the sweetness of her wit, communicated these qualities to those who had them not; she was besides extremely good, and knew thoroughly many things without ever wishing to appear as though she knew anything.[51]

Saint-Simon himself had enemies, perhaps partly because he was higher in the pecking order and more thoroughly engaged within the court itself. He was also rather discontented with the direction of affairs under Louis XIV. His descriptions of the extremes of punctilious protocol at court, where the highest aristocrats danced attendance on the king, evoke nostalgia for the days of greater freedom and power for the nobility. At the same time, he was a stickler for hierarchy himself, engaging in (unsuccessful) lawsuits to assert the precedence of his own noble title over others he considered upstarts. He was especially disgusted by the prestige and promotion accorded to Louis's illegitimate sons, whom he called "the bastards." His urge to record the events of his own life, along with those he heard about, has preserved some striking instances of the role of laughter in those elite circles of power.

Saint-Simon's memoirs were once criticized by historians as excessively loaded with "gossip," with the implication that this frivolous focus drained them of much historical value. Gossip, with its connotations of feminine irresponsibility and doubtful relationship to facts, was in bad odor. More recently, however, scholars have come to recognize the importance of rumor in a social world where nuances of reputation and status were paramount.[52] Certainly one cannot take everything recounted in the memoirs as reliable, even aside from the author's own prejudices; he often relied on hearsay. For his portrait of Sévigné, for instance, he tells us that he learned of her from the testimony of her grandson. In other cases, he retells events (and jokes) from before he was born, incorporating oral tradition into his written account. With all due caution about the literal truth of individual anecdotes, the memoirs are exceptionally revealing about the effectiveness of the gossip network itself.

A striking example of the rapid spread of gossip emerges from Saint-Simon's account of an occasion when he himself was laughed at. In the period after Louis XIV's death, he had enhanced access to the center of power through his friendship with Philippe d'Orleans, who ruled as regent during the minority of the future Louis XV. Saint-Simon felt free to chide Orleans for what he saw as an irresponsible lifestyle of excessive partying. On this occasion in 1718, Orleans took him aside and delighted him by declaring his intention to turn over a new leaf and lead a more sober life. The following day, however, Saint-Simon learned

> that M. le Duc d'Orleans was no sooner at table than he burst out laughing, and applauded his cleverness, saying that he had just laid a trap for me into which I had fallen full length. He recited to them our conversation, at which the joy and applause were marvellous.

More than one acquaintance heard about this laughter and hastened to tell Saint-Simon about it the very next day.[53] The Duke's memoirs are full of testimony to the ultra-efficient rumor mill of court society. Occasions of ridicule could quickly become public—that is, known to everyone who mattered in these elite circles—far faster than the machinery of print could have spread them. Even when the laughter occurred in the target's absence, he or she was likely to learn of it before its echoes had died down.

Sometimes the laughter was more open, and the shame of being laughed at could result in effective self-banishment. Saint-Simon recounts the story of a friend of his, Montbron (the Marquis de Montbron), who made a fool of himself by dancing poorly at court. The account makes it clear that the courtiers were watching for him to fail. His birth was not quite up to snuff—he was "no more made to dance at Court than his father was to be chevalier of the order (to which, however, he was promoted in 1688)." He made matters worse by claiming to be a good dancer, not once, but twice. When he started to dance he lost the step and, according to Saint-Simon, tried to compensate with ridiculous gestures that elicited "bursts of laughter, which, in despite of the respect due to the person of the king (who likewise had great difficulty to hinder himself from laughing), degenerated at length into regular hooting." Instead of lying low after this first failure, he persisted and "promised marvels for the ball which was to follow." The courtiers were lying in wait, eager to amuse themselves at his expense—including Saint-Simon himself, despite his professed friendship:

> As soon as he began to dance at the second ball, those who were near stood up, those who were far off climbed wherever they could get a sight; and the shouts of laughter were mingled with clapping of hands. Every one, even the King himself, laughed heartily, and most of us quite loud, so that I do not think any one was ever treated so before.[54]

After this, Saint-Simon tells us, Montbron disappeared and was scarcely seen thereafter.

Another self-banishment was likewise the result of some malice aforethought by those looking for a laugh. In this case, however, the laughter was hidden from its victim until after the fact. The Abbé de Caumartin, feeling privileged by his powerful friends, felt entitled to a jest at the expense of the bishop of Noyon. Known for his vanity and his bombastic speaking style, Noyon had been nominated by the king for membership in the prestigious French Academy. Caumartin, the Academy's director, created an elaborate parody for the occasion of Noyon's induction, "full of pompous phrases, turning the prelate into ridicule, while they seemed to praise him." He even went so far as to take his draft to Noyon himself for approval. The unsuspecting victim attended the event in his honor at the Academy with complacency, although others were in on the joke: "The King and the Court were there, all expecting to be diverted." The audience supported the joker by assuring Noyon that the praise was genuine, despite their amusement at the ridiculous speech. For some time Noyon plumed himself on the great accolades, not suspecting the trick that had been played, even though the story of his humiliation had spread, as court gossip so reliably did. When at last he was convinced of the truth, he was enraged and complained to the king of how he had been made "the sport and laughing-stock of all the world." The king was ready to punish the prankster, but Caumartin escaped with a reprimand, since he had so deviously enlisted Noyon himself to approve his speech. Bishop Noyon, however, absented himself from court: he "retired into his diocese to hide his shame, and remained there a long time."[55]

Of course, both here and in the case of Montbron, we have only Saint-Simon's word for it that shame over ridicule was the cause of absence from court. How did he know why they were away? One can see here a projection created by the court's self-concept of the power of its ridicule—fed by its own gossip network of people explaining to each other why someone had left. This idea was also fueled by their sense of the court's powerful attraction as the center of power and promotion. Whether it reflects the real feelings of the targets or not (maybe they were quite happy to be away from the snake pit at court, or perhaps they were absent for other reasons), it reveals how powerful the laughers felt.[56]

Laughter and Protocol

The Montbron incident is a telling one, not only because of the discomfiture and flight of the unhappy young man, but also for its hints about the laughter protocol at court. At first, as Montbron flailed about trying to correct his missteps, laughter erupted "in despite of the respect due to the person of the King." Normally, then, the royal presence inhibited some laughter, demanding control of the impulse. At the first ball, the hooting occurred even though the king managed, with some difficulty, to maintain his usual gravity. But at the second exposure, the laughter burst all bounds and precedents. And what was so funny? As in much of Sévigné's laughter, a lack of the inside knowledge and skills of aristocratic comportment was a great spur to ridicule. In this case, Montbron's lack of the precise physical control needed for the complexities of court dance proved to be too much for the even subtler self-control of the courtiers over their urge to laugh. And in fact, they felt entitled to laugh, even without the king's permission or countenance. Having schooled and disciplined themselves to a demanding comportment that signaled both their superiority and their subjection, the courtiers found the fumbles of an outsider irresistibly absurd.

Saint-Simon describes the Montbron episode as a singular event: "I do not think anyone was ever treated so before." This was not the only occasion when there was general laughter at someone's expense, however, or when the king himself joined in. Some years later, the Prince de Condé played a malicious trick at a court masquerade. He persuaded M. de Luxembourg to wear a costume featuring enormous horns—the sign of the cuckold. Since everyone knew of the loose conduct of Luxembourg's wife, there was laughter throughout the ball, including by the king. In this case the butt of the joke seems to have remained oblivious, flattered by the prince's interest in his costume.[57] On a less grand occasion, the king and his courtiers all laughed at a practical joke played on a number of court ladies. The ladies attended prayers on Thursdays and Sundays, but only when they thought the king would be there to see him. One day when they were awaiting the king's arrival, Major Brissac announced that he wasn't coming, prompting most of them to leave. The king arrived to find the chapel nearly empty of ladies: "At the conclusion of the prayers Brissac related what he had done, not without dwelling on the piety of the Court ladies. The King and all who accompanied him laughed heartily."[58] This story too spread throughout the court—which is surely how Saint-Simon learned of it.

In spaces apart from formal court gatherings, laughter erupted freely. When the king withdrew instead of pressing his advantage against the Prince of Orange in 1693, the Prince de Conti thought it was a huge joke. With only the precaution of sending the servants away, he "told me about the King's retreat, dying with laughter, making great fun of him, despite my youth, for he had confidence in me."[59] This was on campaign, but Saint-Simon heard a lot of people laugh at court, including about the king—in the latter's absence, of course. Philippe d'Orleans was "bursting with laughter" when recounting how Louis XIV didn't want to allow his nephew to go with Orleans' army to Spain, because the young man's father was a Jansenist, member of a puritanical Catholic group; but when assured that the nephew didn't believe in God at all, the king dropped his objection. As this story "ran all through the Court and all over the town," most people laughed "with all their heart" that the king found it better to be an atheist than a sectarian.[60]

The laughter here was not subtle, even though courtesy books had long been criticizing loud laughter as crude. Saint-Simon hints at this restraining attitude in his praise of the salon of Ninon de l'Enclos, the famous courtesan and intellectual who managed to keep a high reputation among the elite despite her free lifestyle. In her company, there was ample wit and repartée, but no loud laughing.[61] On the other hand, the Prince de Conti had a braying laugh[62]—or, as Saint-Simon says, in anyone else it would be called that. The frequency of laughter suggests that faces at the Versailles court were perhaps not as immobile as Jones implies, apart from ceremonial occasions. There certainly was dissimulation at court—courtiers were advised to hide their true feelings—but that is not the same as avoiding all expression of feeling. It might involve the counterfeiting of emotions one did not feel. And, although people had the bad teeth that Jones documents, they did not trouble to hide them and were ready to laugh about it. The Dauphine (wife of the heir to the throne) had teeth that were all rotten, according to Saint-Simon, but "she was the first to talk and jest" about them.[63] In another telling scene, Saint-Simon recounts how Cardinal d'Estrées joked with the king about his bad teeth. The Cardinal, despite his advanced age, had a full and visible set of strong white teeth. When the king complained of his own lack of teeth, d'Estrees said, "Teeth, sire! Who has any teeth?" Jones cites the incident to show the bad dental situation, but he downplays the laughter that follows: "the King laughed at this reply, and all present also, including the Cardinal, who was not in the slightest degree embarrassed."[64] The joke and response became part of the court lore, remembered, retold, and collected by the memoirist. Whether the details of the story are true or not (it was another case of hearsay about an incident in the past), the bad teeth were matter for amusement rather than shameful silence.

It was especially noteworthy when the king laughed on public occasions, as at the ball where Montbron danced. Like his courtiers, he laughed more in private, even though he usually enacted an imposing gravity on formal public occasions. According to the Italian nobleman Jean-Baptiste Primi Visconti,

> When someone speaks to him in too elaborate a style, he privately makes fun of it with [his mistress] Madame de Montespan. But in public he quietly keeps a straight face, with the gravity of a king on the stage.[65]

But, of course, nothing was truly private here. Even the royal bedroom was a ceremonial space where courtiers gathered to attend the king; sotto voce jokes with his mistresses could be observed, if not overheard. According to Saint-Simon, Madame de Montespan was especially dangerous to her enemies because of her powers of ridicule, which she could pour directly into the ear of the king.[66]

★ ★ ★

Saint-Simon thought the Montbron incident was a first; by the late eighteenth century, the French court's reputation for virulent ridicule grew more extreme. The English traveler Arthur Young, visiting the court in 1787, was offended by the mocking laughter of a lady whom he asked a question, "as if he had said the stupidest thing in the world," because he was unaware of a French custom. In her later memoirs, the Comtesse de Boigne criticized the ridicule practiced at the court of Louis XVI, asserting that courtiers used it mercilessly against those seen as outsiders, and even against their own. One of the victims the countess pitied, the young M. De Lusson, was of lesser birth, like Montbron. Handsome, rich, and accustomed to the best company in Paris, he ventured to show himself at one of the balls at Versailles: "He was driven out with such harshness that, made desperate by the constant ridicule at a time when ridicule was the worst of ills, he killed himself on arriving in Paris."[67] A less extreme but still humiliating fate befell M. de Chabannes, the man who fell while dancing on his first appearance at a royal ball. He happened to exclaim as he fell, "Jésus, Maria"—and no matter his later brilliant exploits as an officer, according to the countess he was ridiculed with this phrase ever after. These stories were born of post-Revolutionary hindsight, of course; the countess herself was only eight years old at the revolution in 1789. But they testify to the growing reputation for heartless laughter that was already beginning to brew in the time of Saint-Simon. Perhaps the status anxiety of Old Regime court nobles, no longer wielding their own independent power and surrounded by upstarts, enhanced the power of ridicule in a way similar to what Peter Jones found in the twelfth-century English court. There, the rising "new men" from the ranks of educated non-nobles gave new prominence to personal factors like wit, challenging the more stable pillar of noble birth.[68]

There is an irony in the apparent pre-revolutionary pinnacle of courtly derision, since it was also in the eighteenth century that theorists began emphasizing the positive qualities of laughter. Perhaps this change was partly in reaction against perceived abuses, just as the early advocates of courtliness were reacting against rough buffoonery. The Earl of Shaftesbury, writing in 1709, saw laughter as an element of social bonding, rather in the way we saw it operating for Felix Platter. Another irony of courtly laughter, and probably another contributor to the ideas of Shaftesbury and other pro-laughter thinkers, was how charming it could be for those who were not ridiculed and excluded. The British conservative Edmund Burke regretted the loss of French courtly manners after the Revolution, and he was far from alone. The reputation of this courtly milieu for gaiety and delight harks back to the ideal of Castiglione. The courtier's skills of wit were supposed to spread enjoyment and good feeling among his company.

Madame de Sévigné offers a link to both the warm glow of courtly sociability and its exclusionary elitism. She used laughter and humor to foster intimacy among her circle of family and friends, and to preserve emotional ties across distance in her letters. At the same time, even in this relatively gentle version of elite humor, people who lacked the right kind of manners and speech were ridiculous. One can see her targeted laughter as exclusive, but not aggressive; the Bretons and peasants were already outsiders to Parisian high society, not branded as such by the ridicule itself. When she laughed at her neighbors or at a courtier who breached protocol, she could still maintain friendly relations with them. Among the men and women of the Versailles court, however, ridicule went far beyond these bounds. The courtiers had distanced themselves from crude practical joking of the physical kind, but delivered sharper wounds that could not easily be laughed off.

Notes

1 Alexandre Maral, *Le roi, la cour et Versailles: le coup d'éclat permanent 1682–1789* (Paris: Perrin, 2013), 357.
2 Norbert Elias, *The Court Society*, trans. Edmund Jephcott (New York: Pantheon, 1983), 111.
3 Colin Jones, *The Smile Revolution: In Eighteenth-Century Paris* (Oxford, UK: Oxford University Press), 11.
4 See Peter Burke, *The Fortunes of the Courtier: The European Reception of Castiglione's 'Cortegiano'* (University Park: Penn State University Press, 1996).
5 Baldesar Castiglione, *The Book of the Courtier: The Singleton Translation*, ed. Daniel Javitch (New York and London: Norton, 2002); for the quotations I have also consulted Baldassarre Castiglione, *Il Libro del Cortegiano*, ed. Giulio Preti (Torino: Einaudi, 1965), http://www.letteraturaitaliana.net/pdf/Volume_4/t84.pdf; and the translation by Leonard Epstein Opdycke (New York, 1903), https://archive.org/stream/bookofcourtier00castuoft/bookofcourtier00castuoft_djvu.txt.
6 Castiglione, *Book of the Courtier*, 12 (Book 1, chap. 4).
7 See JoAnn Cavallo, "Joking Matters: Politics and Dissimulation in Castiglione's Book of the Courtier," *Renaissance Quarterly* 53, no. 2 (Summer 2000): 402–24.
8 Similarly, Cathy Shrank has recently observed that in dialogues like Castiglione's, laughter in action was far more positive than in theories about laughter; Cathy Shrank, "Mocking or Mirthful: Laughter in Early Modern Dialogue," in *The Power of Laughter and Satire in Early Modern Britain: Political and Religious Culture, 1500–1820,* ed. Mark Knights and Adam Morton (Woodbridge, Suffolk: Boydell & Brewer, 2017), 48–66, esp. 58–61.
9 Castiglione, *Book of the Courtier*, 102 (Book 2, chap. 41).
10 Castiglione, *Book of the Courtier*, 210 (Book 4, chap. 4).
11 Castiglione, *Book of the Courtier*, 210 (Book 4, chap. 5).
12 Castiglione, *Book of the Courtier*, 194 (Book 3, chap. 59); 153 (Book 3, chap. 6).
13 Castiglione, *Book of the Courtier*, 106 (Book 2, chap. 46).
14 Castiglione, *Book of the Courtier*, 94 (Book 2, chap. 32).
15 Castiglione, *Book of the Courtier*, 114, 103 (Book 2, chaps. 57, 43).
16 Quoted in Chris Holcomb, *Mirth Making: The Rhetorical Discourse on Jesting in Early Modern England* (Columbia, SC: University of South Carolina Press, 2001), 132.
17 *Oxford English Dictionary*, s.v. wit.
18 Holcomb, *Mirth Making*, 138.
19 See Norbert Schindler, "Ein bäuerlicher Münchhausen? Die Memoiren des Zillertaler 'Hoftirolers' Peter Prosch (1789)," *Österreichische Zeitschrift für Volkskunde* 72, no. 1 (2018): 85–110; Dorinda Outram, *Four Fools in the Age of Reason: Laughter, Cruelty, and Power in Early Modern Germany* (Charlottesville and London: University of Virginia Press, 2019), 86–105.
20 Laurent Joubert, *Traité du Ris, Contenant ses causes, et mervelheus effais, curieusemant recerchés, raisonnés et observés* (Paris, 1579), https://babel.hathitrust.org/cgi/pt?id=ucm.5309454426&view=1up&seq=5&skin=2021.
21 See Jones, *The Smile Revolution*, 3.
22 *Le Dictionnaire de l'Académie française* (1694), s.v. rire, https://artflsrv03.uchicago.edu/philologic4/publicdicos/query?report=bibliography&head=rire.
23 References for quotations are from Marie de Rabutin-Chantal, Marquise de Sévigné, *The Letters of Madame de Sévigné*, ed. A. Edward Newton, 7 vols. (Philadelphia: J. P. Horn, 1927); Sévigné, *Correspondance*, ed. Roger Duchêne, 3 vols. (Paris: Gallimard, 1972). Here Sévigné, *Correspondance*, 2:317, 11 June 1676.

24 Eckhard Schörle, *Die Verhöflichung des Lachens* (Bielefeld: Aisthesis Verlag, 2007), 154; Sévigné, *Letters*, 1:95, 11 February 1671.

25 Sévigné, *Letters*, 1:324, 23 December 1671.

26 Sévigné, *Letters*, 1:120, 11 March 1671; *Correspondance*, 1:181.

27 Sévigné, *Letters*, 1:144, 8 April 1671; *Correspondance*, 1:209.

28 Sévigné, *Letters*, 1:324, 23 December 1671; *Correspondance*, 1:398.

29 Sévigné, *Letters*, 1:145–6, 8 April 1671; *Correspondance*, 1:211.

30 Sévigné, *Letters*, 1:214; *Correspondance*, 1:288. Marie-Anne du Plessis, member of a noble Breton family with a chateau near Sévigné's; see Roger Duchêne, *Madame de Sévigné ou la chance d'être femme* (Paris: Fayard, 1982), 164.

31 Sévigné, *Letters*, 1:172–73; 1 May 1671; *Correspondance*, 1:241.

32 Sévigné, *Letters*, 1:153, 15 April 1671; *Correspondance*, 1:221.

33 Sévigné, *Letters*, 1:207, 28 June 1671; *Correspondance*, 1:281.

34 François duc de La Rochefoucauld, *Reflections; or Sentences and Moral Maxims,* ed. and trans. J.W. Willis Bund and J. Hain Friswell (London, 1871), https://www.gutenberg.org/files/9105/9105-h/9105-h.htm.

35 Sévigné, *Correspondance*, 2:981, 21 June 1680.

36 Sévigné, *Correspondance*, 1:480, 15 April 1672.

37 Sévigné, *Letters*, 1:157, 17 April 1671; *Correspondance*, 1:226.

38 Sévigné, *Letters*, 1:159–60, 22 April 1671; *Correspondance*, 1:228.

39 Sévigné, *Letters*, 1:264, 283, 6 September 1671, 4 October 1671; *Correspondance*, 1:339, 358.

40 Sévigné, *Letters*, 1:250, 19 August 1671; *Correspondance*, 1:326.

41 Sévigné, *Letters*, 1:249, 19 August 1671; *Correspondance*, 1:325.

42 Sévigné, *Letters*, 1:230, 26 July 1671; *Correspondance*, 1:305.

43 Sévigné, *Correspondance*, 2:212–13, 5 January 1676.

44 Sévigné, *Letters*, 1:233–34, 29 July 1671; *Correspondance*, 1:309.

45 Sévigné, *Letters*, 1:214, 5 July 1671; *Correspondance*, 1:289.

46 Sévigne, *Correspondance*, 2:953, 31 May 1680.

47 Sévigné, *Letters,* 1:104, 20 February 1671; *Correspondance*, 1:166.

48 Elias, *The Court Society*, 110–11.

49 Sévigné, *Letters*, 1:303, 11 November 1671; *Correspondance*, 1:378.

50 Sévigné, *Correspondance*, 1:669, 15 January 1674.

51 Louis de Rouvroy, duc de Saint-Simon, *The Memoirs of Louis XIV, His Court and the Regency*, trans. Bayle St. John, https://www.gutenberg.org/files/3875/3875-h/3875-h.htm#link2H_INTR, chap. 9; Saint-Simon, *Mémoires de Saint-Simon*, ed. Arthur de Boislisle (Paris, 1879–1919), 3:77–78 (cited below as Boislisle, *Mémoires de Saint-Simon*). I have also consulted *Historical Memoirs of the Duc de Saint-Simon*, ed. and trans. Lucy Norton, 3 vols. (London: Prion Books, 2000).

52 See, for example, the discussion and references in Rudolf Dekker, *Family, Culture and Society in the Diary of Constantijn Huygens Jr, Secretary to Stadholder-King William of Orange* (Leiden and Boston: Brill, 2013), esp. 119; Nicholas Hammond, *Gossip, Sexuality and Scandal in France (1610–1715)* (Oxford and New York: Peter Lang, 2011).

53 Saint-Simon, *Memoirs*, chap. 89; Boislisle, *Mémoires de Saint-Simon*, 33:83.

54 Saint-Simon, *Memoirs*, chap. 2; Boislisle, *Mémoires de Saint-Simon*, 1:97–99.

55 Saint-Simon, *Memoirs*, chap. 6; Boislisle, *Mémoires de Saint-Simon*, 2:194–201.

56 For a similar assumption by court elites of their power to police others' behavior with ridicule, see Antoine de Baecque, *Les éclats du rire: la culture des rieurs au XVIIIe siècle* (Paris: Calmann-Lévy, 2000), 21–55.

57 Saint-Simon, *Memoirs*, chap. 16; Boislisle, *Mémoires de Saint-Simon,* 7:57–60.

58 Saint-Simon, *Memoirs*, chap. 40.

59 Saint-Simon, *Memoirs*, chap. 4; Boislisle, *Mémoires de Saint-Simon*, 1:233.

60 Saint-Simon, *Memoirs*, chap. 39.

61 Saint-Simon, *Memoirs*, chap. 33.

62 Saint-Simon, *Memoirs*, chap. 45; Norton, *Historical Memoirs,* 1:420.

63 Saint-Simon, *Memoirs*, chap. 59.

64 Saint-Simon, *Memoirs*, chap. 69; Boislisle, *Mémoires de Saint-Simon*, 25:182; cf. Jones, *Smile Revolution*, 17.

65 Quoted in Maral, *Le roi, la cour et Versailles*, 341–42.

66 Saint-Simon, *Memoirs*, chap. 75.

67 Maral, *Le roi, la cour et Versailles,* 356–57.

68 See Peter J. A. Jones, *Laughter and Power in the Twelfth Century* (Oxford: Oxford University Press, 2019), esp. 103.

FIGURE 6.1 Samuel Pepys as a young man, portrait by John Hayls

Source: © Niday Picture Library/Alamy Stock Photo

6

LAUGHTER AND THE RISING MAN

Samuel Pepys

The affair of the tankard was an awkward episode for Samuel Pepys. Meant as a harmless practical joke, it marked a permanent estrangement between him and his senior colleague at the Navy Office, Sir William Penn. This gentleman, father of the more famous founder of Pennsylvania, was not amused.

Their relationship had begun on a friendly footing, with Pepys delighted at the elder man's entertaining company, including his ribald humor. On a walk together in October 1660, they "in our way had a great deal of merry discourse, and find him to be a merry fellow and pretty good-natured and sings very bawdy songs."[1] It was a different story the following year, when he and Sir William Batten staged a fake theft of Penn's tankard. Batten spirited it away, and Pepys wrote ransom letters purporting to come from the thief. He gloated about the jest in August 1661: "This day I counterfeited a letter to Sir W. Penn, as from the thief that stole his tankard lately, only to abuse [deceive] and laugh at him." The following week, they "were very merry with Sir W. Penn about the loss of his tankard, though all be but a cheat, and he do not yet understand it." The joke was carried pretty far: the conspirators actually collected 30 shillings from Penn and used the money to fund a night of convivial drinking at the Dolphin tavern, with Penn himself and a crowd of friends. Penn was too fuddled to grasp what was going on:

> But so much the better; for I believe when he do come to understand it, he will be angry; he has so talked of the business himself and the letters, up and down, that he will be ashamed to be found abused in it.

Pepys thought it all "very good sport," though to be sure there was a touch of malice in it. He later learned "that Sir W. Penn do take our jest of the tankard very ill—which I am sorry for."[2] The two were often at odds after that. Likely they would not have gotten along anyway, but the tankard episode did not help.

DOI: 10.4324/9781003247517-7

Pepys's diary offers a remarkably rich look at the laughing relations of a young man climbing the social scale with the bourgeois tools of education and ability. It is full of laughter across lines of status difference, in a society that combined sharp hierarchies with rising social mobility. Pepys loved to laugh with everyone, yet his laughter highlights the distinctiveness of his own social position as well as his concept of the place of others. Laughter flowed across boundaries of status and gender, public and private, in ways that shed light on laughter as both social lubricant and source of potential conflict.

In the Penn episode, the other participants in the joking were both senior to him; both had been knighted (and he regularly names them with their titles of "Sir," even in the private diary he wrote in cryptic shorthand); both were seasoned naval commanders who had navigated the rocky political terrain of the Interregnum and Restoration. Pepys, at 28, was a sharp young civilian, with a Cambridge education, already in a highly responsible position as clerk of the Navy Office and on his way up. None of these men were of high birth; the knighthoods had come of rough-and-tumble service in a time of political upheaval. Pepys himself clearly thought he might well gain the same honor through his alternate path of ascent through education and intellect. He was annoyed, already in 1660, when he learned that his relations the Joyces (another set of social climbers) were laughing at the idea that Pepys might be knighted by the king.[3] How much of Penn's resentment came of being laughed at by a junior whippersnapper along with the old salt Batten? And the mode of the jest—a clever forgery by a youngster who owed his advancement to exceptionally fine pencil-pushing—must have rankled. Questions of status arise in other Pepysian laughter as well—with superiors, with inferiors, and in socially doubtful circumstances. How did laughter operate in the negotiation of social hierarchies, for Pepys and for others?

A Restoration of Merriment

The Restoration of the English monarchy in 1660—scene of Pepys's rapid rise—followed the famously puritanical Interregnum ruled by Oliver Cromwell and then, briefly, his son Richard. Notorious for doing away with Christmas among other unruly celebrations, the era of Puritan dominance has been linked with the death of what became known, nostalgically, as "merry old England." Ronald Hutton has documented a decline in popular festivities already in the 1560s and 1570s, driven by the campaigning of the godly. To be fair, we should note that Christmas merriment involved a lot more alcohol than modern Americans might imagine. The pious reformers worried about drunkenness and other vicious behaviors born of idleness, such as the sexual license they saw promoted by the risqué play of May Day games. At the same time, reformers sought to cleanse Sunday, the Sabbath devoted to God, of all worldliness. Laughing, along with dancing, was among the proscribed activities on the Sabbath in a 1560 catechism by the Protestant evangelical Thomas Becon.[4]

Pepys was raised in an atmosphere of Sabbath observance, and he scrupulously labels each "Lord's day." But laughing and social merriment were part of what he considered appropriate Sunday amusements, alongside regular attendance at church. Ridicule of silly sermons was also allowed. Sundays were officially honored under the Restoration: Pepys observed in November 1662 "that in the streets and churches the Sunday is kept in appearance as well as I have known it at any time."[5] Pepys was not a zealous religionist, of course. But there is reason to think that the humorless image can be overdrawn even for Puritans and other religious enthusiasts. Laughing at the ungodly was a legitimate brand of fun—though not in church, perhaps. Pepys's contemporary further down the social scale, the Lancashire shopkeeper's apprentice Roger Lowe, adhered to the Puritan clergy who refused to comply with the new Act of Uniformity in 1662. Yet he relished the comic and sexually suggestive stories he told among male friends at the minister's house, recounting them in his diary complete with dialogue.[6] Even evangelicals sought to persuade youth that religion was not "an enemy to your mirth, pleasure, and delight."[7]

A Lover of Laughter

Like his contemporary Madame de Sévigné, Samuel Pepys loved to laugh, and he recorded many instances of jollity in the daily record that he kept from 1660 to 1669. The son of a tailor, Pepys gained his elite education and advancement through a combination of scholarship and patronage. In 1660, he was just taking up his first position at the Navy Office, gained through the patronage of his cousin Sir Edward Montagu, first Earl of Sandwich. The post came with a house and a definite boost in rank. Pepys's professional acumen more than repaid his patron's trust. Long before his secret diary became known, he gained fame for his achievements in naval administration and beyond. He eventually became Secretary of the Admiralty, a Member of Parliament, and president of the prestigious Royal Society. His youthful diary belongs to the early years of the Restoration era, as the fun-loving Charles II ended the more austere atmosphere of the Cromwellian Interregnum. This king sometimes even appeared too frivolous to Pepys himself—a sharp contrast with the sober Louis XIV, as well as with his English predecessor.

Pepys laughed enthusiastically and inclusively—with superiors, inferiors, friends, family, men, and women, in private and in public. At the same time, his laughing sociability was calibrated for purposes of social advancement. Usually adept at suiting his humor to the company he was in, Pepys seldom fell into laughter trouble. Yet he had definite ideas about good and bad laughter. In addition to laughter across status lines, his diary offers insights into laughter's place in mixed-gender sociability and evolving concepts of public and private life. As an aspiring gentleman, an official, and an intellectual, Pepys expected laughter in public spaces, such as the theater or the king's entourage, to meet certain standards of wit and decorum (expectations that were sometimes disappointed). In scenes of sociability, the matter for laughter was less scrutinized, with shared merriment the main focus.

Something of a connoisseur of laughter, Pepys frequently took note of it. His entries often speak of the degree of hilarity enjoyed in social gatherings— with other men and also in mixed company or as the only man among groups of women. He and his companions were "very merry," "mighty merry," "pretty merry," or sometimes just merry, but the amount of laughter was regularly a matter of interest. Similarly, the quality of an especially hearty laugh was worth recording. Pepys was in a sour mood on the evening of 1 January 1664, having seen a disappointing play and apparently annoyed by his aunt. But a mistake of his uncle's in saying grace after their meal sent him into "a mighty laugh (the greatest I have had these many months)."[8] Here the great laugh was roused by a small thing, perhaps by contrast to the annoyances that came before. The best laughter of all came instead at a time of more general delight at news of the navy's victory over the Dutch in September 1665:

> this news did put us all into such an ecstasy of joy, that it inspired into Sir J. Mennes and Mr. Evelyn such a spirit of mirth, that in all my life I never met with so merry a two hours.

The impromptu verses of John Evelyn "did make us all die almost with laughing." The occasion was "one of the times of my life wherein I was the fullest of true sense of joy."[9]

In some cases merriment was explicitly or implicitly heightened by consumption of alcohol. At a dinner with relatives for which Pepys supplied 18 bottles of wine, he talks of "when the women were merry and rose from table," implying a process of induced merriment.[10] At an event he learned of by hearsay, a visit by the king to the Dutch ambassador, "after dinner they drank, and were pretty merry." In March 1668, he thoroughly enjoyed the effect of alcohol on the usually sedate Thomas Hollier, surgeon at St. Thomas Hospital. At dinner he was "a little fuddled and so did talk nothing but Latin and laugh, that it was very good sport to see a sober man in such a humour, though he was not drunk to scandal."[11] But there was often no need of stimulants to spark merriment.

Laughing with Superiors—or at Them

How did Pepys laugh with people at different social levels? We can start with his social superiors. Like Benvenuto Cellini, Pepys needed patrons to get ahead— people with more status and power who could distribute favor. It was a different kind of patronage relationship from the hiring of artistic talent, however. The young Pepys relied on his wealthy and well-connected cousin Edward Montagu, later Earl of Sandwich, for both the start of his career and its substantial boost in 1660 with his appointment to the clerkship of the Navy Office. His education at Cambridge was facilitated by family connections, and as a young graduate he took up a position of factotum that brought him into intimate relations with the

Montagu family. The shared sociability and laughter of these ties continued after Pepys had set up a household of his own. While careful to maintain respect—Sandwich and his wife were always "my Lord" and "my Lady" in the diary—Pepys had fun with them. He often played games with their children or ate meals with them. On 30 August 1661, he went with his wife, "dined with the children, and after dinner up to my Lady's bedside, and talked and laughed a good while."[12] In November, his wife went without him, but with his Aunt Wight and another woman, to visit Lady Sandwich, where they "danced and were very merry; and my Lady very fond, as she is always of my wife."[13]

He enjoyed, too, occasions when the Earl was ready to share merriment with him, as in May 1662, at dinner together with Sandwich, Mr. Browne (clerk of the House of Lords), and Browne's wife and mother. Browne and Sandwich were "mighty merry—among other things, saying that the Queen is a very agreeable lady, and paints still."[14] Possibly Pepys's greatest coup was his success in negotiating a marriage between the Montagus' daughter Jemima and Philip, son of Sir George Carteret. There was "mighty mirth" at Pepys's account of the good news, and after the wedding they were "Very merry at Dinner, and so to talk and laugh after dinner, and up and down, some to [one] place, some to another—full of content on all sides."[15] The initiative was always scrupulously left in the hands of his patrons, however. Pepys, for all his close association—having often looked after young Jemima and played games with her, besides his activity in the wedding arrangements—did not venture to kiss the bride until expressly invited to do so by Lady Sandwich.[16]

Pepys was content to acknowledge his own lower status in relation to the Montagus; he respected their intelligence and was grateful for their aid and favor. With his middle-class notions of meritocracy, however, he was contemptuous of the incompetence he often found in colleagues at the Navy Office, particularly some of his bosses. Unlike Cellini's aggressive laughter in the face of rivals, however, his derision was typically in the target's absence. He and his coworkers laughed readily at absent superiors when they did not meet their professional standards. Pepys was scathing about the lapses of Sir John Mennes, a clueless superior at the Navy Office. On 10 January 1663, he was in the office with a coworker when Mennes came in,

> which at last he did; and so, beyond my expectation, he was willing to sign his accounts, notwithstanding all his objections, which really were very material; and yet now like a doting coxcomb [a fool] he signs the accounts without the least satisfaction—for which we both sufficiently laughed at him and Sir W. Batten after they had signed them and were gone.[17]

The following year they were laughing at Mennes again. When Sir George Carteret was awarded a handsome lodging by the Council, Mennes

> took occasion, in the most childish and most unbeseeming manner, to reproach us all; but most himself, that he was not valued as Controller among

us, nor did anything but only set his hand to paper (which is but too true); and every body had a palace, and he no house to lie in. . . . It was to no end to oppose, but all bore it, and after laughed at him for it."[18]

Sir William Batten was again a figure of fun in 1665 because of his untutored writing style. The Cambridge-educated Pepys was amused by the literary failings of men like Batten, who had come up through the navy with far less education. In June 1665, while England was engaged in naval conflict with the Dutch, they received word of victory from Batten. Pepys did not have much confidence in this news, since Batten was not actually with the fleet, and besides, his letter was "writ so simply that we all made good mirth of it."[19] This was at dinner at Sir George Carteret's house, where the whole Navy Board was in attendance. Here Pepys was able to join with superiors as well as peers in laughter at Batten's expense.

As a brilliant and efficient young official, Pepys was regularly amused by those less competent, and he enjoyed opportunities to laugh about them with his seniors. He shared more laughter at ineptitude with his superior, William Coventry (later Sir William), over the doings of Commissioner Peter Pett, whose complaints "did make us laugh mightily; and was good sport to think how awkwardly he goes about a thing that he has no courage of his own nor mind to do." Pett had wanted their support in suspending two pursers, apparently unable to do it on his own.[20] Together with his patron Sir Edward Montagu, Pepys laughed at the poor arguments of Captain George Cocke, as they stopped to dine along the way while traveling. The men were "very merry," but got into disagreement about the Dutch war,

> Cocke undertaking to prove that they were able to wage war with us three year together—which, though it may be true, yet, not being satisfied with his arguments, my Lord and I did oppose the strength of his arguments, which brought us to a great heat—he being a conceited man but of no Logic in his head at all, which made my Lord and I mirth. Anon we parted, and back again, we hardly having a word all the way, he being so vexed at our not yielding to his persuasion.[21]

It was especially in relations with his betters that Pepys took some care in jesting, sometimes worrying that a joke might work to his disadvantage if heard by the wrong person. In the incident of Penn's tankard, of course, he came to regret the joke that he had so much enjoyed in the making. In some other cases too, he felt that he might have jested in the wrong way or with the wrong person. In 1668, while on his way to Westminster Hall on dealings with Parliament,

> the Duke of York called to me whither I was going and I answered aloud, "To wait on our Masters at Westminster!" at which he and all the company laughed; but I was sorry and troubled for it afterward, for fear any Parliament-man should have been there, and will be a caution to me for the time to come.[22]

Pepys, as a civil servant who had grown up under the Interregnum of Cromwell, knew the danger of becoming embroiled in combative political allegiances. He had to deal with Parliament in managing day-to-day naval business and did not want to get on their bad side. In the longer term, the political winds might blow power over his very position into parliamentary hands—a danger that actually came to pass twenty years later, with the "Glorious Revolution" of 1688. So he put himself on guard against rash political joking.

On the other hand, Pepys sometimes expected more license for jest than he received, especially where the lines of status were murky. Lord Brouncker, another titled colleague at the Navy Office, maintained a long-term relationship with his mistress, Abigail Williams. The bond persisted throughout Brouncker's life, and Williams inherited his property. Pepys, however, after having been merry in her company on several occasions, misjudged the degree of respect that she would demand. In 1665, he was "somewhat vexed at a snappish answer Madam Williams did give me to herself, upon my speaking a free word to her in mirth, calling her a mad jade. She answered, we were not so well acquainted yet."[23] As the mistress of Lord Brouncker, Williams likely felt offended at the liberty he was taking. "Jade" was a term of insult for women, comparable to "hussy" or "minx."[24] Pepys's description of her words as "snappish" suggests that he thought his jest was perfectly fine and should have been taken in good part. But would he have used this language to her if she had been Brouncker's wife and titled "my lady" rather than the semi-honorific "madam"? It seems unlikely, especially as he had been privately labeling her a "doxy" and "whore" in his diary. Lord Brouncker was obviously a social superior, but Pepys did not feel deferential toward Williams. She was probably right to take offense.

Jests about religious matters also could raise concern, but again, it was a concern about who might hear the joke and take it the wrong way. In April 1660, while sailing for Holland, Pepys had qualms about his behavior to the ship's minister: "It comes now in my mind to observe that I am sensible that I have been a little too free to make mirth with the Minister of our ship, he being a very sober and an upright man."[25] When he was with safe company, however, he did not shy from joking that touched on religion. He recorded with some delight the fun at his own garbling of a gravestone inscription, with "much mirth at a tomb on which was 'Come sweet Jesu' and I read 'Come sweet Mall [Moll, a girl's nickname],' &c., at which Captain Pett and I had good laughter."[26] On another occasion he shocked his aunt by praising the Catholic religious service—quite a touchy subject in an English cultural and political climate that was strongly anti-"papist." Dining at the house of his Uncle and Aunt Wight, Pepys "all supper did vex my aunt talking in commendation of the mass which I had been at today. But excused it afterwards, that it was only to make mirth."[27] Such joking likely did not help Pepys years later, when suspicions arose that he might have Catholic tendencies and excessive loyalty to the banished Stuart king. He also enjoyed "talking merrily about the difference in our religions" with the Catholic Lord Almoner Howard, after a pleasing monastery tour.[28]

If one had to be careful about making the wrong joke to the wrong person, it might also be politic to laugh even when one didn't feel like it. Pepys had fraught and sometimes hostile feelings about both Sir William Batten and Sir William Penn. But he was obliged not only to work with them at the Navy Office but to live in close proximity, as they all had adjacent houses that went with their posts. They and their families were frequently socializing and visiting each other. Pepys enjoyed Penn's merry company when they were first acquainted, but a few years later he was laughing only for appearance's sake: "At noon dined with Sir W. Penn, a piece of beef only, and I counterfeited a friendship and mirth which I cannot have with him."[29] By April 1666 he was not bothering to act amused at Penn's "talking simply and fondly [foolishly] as he used to do." His own social ascent, he felt, had made it possible to take a different attitude: "I find myself to slight him and his simple talk, I thank God, and that my condition will enable me to do it."[30] But later that year, Penn's growing reputation as a naval commander made Pepys think he had better laugh with him again. He invited Penn's wife and daughter to dine with him,

> which at noon they did, and Sir W. Penn with them, and pretty merry we were. And though I do not love him, yet I find it necessary to keep in with him—his good service at Sheerness in getting out the fleet being much taken notice of, and reported to the King and Duke even from the Prince and Duke of Albemarle themselves, and made the most of to me and them by Sir W. Coventry. Therefore, I think it discretion, great and necessary discretion, to keep in with him.[31]

The following March, he received news that his mother was on the verge of death "yet was obliged to sup at Sir W. Penn's, and my wife; and there counterfeited some little mirth, but my heart was sad."[32] A few days later, he was in company with both Penn and Batten, traveling to review the repair of ships, but also being entertained at a house where they were

> mighty extraordinary merry (too merry for me, whose mother died so lately; but they know it not, so cannot reproach me thereon, though I do reproach myself); and in going home had many good stories of Sir W. Batten, and one of W. Penn, the most tedious and silly and troublesome (he forcing us to hear him) that ever I heard in my life.[33]

The men were constantly in company, both at work and at home; yet Pepys did not tell them that his mother had died, instead forcing himself to join in the feigning of convivial laughter. (He may have been waiting for his "very handsome" mourning clothes, which arrived some days later.)

The duties of sociability sometimes called for merriment even apart from concern for professional advancement. Pepys was not fond of his relatives the Joyces, likely associating them with the lower social level he sought to transcend. Still, he made merry with them: "to dinner, and in comes Uncle Fenner and the two Joyces; I sent for a barrel of oysters and a breast of veal roasted, and were very merry but I cannot down with their dull company and impertinent."[34] Laughter could be used to cover his dislike, or, as in another case in 1663, his jealousy. Pepys had conceived suspicions of his wife's relations with her dancing instructor Pembleton. Ashamed of his own jealousy, he was chagrined when his wife mentioned in front of her maid that she would not let Pembleton in when Pepys was away from home. On 27 May Pepys joined his wife in the dancing and paid the master for his month's services. Then they invited him to supper: "After dancing, we took him down to supper and were very merry; and I made myself so and kind to him as much as I could, to prevent his discourse; though I perceive to my trouble that he knows all."[35]

Laughing with Inferiors

In relations with those below him on the social spectrum, Pepys was markedly at ease in laughing. He liked to laugh with his servants and other employees, as well as with service workers he met in the course of his days. In 1660, he was renovating his new house near the Navy Office, improving it to fit his rising resources. He had a good time with the men working on the house, as he recorded on 28 September: "All the afternoon at home among my workmen; work till 10 or 11 at night; and did give them drink and were very merry with them—it being my luck to meet with a sort of Drolling workmen upon all occasions."[36] The "drolling"—joking—was a delight to him when he encountered readiness in jest. On 4 August 1662 he went with Captain Cocke and two men in a coach to Gravesend, where they encountered an acquaintance, "an old waterman of mine." They had supper together, "being very merry with the drolling drunken coachman that brought us," before heading back.[37] Similarly, in August 1663, he

> went by water to the Old Swan by a boat; where I had good sport with one of the young men about his travels as far as Fox-hall [Vauxhall, just upriver]—in mockery; which yet the fellow answered me most prettily and travellerlike unto my very good mirth.[38]

Laughter across barriers of class was not new in Pepys's time, and we should not be too quick to take it as a sign of social bonding. A cautionary reminder of its limits emerges from the distant past, in a manual on agricultural management by the ancient Roman author Columella. Here the master finds it useful to laugh and joke with his slaves on the farm, to put them at their ease and make them more willing to work.[39] Dignified distance versus camaraderie—which is the best management tool? Advice givers and moralists have differed on these points even within the same time and place. But the potential fluidity of status in early modern Europe made some see laughter as a field of risk.

Arguably, the freedom to laugh and joke with inferiors implies secure confidence in one's own status. The slave master of late antiquity did not worry that laughing with the slaves would lower his own position. By contrast, early modern commentators warned of danger, as in the sixteenth-century advice book *Court of Civil Courtesy*:

> I would not advise any man to jest much with his inferiors, unless they be such as he knoweth, both can and will use restraint of over malapertness. For if a Gentleman should be saucily used by jest, by his inferior, he cannot escape disgrace, whether he bear with it, or quarrel for it.[40]

The inferior here might talk back, might mock and be "saucy" or "malapert [impudent]." Opening the disorderly space of jest among social subordinates was safe only if they could be trusted to be deferential—to laugh at the superior's jokes without presuming to turn the tables against him. Joking back could lay a claim to equality that the jesting gentleman could not well combat. Honor, that precious and vulnerable commodity, could suffer damage. As we have seen in previous chapters, legal claimants might even collect damages for the wrong sort of laughter, a recourse that was mainly open to the prosperous.

Other Renaissance advice-givers also worried about improper jesting by inferiors that could endanger the dignity of social superiors. Henry Peacham, in his 1593 *Garden of Eloquence*, thought irony and derision should be off limits for people of lower station; they might turn them against their betters. Such verbal mockery was "not a meet form of speech for every sort of person to use, especially of the inferior toward the superior."[41] This was wishful thinking, of course. But for people who aspired to the advancing standards of politeness and civility, it was important to know how to modulate jesting and laughter according to the hierarchies of status. Traditional laughter rules, going back to the thirteenth-century theologian Thomas Aquinas, had long advised attention to time, place, and person to be sure of appropriate joking. Castiglione, in *The Courtier*, added the significant variable of attention to one's own standing: the courtier should heed "time, person, and his own rank" in his "banter and witticisms."[42] It mattered who you were as well as who you were with.

Pepys was aware of such issues in his laughing relations, but he was largely free of the advice-givers' anxieties. He felt completely comfortable jesting downward with servants and workmen, a measure of confidence in his own abilities and growing success. His distinctive middling but rising status appears clearly in the way he made fun—in their absence—of superiors he found violating his own standards of merit. The points where his jesting went awry were moments when he expected more freedom from superiors than they would allow. He embraced a subordinate role with his respected patrons, but his modern ideas of meritocracy put him at odds with some placed above him whom he found unworthy of deference—such as incompetent navy bosses and the "doxy" Madam Williams.

Pepys in Mixed Company

Like most men of his day, Pepys believed in male superiority. As his low respect for Madam Williams attests, he also held to a double standard of sexual conduct for women, in spite of all his own dalliances. He has become well known for his sexual play with various women, which he recorded cryptically in his diary. Apart from the frequent groping, however, he enjoyed women's company and often appreciated the laughter sparked by their wit. Unlike some moralists, he did not assume that women who were ready to laugh in male company were likely to be sexually available. On first meeting her, he greatly enjoyed the wit of Judith Penington and perceived her to be a modest lady. Dining with her and four other men at the home of Captain Cocke, he found her to be "a very fine witty lady, one of the best I ever heard speak—and indifferent handsome."[43] A couple of weeks later, he again had occasion to dine with her in the company of some other men, where they were "mighty merry with only Madam Penington, who is a fine witty lady."[44] They stayed late into the evening, "with great mirth." A few weeks later still, he was sincerely shocked to find that she was willing to engage in sexual play as well: he and a colleague

> sat talking and playing with Mrs. Penington, whom we found undressed in her smock and petticoats by the fireside; and there we drank and laughed, and she willingly suffered me to put my hand in her bosom very wantonly, and keep it there long—which methought was very strange, and I looked upon myself as a man mightily deceived in a lady, for I could not have thought she could have suffered it, by her former discourse with me—so modest she seemed, and I know not what.[45]

While Madam Penington enjoyed sociability as the only woman in a group of men—first modestly and then less so—Pepys also liked to make merry among groups of women. In 1664, Pepys and his wife were beginning to be uneasy about having children, since after nearly nine years of marriage Elizabeth had not conceived, and their marriage indeed proved childless. At a "gossips' dinner" with his relatives the Joyces, everyone was "very merry," men and women both; Pepys himself had supplied plenty of wine for the event. The merry women left the table and Pepys went with them, "ne'er a man but I," to go upstairs. There he asked their advice on the begetting of children, and they "freely and merrily" gave him ten precepts, including keeping the stomach warm and the back cool, wearing cool underwear, avoiding late suppers, and not hugging his wife too hard or too much. When he asked whether night or morning was the best time, "they answered me neither one nor other, but when we had most mind to it." In short, it was "very merry all"; he did not think highly of the Joyces, but still enjoyed the lighthearted sharing of feminine wisdom about sex and fertility.[46]

There was similar frolicking at another scene of female-centered sociability, the christening of a friend's child:

> In the afternoon with my Lady Batten, Penn and her daughter, and my wife to Mrs. Poole's, where I mighty merry among the women, and christened the child, a girl, Elizabeth; which though a girl, yet my Lady Batten would have me to give the name. After christening comes Sir W. Batten, W. Penn and Mr. Lowther, and mighty merry there, and I forfeited for not kissing the two godmothers presently after the christening, before I kissed the mother—which made good mirth.[47]

Pepys's description highlights several assumptions about customary practices at christenings in this social milieu. The women gathered and ran the show; Lady Batten declared that Pepys should bestow the name. Pepys's comment implies that normally a woman would have this honor for a girl child, and that the choosing of him was something of a joke, in keeping with the general merriment. More laughter arose when he violated an unwritten rule by kissing the mother out of turn.

Opportunities for kissing were frequently attended by laughter, and perhaps vice versa, as on this occasion in September 1660 of mixed-gender sociability at a tavern:

> In the afternoon Luellin comes to my house and takes me out to the Miter in Wood Street, where Mr. Samford, W. Symons and his wife, and Mrs. Scobell, Mr. Mount and Chetwind. Where we were very merry—Luellin being drunk, and I being to defend the ladies from his kissing them, I kissed them myself very often with a great deal of mirth.[48]

These were more people he knew through his work, clerks and other members of the growing bureaucracy, along with their wives.

Pepys's diary goes beyond most of our other sources in documenting occasions for women and men to enjoy laughter in each other's company. Here it was not only intimate partners who laughed together—although these certainly did too. As the early fun with Madam Penington indicates, there was no assumption that women would or should curb their laughter in the presence of men, even if they aspired to a reputation for modesty. One suspects, in fact, that the idea of the chaste woman's suppression of laughter, like the idea of her silence, was largely a fantasy of male moralists. Customs of kissing on greeting were common in England, and playful imitations of male–female love relations were a source of fun. Pepys recounts mock weddings among his associates, as well as a Valentine's Day tradition of choosing a random member of the opposite sex for a valentine—a game that involved the giving of gifts, especially gloves, and some light banter. No doubt such laughing sociability was the kind of thing the Quaker William Stout had in mind some years later, when he complained of

> what's too common with not only youth but also married men and women with each other . . . to entertain each in a bantering way in such terms as could only tend to beget evil thoughts and excite to lewdness.[49]

Pepys was the first diarist ever to delve so deeply into his social activities and relationships, but we should not assume that all such enjoyment of mixed-gender sociability was new. Already in Castiglione, of course, we find the assumption that men and women should play and joke with each other, though according to courtly etiquette. One of the hallmarks of elite refinement was a knowledge of the rules of social engagement across gender and status lines. Notable among attempts to raise the tone of sociability in the seventeenth century is the *Frauenzimmer Gesprächspiele*—"Ladies' Conversation Games"—of the Nuremberg patrician Georg Philipp Harsdörffer. These little volumes offered word games, rhymes, stories, and riddles—morally acceptable and semi-intellectual play for the increasing occasions of mixed sociability, including fun, among classes possessed of education and leisure.[50]

Pepys takes us into everyday laughter at a "middling" social level, and his sociability was not nearly so refined or structured, even with his social superiors. Exchanges of conversation and laughter appear remarkably free, as in the occasions with Pepys, his friends, and the "fine witty lady" Madam Penington. He was certainly not alone in his relish for playful female company. Roger Lowe, the shopkeeper's apprentice, not only regaled his male friends with funny stories, but also enjoyed chatting and drinking with young female friends at the alehouse—and the girls' reputations suffered no harm.[51] A few decades later, in 1715, the young diarist and lawyer-in-training Dudley Ryder described a London youth culture in which skills at banter were in high demand. The young women of his acquaintance expected fun, and Ryder envied men who could get them laughing. He himself often felt awkward and bashful, but was pleased on an occasion when "I luckily got into a vein of mirth and raillery which I kept up, I think the best I ever did in my life."[52] This demand for laughter skills in social performance will concern us more in the next chapter.

Private Laughter

Jesting sociability was part of Pepys's daily habit in his life at home, with servants as well as with his wife Elizabeth. A pleasant Sunday in 1663 was spent talking and laughing all afternoon in his own chamber with his wife and her maid Mary Ashwell.[53] Pepys also appreciated the laughter Elizabeth and Mary got out of the spilling of a chamber pot, and the cleaning up after.[54] Even the more ordinary washing of a wainscot, done handily by their young maidservant, became cause for mirth.[55] He was delighted when he found that a young servant could be funny: on 23 July 1660, he came home after drinking with some friends at a tavern, "Where we supped merrily among ourselves (our little boy proving a droll); and so after prayers, to bed." (This footboy, Will, was later dismissed for stealing, despite his amusing qualities.)[56]

Pepys had times of friction with his wife, but he cherished their moments of laughing intimacy. Especially on Sunday mornings, they stayed in bed late to enjoy each other's company, as on 21 January 1666: "(Lord's day). Lay almost till noon merrily and with pleasure talking with my wife in bed." Similarly on 3 March 1667, "Lay long, merrily talking with my wife, and then up and to church."[57] This was likely really talking and not sex; obviously sex between the married couple was legitimate, but Pepys is explicit here. He may well have had qualms about Sunday sex left over from his puritanical upbringing—but although some rigorists even objected to laughter on a Sunday, he had clearly overcome those inhibitions. The pair shared many sources of amusement, including their critical eye for literature from drama to biography. Literary parody engaged and entertained them both on a Sunday when Elizabeth had been ill in bed. After church Samuel went "up to my wife and with great mirth read Sir W. Davenant's two speeches in dispraise of London and Paris, by way of reproach one to the other."[58] On this and other occasions, Elizabeth was an active partner in the merriment. They were both mightily amused at a biography of the queen, "which I read at home to my wife; but it was so sillily writ that we did nothing but laugh at it: among other things, it is dedicated to that Paragon of virtue and beauty, the Duchess of Albemarle."[59]

Pepys enjoyed real sex play with various women, especially taking advantage of opportunities with women of lesser status. He was surprised, as we have seen, that a lady of the caliber of Judith Penington would allow it so freely. He seldom explicitly mentions laughter in his sexual encounters, though it probably occurred. As we have seen in Chapter 4, laughter and sexual intimacy were closely enough linked that he may have taken it for granted. There was also joking about sex. In the right company it was possible to get away with daring jokes, somewhat reminiscent of the one that got Edward Peckett into such trouble for defamation. At a merry late-night dinner in mixed company, Pepys joked about fathering Captain Pett's child, to the latter's great amusement:

> Captain Pett was saying that he thought that he had got his wife with child since I came thither. Which I took hold of and was merrily asking him what he would take to have it said for my honour that it was of my getting? He merrily answered that he would, if I would promise to be godfather to it if it did come within the time just; and I said that I would. So that I must remember to compute it when the time comes.[60]

Another daring episode proved less amusing, when Pepys's Uncle Wight proposed to Elizabeth Pepys that he father a child for their barren marriage. Elizabeth repulsed the suggestion, and the uncle tried to pass it off with "a kind of counterfeit laugh."[61] But neither Elizabeth nor Samuel believed that it was really a joke, and the incident shattered their trust in the uncle's character.

Public Laughter

These various scenes of sociability—in workplaces, homes, taverns—were private in the sense of involving face-to-face interchange rather than performances aimed at eliciting laughter. Pepys was also an avid consumer of public entertainment. He often recounted his attendance at plays, with judgments about their quality. He expected real laughs from a comedy, both for himself and from others in the audience. Possibly the most outstanding for Pepys was John Dryden's play *Sir Martin Mar-all*, which premiered in the summer of 1667: "I never laughed so in all my life; I laughed till my head [ached] all the evening and night with my laughing, and at very good wit therein, not fooling."[62] As this judgment implies, Pepys thought comedy should show wit and was contemptuous of what he regarded as cheap laughs. In a new play in March 1668, *The Man is the Master* by Sir William Davenant, "most of the mirth was sorry, poor stuff, of eating of sack-posset and slabbering themselves, and mirth fit for Clowns."[63]

Pepys paid close attention not only to the play and his own enjoyment (or lack thereof) but also to the response of others. At *The Man is the Master* Pepys noticed, and was influenced by, the reaction of the king, who was at the same performance: "I found the King and his company did think meanly of it, though there was here and there something pretty." Still worse was Sir Charles Sedley's *The Mulberry Garden* in May 1668, which opened to great expectations and a packed house that included the king and his courtiers. It was a great disappointment,

> insomuch that the King I did not see laugh nor pleased the whole play from the beginning to the end, nor the company; insomuch that I have not been less pleased at a new play in my life I think."[64]

On the other hand, audience laughter enhanced his pleasure, as on 16 September 1667, when Pepys and his party attended a play that was not their favorite: "But one of the best parts of our sport was a mighty pretty lady that sat behind us, that did laugh so heartily and constantly that it did me good to hear her."[65]

Laughter in the playhouse was not always positive, however. Pepys found his enjoyment spoiled when some of his companions laughed at a stage mishap in the midst of a serious performance.[66] But Pepys himself could also laugh at things that were not meant to be funny. He recounted at length the mortifying end of a performance of *The Black Prince* by Roger Boyle, Earl of Orrery. Here too the king was in attendance, and the play went swimmingly until near the end, when the playwright saw fit to reveal key points of the plot "by the reading of a long letter; which was so long and some things (the people being set already to think too long) so unnecessary, that they frequently began to laugh, and to hiss twenty times." If the king had not been present, he says, they would have hissed the play right off the stage. Despite his admiration of Orrery's other works, Pepys himself could not stop laughing at the absurdity of that seemingly endless letter: he

> could not forbear laughing almost all the way home, and all the evening to my going to bed, at the ridiculousness of the letter; and the more because my wife was angry with me and the world for laughing, because the King was there, though she cannot defend the length of the letter.[67]

Audiences laughed in scorn at failure, as at the second performance of a new play that was "so mean a thing, as when they came to say it would be acted again tomorrow, both he that said it . . . and the pit fell a-laughing—there being this day not a quarter of the pit full."[68]

Pepys had standards for appropriate laughter, especially in public places, where the laughter should suit the occasion. He was contemptuous of slapstick buffoonery on the stage, where he expected real wit. Conversely, laughers should use some discrimination in the subjects of their mirth. In 1662, Pepys admired the exotic finery of the Russian ambassador's entourage, but his countrymen were less discerning: "Lord," he exclaimed, "to see the absurd nature of Englishmen, that cannot forbear laughing and jeering at everything that looks strange."[69] These were ordinary people in the street, but Pepys found unworthy laughter among their betters as well. At the launching of a new ship in 1664, the courtiers surrounding the king had nothing but "sorry talk and discourse." On the arrival of the queen and her ladies, some of whom were seasick from traveling over rough water, the "silly sport they made with them, in very common terms, methought, was very poor, and below what people think these great people say and do."[70] Later that same year, he was disgusted by Lord Craven, who, as chairman of a government committee and "before many persons of worth and grave," compared the granting of a Virginia lottery to the taking of a maidenhead. Pepys was not amused: "They made mirth, but I and others were ashamed of it."[71]

For Pepys, laughter about sex and the body belonged in private spaces, not public occasions among persons of power who should embody dignity. He loved sex play with women—but he recorded it in his diary in code and foreign languages for extra privacy. He could find humor in the overturning of a chamberpot or the bawdy songs of Sir William Penn. But the jests of the courtiers about seasickness—presumably involving vomit—and the crude intrusion of sex talk into the affairs of state, were to him jarring and unfunny. One can trace here the trend toward bodily containment and privacy—the "civilizing process" highlighted by Elias—not trickling from courtiers downward, but in a bourgeois critique of aristocratic looseness. Similarly, the demand for clever wit rather than slapstick comedy reflects a development in humor standards that was elite in one sense—associated with the spread of educational privilege—but not strictly aligned with social class. We will see further development of these ideas about wit in the eighteenth century (Chapter 7).

Perceptions of misplaced frivolity also colored Pepys's view of the Restoration government of Charles II—in which, of course, he was not alone. He and his office colleagues might laugh at the foibles of Mennes and Batten, but when high mismanagement had increasingly serious consequences, especially in war with the Dutch, any humor took on a darker edge. In Charles's case, Pepys saw it as lack of will rather than lack of ability—much less funny than simple bumbling. His diary is full of complaints about Charles's neglect of state business and devotion to pleasure, particularly sexual dalliances. In this light, the king's witticisms hardly redounded to his credit—as, for instance, when he made sexually suggestive jokes to a pretty Quaker petitioner.[72] Pepys was displeased as well when, in the midst of serious questions about naval management during a disastrous phase of the war, the king and the Duke of York were diverted for "a good while" with making "mighty sport" at the sexual activities of the geese in the park.[73] The love of laughter could go too far.

★ ★ ★

Seventeenth-century society was built on hierarchies, especially of class and gender. And yet the rise of men like Pepys, and even Penn and Batten, reminds us that social categories were hardly static. In addition to the potentially changing status of individuals, the intertwining of familial and professional life involved a daily negotiation of complex relationships. Servants lived in intimate domestic environments with their masters, colleagues shared neighborhood space and sociability, clients like Pepys assumed quasi-familial status with their wealthier relatives and patrons. Managing laughter across status lines was one of the skills in daily use.

Emerging from the humble background of a tailor's family, Pepys aspired to the status of gentleman. Having gained an elite education through fortunate patronage, he followed up that advantage with brilliant professional acumen. His fame as a naval administrator belonged to later years, but already as a young man he felt superior in manners to the rough-hewn Penn, whom he considered no gentleman, despite his title.[74] Pepys's skills in managing laughter were only one aspect of his adept social negotiation. But his intense awareness of his own status—something he was constantly re-assessing and documenting from year to year—helped him train and attune his laughter to the demands of the myriad social settings in which he operated. Both in relations across status lines and across gender lines, the sharing of laughter could smooth the edges of hierarchy. On the other hand, the laughter of an underling—such as Pepys's ridicule of incompetent superiors—could subtly undermine their authority. Perhaps Penn was not so wrong in his rage about the tankard, after all.

Notes

1   Samuel Pepys, *The Diary of Samuel Pepys*, ed. Robert Latham and William Matthews, 11 vols. (Berkeley and Los Angeles: University of California Press, 1970–1983), 1:262, 9 October 1660. Some spellings modernized.

2 Pepys, *Diary*, 2:164, 169, 175–76, 178; 28 August 1661, 1 September 1661, 9 September 1661, 12 September 1661.
3 Pepys, *Diary*, 1:166, 1 June 1660.
4 Ronald Hutton, *The Rise and Fall of Merry England: The Ritual Year 1400–1700* (Oxford: Oxford University Press, 1994), 119–32; Thomas Becon, *The Catechism of Thomas Becon*, ed. John Ayre (Cambridge, 1844), 80.
5 Pepys, *Diary*, 3:252, 9 November 1662.
6 Roger Lowe, *The Diary of Roger Lowe, of Ashton-in-Makerfield, Lancashire, 1663–74*, ed. William L. Sachse (New Haven: Yale University Press, 1938), 38–39.
7 Henry Hesketh (1683), quoted in Griffiths, *Youth and Authority*, 179.
8 Pepys, *Diary*, 5:2, 1 January 1663/4.
9 Pepys, *Diary*, 6:220, 10 September 1665.
10 Pepys, *Diary*, 5:222, 26 July 1664.
11 Pepys, *Diary*, 9:142, 31 March 1668.
12 Pepys, *Diary*, 2:165, 30 August 1661.
13 Pepys, *Diary*, 2:221, 27 November 1661.
14 Pepys, *Diary*, 3:89, 23 May 1662.
15 Pepys, *Diary*, 6:179, 1 August 1665.
16 Pepys, *Diary*, 6:176, 31 July 1665.
17 Pepys, *Diary*, 4:11, 10 January 1662/3.
18 Pepys, *Diary*, 5:278, 23 September 1664.
19 Pepys, *Diary*, 6:119, 6 June 1665.
20 Pepys, *Diary*, 4:275, 13 August 1663.
21 Pepys, *Diary*, 6:282, 29 October 1665.
22 Pepys, *Diary*, 9:171, 22 April 1668.
23 Pepys, *Diary*, 6:337, 22 December 1665.
24 *Oxford English Dictionary*, s.v. jade.
25 Pepys, *Diary*, 1:107, 11 April 1660.
26 Pepys, *Diary*, 2:70, 10 April 1661.
27 Pepys, *Diary*, 3:202–3, 21 September 1662.
28 Pepys, *Diary*, 8:26, 23 January 1667; this was Philip Howard, the queen's Lord Almoner, later a cardinal.
29 Pepys, *Diary*, 5:232, 4 August 1664.
30 Pepys, *Diary*, 7:90, 4 April 1666.
31 Pepys, *Diary*, 7:189, 1 July 1666.
32 Pepys, *Diary*, 8:129, 25 March 1667.
33 Pepys, *Diary*, 8:135, 28 March 1667.
34 Pepys, *Diary*, 3:62, 8 April 1662.
35 Pepys, *Diary*, 4:161, 27 May 1663.
36 Pepys, *Diary*, 1:255, 28 September 1660.
37 Pepys, *Diary*, 3:156, 4 August 1662.
38 Pepys, *Diary*, 4:262, 4 Aug 1663.
39 Columella, *On Agriculture*, in Brent D. Shaw, ed., *Spartacus and the Slave Wars: A Brief History with Documents* (Boston and New York: Bedford/St. Martin's, 2001), 34.
40 Simon Robson, *The Courte of Civill Courtesie* (1591), quoted in Chris Holcomb, *Mirth Making: The Rhetorical Discourse on Jesting in Early Modern England* (Columbia, SC: University of South Carolina Press, 2001), 75.
41 Quoted in Holcomb, *Mirth Making*, 75.
42 Baldassare Castiglione, *The Book of the Courtier*, ed. Daniel Javitch, trans. Charles S. Singleton (New York: Norton, 2002), 131.
43 Pepys, *Diary*, 6:257, 8 October 1665.
44 Pepys, *Diary*, 6:273, 22 October 1665.
45 Pepys, *Diary*, 6:297, 13 November 1665.
46 Pepys, *Diary*, 5:222, 26 July 1664: "Very merry all, as much as I could be in such sorry company."

47 Pepys, *Diary*, 8:404–5, 28 August 1667.

48 Pepys, *Diary*, 1:244, 14 September 1660.

49 William Stout, *Autobiography of William Stout of Lancaster*, quoted in Paul Griffiths, *Youth and Authority: Formative Experiences in England, 1560–1640* (Oxford: Clarendon Press, 1996), 240.

50 Georg Philip Harsdörffer, *Frauenzimmer Gescprächspiele*, 8 vols., ed. Irmgard Böttcher (Tübingen: Max Niemeyer, 1968).

51 See Lowe, *Diary of Roger Lowe*, 7, 44.

52 Dudley Rider, *The Diary of Dudley Ryder 1715–1716*, ed. William Matthews (London: Methuen & Co., 1939), 73.

53 Pepys, *Diary*, 4:88, 29 March 1663.

54 Pepys, Diary, 4:155, 25 May 1663.

55 Pepys, *Diary*, 1:243, 11 September 1660.

56 Pepys, *Diary*, 1:206, 23 July 1660.

57 Pepys, *Diary*, 7:19, 21 January 1665/6; 8:91, 3 March 1666/7.

58 Pepys, *Diary*, 5:40, 7 February 1664.

59 Pepys, *Diary*, 1:275, 26 October 1660. Anne Clarges Monck became a duchess when her husband, General George Monck, was named Duke of Albemarle for his role in bringing about the Restoration of Charles II; she was widely disrespected for her low birth and education.

60 Pepys, *Diary*, 2:71, 10 April 1661.

61 Pepys, *Diary*, 5:145–46, 11 May 1664.

62 Pepys, *Diary*, 8:387, 16 August 1667.

63 Pepys, *Diary*, 9:134, 26 March 1668.

64 Pepys, *Diary*, 9:203, 18 May 1668.

65 Pepys, *Diary*, 8:440, 16 September 1667.

66 Pepys, *Diary*, 8:421, 4 September 1667.

67 Pepys, *Diary*, 8:488, 19 October 1667.

68 Pepys, *Diary*, 9:307, 15 September 1668.

69 Pepys, *Diary*, 3:268, 27 November 1662.

70 Pepys, *Diary*, 5:306, 26 October 1664.

71 Pepys, *Diary*, 5:323, 18 November 1664.

72 Pepys, *Diary*, 5:12, 11 January 1664.

73 Pepys, *Diary*, 8:68, 17 February 1667. Also see 8:420–21, 4 Sept 1667: observing proceedings in the Council, "All I observed there is the silliness of the King, playing with his dog all the while, or his codpiece, and not minding the business, and what he said was mighty weak."

74 He was "a man of very mean parts, but only a bred seaman" and his family of "low, mean fashion." Pepys, *Diary*, 5:293, 10 October 1664; 8:217, 15 May 1667.

FIGURE 7.1   Hester Lynch Thrale, engraving by T. Holloway of portrait by Robert Edge Pine

Source: © Granger Historical Picture Archive/Alamy Stock Photo

7

LAUGHTER AS SOCIAL COMMODITY

Hester Thrale and Friends

One day in 1778, Hester Thrale drew up a table rating the qualities of her male acquaintances. They were assessed on a 20-point scale in each of nine categories, in a table that looked something like this:

Religion	Morality	Scholarship	General Knowledge	Person & Voice	Manner	Wit, Humor, Good Humor

The ratings were an idle amusement, she said—nothing serious. And yet the table marks a significant historical moment. This quantification of social performance was the product of a competitive eighteenth-century society fascinated with measurement. Thrale's criteria listed a range of desirable social qualities, perhaps intended as an order of importance. Religion and morality came first, followed by knowledge and manners. Especially noteworthy for our purposes, however, are the final three categories, rated separately but set off by Thrale in their own column: wit, humor, and good humor. These were terms of shifting meanings in the eighteenth century, but all were bound up with the history of laughter. Laughter-related performance, in effect, formed a third of the criteria of social approval. She set different standards in her separate ratings of women—more on that later.[1]

Thrale offers us an entry point into the longer-term history of laughter as a valuable commodity, both in social interaction and in the marketplace. Her story intersects with the professional selling of laughter and allows us to see links between the market value of laughter materials and the demand for certain kinds of social performance. In the eighteenth century, the rise of new laughter-friendly theories—rebuttals to the harsher view of Hobbes—promoted the idea of laughter

DOI: 10.4324/9781003247517-8

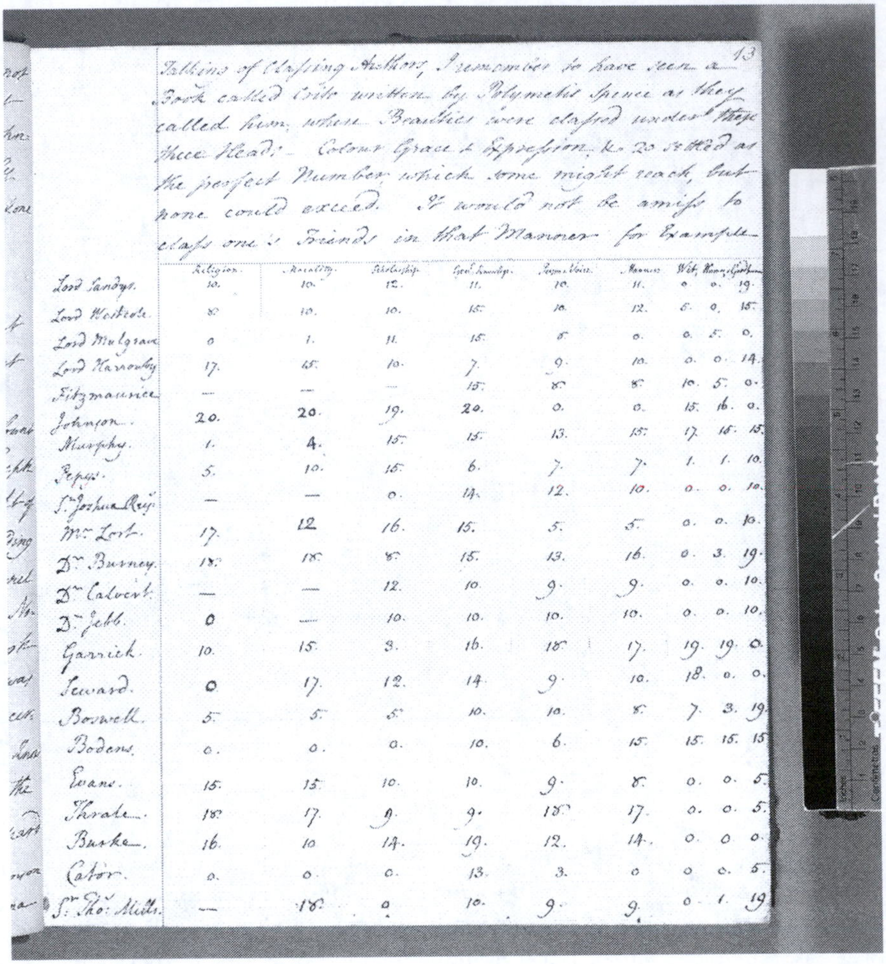

13

Talking of Classing Authors, I remember to have seen a Book called Critic written by Polymetis Spence as they called him, where Beauties were classed under these Three Heads;– Colour Grace & Expression, & 20 settled as the perfect Number, which some might reach, but none could exceed. It would not be amiss to class one's Friends in that Manner for Example

	Religion	Morality	Scholarship	Gen. Knowledge	Person & Voice	Manner	Wit	Humour	Good Humour
Lord Sandys	10.	10.	12.	11.	10.	11.	0.	0.	19.
Lord Westcote	8.	10.	10.	15.	10.	12.	6.	0.	15.
Lord Mulgrave	0	1.	11.	15.	8.	0.	0.	5.	0.
Lord Harrowby	17.	15.	10.	7.	9.	10.	0.	0.	14.
Fitzmaurice	—	—	—	15.	8.	8.	10.	5.	0.
Johnson	20.	20.	19.	20.	0.	0.	15.	16.	0.
Murphy	1.	4.	15.	15.	13.	15.	17.	15.	15.
Pepys	5.	10.	15.	6.	7.	7.	1.	1.	10.
Sr Joshua Reyn:	—	—	0.	14.	12.	10.	0.	0.	10.
Mr Lort	17.	12	16.	15.	5.	5.	0.	0.	10.
Dr Burney	18.	18.	8.	15.	13.	16.	0.	3.	19.
Dr Calvert	—	—	12.	10.	9.	9.	0.	0.	10.
Dr Jebb	0	—	10.	10.	10.	10.	0.	0.	10.
Garrick	10.	15.	3.	16.	18.	17.	19.	19.	0.
Seward	0	17.	12.	14.	9.	10.	18.	0.	0.
Boswell	5.	5.	5.	10.	10.	8.	7.	3.	19.
Bodens	0.	0.	0.	10.	6.	15.	15.	15.	15.
Evans	15.	15.	10.	10.	9.	8.	0.	0.	5.
Thrale	18.	17.	9.	9.	18.	17.	0.	0.	5.
Burke	16.	10	14.	19.	12.	14.	0.	0	0.
Cator	0.	0.	0.	13.	3.	0	0	0.	5.
Sr Tho: Mills	—	18.	0	10.	9.	9.	0.	1.	19.

FIGURE 7.2 Hester Thrale's table of numerical ratings

Source: Thraliana, manuscript, vol. 3, 13, The Huntington Library, San Marino, California.

as a positive social good. We know, of course, that people had long enjoyed laughter in practice, even among elites where anti-laughter prescriptions might thrive. But laughter's stock was rising among intellectuals. Thrale's social circle was marked by convergence of these trends toward valuing as well as selling. Her friends and acquaintances included the comic virtuoso Arthur Murphy, as well as the formidable Samuel Johnson and his laughter-prone biographer, James Boswell. It was an age of changing and contested social valuation of laughter: increased appreciation of its benign qualities combined with policing of its unruliness among aspirants to class-based respectability.

A Life as Jestbook

Hester Lynch Thrale, best known as the valued confidant of Samuel Johnson but also an author herself, came of landed gentry in Wales. With a decline in the family fortunes, she married the wealthy brewer Henry Thrale. The couple were not well matched in temperament, but the prosperous marriage enabled her to interact with the leading lights of London's literary society. Her friendship with Johnson became a central pillar of both their lives. After her first husband's death, however, her marriage to the Italian musician Gabriel Piozzi—a foreigner as well as a social inferior—led to quarrels with both Johnson and her disapproving daughters.[2]

Thrale produced a distinctive type of "ego document" in her journal, the *Thraliana*. With encouragement from her husband and Johnson, she began keeping a notebook of memorable things that came to her notice. Unlike the older genre of commonplace book, usually made up of extracts from published wisdom, her journal combines personal experiences with bits of poetry (her own and others'), stories she heard, character sketches of her acquaintances, and other oddments. In addition to Johnson's advice, she was inspired by French compilations of anecdotes. Gradually the collection took on the character of a diary.[3]

The memorable in this context largely meant the amusing, especially at the outset of the enterprise, as she searched her memory for bon mots delivered by her mother, her daughter, her wider acquaintance, and herself. Thrale was good at raising laughter, known for her amusing conversation and witty letters. The journal provides fascinating evidence about the influence of the laughter market on practices and reception of laughter in her social circle. What Boswell called "good things" said by family and friends become fodder for what she facetiously termed a "Jest Book."[4] In effect, in launching this anecdotal record, she saw the materials of laughter as the elements that were memorable and worthy of preservation. As an author herself, Thrale may well have been thinking of grist for future publications, although she did not publish the *Thraliana*. After her controversial second marriage to the Italian musician Piozzi, she published accounts of her travels in Europe, as well as a volume of anecdotes—a "Johnsoniana"—drawn from the life of Samuel Johnson. The raw materials of amusing social interaction could be turned into products for future exchange.

The laughs of this life story were born in the course of daily experience, at least in so far as we trust Thrale's narration. But the recording and its motivation transformed them into something else. Flashes of wit should not be allowed merely to sparkle and die in the moment. They had a value—an exchangeable value—to be preserved beyond the circle of the original laughers. They were products of social interaction but not bound to time, place, and relationships. Whether eventually published or not, their production as text grew out of the perceived commodity value in the spurs to laughter. At the same time, by taking on the character of a diary, Thrale's journal gave laughter a prominent role in the portrayal of her own life.

Among the bon mots worthy of memory, plays on words were seen as especially witty. Thrale proudly recorded the precocious wit of her daughter Hester: on being told that the Burneys were Irish, formerly called MacBurney, and "were remarkably tall Folks, Highbernias then to be sure cries Hester merrily—this was at the latter end of 1776 when She was just turn'd twelve Years old."[5] The pun on "high" Burneys/Hibernia (the Latin name for Ireland and a familiar term to eighteenth-century elites) marked the young Hester's quickness and invention. Later, in 1799, at a period when Thrale's journal was mostly taken up with family matters, reflections on her reading, and news of the day, she paused to record "The best Joke I have lately heard," which "was on Mr Gunter the *Confectioner* getting so much Money last Winter—Twas a Shame says *one*, not at all replies another, He gained it by his *Desserts*."[6]

The *Thraliana* often does not state explicitly when and how much laughter succeeded such sallies. But there was no hint here of the aristocratic disdain for audible laughter famously laid down by Lord Chesterfield in the *Letters to His Son*, published just a couple of years before Thrale began her journal. The "laugh was loud" when Colonel Bodens made a joke about the resemblance between two tall young ladies they knew and a dish of rabbits at dinner.[7] Other accounts of the company at the Thrales' house at Streatham testify to the sounds of hilarity. A visitor remembered an occasion when young Hannah More and Dr. Johnson exchanged so many "good things" that "you would have imagined we had been at some comedy, had you heard our peals of laughter."[8] Thomas Davies, who had heard Johnson, said that he "laughs like a rhinoceros."[9] Later in life, after her second marriage, Hester valued her home in Wales as a place where the "Days were always consecrated to Mirth, & we have been happy & merry here."[10]

This high valuation of laughter had increasing support from philosophy. The negative view of laughter put forward by Thomas Hobbes in the seventeenth century roused significant opposition by the eighteenth. Early in the century, the influential Lord Shaftesbury skewered Hobbes's ideas about many things, notably human nature and the origins of civil society; he also dismissed his notion of laughter. Instead of an implied hostility, laughter was a means of encouraging the pursuit of truth: "For nothing is ridiculous, but what is deform'd: Nor is any thing proof against *Raillery*, but what is handsome and just."[11] To those worried about introducing levity into discussion of serious subjects like religion and morality, he argued that freedom to jest would pose no danger: "I can very well suppose Men may be frighted out of their Wits: But I have no apprehension they should be laugh'd out of 'em."[12]

Another strong voice in laughter's favor was that of the philosopher Francis Hutcheson, who like Shaftesbury was read widely across Europe. His *Thoughts on Laughter*, published in 1750, roundly dismissed Hobbes's idea of laughter as a "sudden glory" in one's own superiority: it was typical of the man's "palpable absurdity" and "ill-natur'd nonsense."[13] Instead, Hutcheson pointed to the role of laughter in sociability. A source of pleasure and easer of sorrow, laughter also bound people together in positive relationships:

> We are disposed by laughter to a good opinion of the person who raises it, if neither ourselves nor our friends are made the butt. Laughter is none of the smallest bonds of common friendships, tho' it be of less consequence in great heroic friendships.[14]

He even found a good word to say for ridicule. Malicious ridicule was nasty; but if reasonably good-natured, ridicule had the power to curb the passions, which otherwise could tend to excess. When our desires lose their proportion, said Hutcheson, the deft application of ridicule can help: "Ridicule gives our minds as it were a bend to the contrary side; so that upon reflection they may be more capable of settling in a just conformity to nature."[15]

Of course, not all laughter fit these ideals. In the wake of her second marriage, Thrale developed a strong sense of the dangers of irresponsible laughter, built on bitter personal experience. The marriage met with widespread disapproval and ridicule—from her intimate family and friends, and more publicly from rivals, enemies, and frenemies in print. The public gibes targeted other purported foibles of hers as well—but it is striking that people seem to have discovered these only after she had married a man whom so many considered unsuitable. Gabriel Piozzi had taught music to her daughter, and Thrale had helped further his concert career as well while her first husband was alive. She hesitated for a long time over the possibility of marrying Piozzi. She recorded in her journal a long list of possible objections and sought to refute each one. The most troubling opposition she feared was from her daughters—and in fact, the marriage did lead to a painful estrangement from them. She drily remarked, when her eldest daughter Hester married at age 44, that Hester was several years older than she herself had been at her second marriage, when the girl had "hooted me" for being "superannuated."[16]

In her decision to remarry, Thrale sought to put aside considerations of how outsiders would react, focusing on her own happiness and that of her family. She dismissed fears "of being censured by the World as it is called—a Composition of Vice & Folly. Though 'tis surely no good Joke to be talked of" with disparagement.[17] Even with her knowledge of the world, she was surprised by the strength of negative reaction both private and public. At one point she thought she would be able to reconcile both her daughters and Johnson to this new reality, but no. In public, rumors flew of her being locked up by her new Catholic husband in an Italian convent, and she was pilloried in satirical print. In 1790 she wrote:

> I love not that scoffing Spirit so rife among the English. . . . Derision is to me—perhaps because I have suffered so much by it—particularly offensive; and I now find that it is dangerous too. It creates a general Cowardice, &

produces perpetual Hypocrisy—it terrifies those who have any Feeling out of many Duties, & hinders many a happy Hour to us all.

People were even laughing, she complained, at the man who offered a reward for capture of a villain who had been stabbing the buttocks of pretty girls in London. "All the merry Fellows" had made his chivalry matter for ridicule and "sett all the Town o' laughing" at him.[18] The high appreciation for good laughter had not banished the dangers of the bad.

How Do Your Friends Rate?

In contemporary society we are used to rankings. A search for any item online leads to lists of the "10 best," or some other number of the best. (A search for "search engines" instantly produces lists of 10, 12, 14, 15, or 40 top contenders.) We are measured, tested, and scored from infancy onward; individuals, products, organizations, all can expect to be rated. But this was not the case in the eighteenth century. Testing was not yet a staple of education; only in the following century did Europeans begin to imitate the Chinese model for measuring merit through civil service examinations, for instance. The prestige of quantification had been growing with the Scientific Revolution, and in the seventeenth century there were increasing efforts to extend numerical measurement from the natural world to society. Early statisticians focused on demographic data for political and economic purposes, serving the growth of modern states. Numerical rating of individuals was something else, a further extension of quantification into the social realm. Thrale borrowed the idea of 20 points as a measure of excellence from a work about beauty by Joseph Spence, but the elaboration into tabular form was all her own.[19]

Thrale's criteria for the assessment of (male) individuals were a combination of intrinsic qualities—religion, morality, scholarship, knowledge—and elements of social presentation and performance—person, voice, manner, wit, humor, good humor. And yet, of course, since the "testing" environment for judging these qualities was in everyday sociability, all of them were connected to social performance. If the more serious aspects of personal attainment got first billing, the criteria quickly moved away from the inner man and to the impression made on others by gesture, voice, and appearance. That last column, the trinity of wit, humor, and good humor, was all about social performance. These were terms whose meanings were contested and shifting in the eighteenth century, a subject explored in more detail shortly. For the moment, it is important to note that they were increasingly becoming associated with comedy and laughter. Thrale clearly felt them to be important aspects of social interaction and distinct enough to be assessed separately, as three ratings out of the total of nine.

Although she called the drawing up of her table a "foolish amusement," Thrale carried it pretty far, recording ratings for 38 men of her acquaintance. In a few cases she felt unable to assess an individual's inner qualities and marked such columns as religion and morality with a stroke—clearly distinguishable from the zeroes marked for other people. The individuals, she said, "are very fairly rated: those that have 0s have none of the Quality mentioned." Once she got to the fifth column, on person and voice, there was no more need for blanks—she was always able to judge the last five criteria. How did men's wit, humor, and good humor fare in the ratings? Though these qualities were grouped together to underline their connection, almost nobody had all of them. There were men with lots of good humor who had zero wit or humor. In fact, good humor was often in an inverse relationship with the other two. Good humor was a much more common quality than either wit or humor. Of the 38 evaluated, 24 had at least some good humor. But wit was rare: 24 had none at all, while 22 lacked humor. Yet only five men had zeroes straight across these three categories. Of the five men with high marks for wit (15 or above out of 20), three had zero good humor. These three qualities were important enough to rate, but not so easy to come by or to combine. Almost everyone had at least some credit for manners, appearance, and knowledge; almost everyone lacked some quality in that final column; only four of the 38 escaped a zero in one of those three sociable abilities.[20]

Thrale's judgments of some of her closest associates are particularly noteworthy. Her intimate friend Samuel Johnson received stellar marks for religion, morality, and scholarship, and also a high 15 and 16 for wit and humor; but for person/voice, manner, and good humor, zero. There was evidently little laughter with her first husband, the brewer Henry Thrale. Among the character sketches in the journal is a description of him as reserved—civil and thoughtful, not given to jest. In the table she assigned Thrale a scanty 5 for good humor—but for wit and humor, zero. Arthur Murphy, the playwright whose laughter lore we will explore later, was one of the very few who were good at all three sociable skills. Thrale thought little of his religion and morality—1 and 4 respectively—but he scored a 17 for wit and 15 each for humor and good humor. James Boswell, another notable laugher to whom we will return, did not get any zeroes, but Thrale did not think highly of his religion, morality, scholarship, wit, or humor (scores averaging 5). His manner was unimpressive too, with a rating of 8. But no one outdid him in good humor: 19 out of 20.

Turning to her female acquaintances, Thrale went on to rate 46 women, including herself. Strikingly, her categories for assessing female qualities were quite different from those for men. Here there were six columns: Worth of Heart; Conversation Powers; Person, Mien, and Manner; Good Humor; Useful Knowledge; and Ornamental Knowledge (accomplishments such as singing, dancing, or painting). The gender difference aligned with the conventional application of more objective and abstract standards to men, more emotive and relational qualities for women—and this in spite of Thrale's clear and even explicit pride in her own wit and that of other women like her mother and her daughter Hester. The category "worth of heart" had something to do with religion and morality, but the emphasis is far more on genuineness of feeling rather than the adherence to principle implied in the male categories. Women should have good "conversation powers"—an undifferentiated category—but it was the men who were rated on displays of wit and humor and, implicitly, the ability to arouse laughter. "Good humor," a rather vague quality, appeared in the lists for both sexes but was not really of the highest value for Thrale. As we have seen, her much-admired friend Dr. Johnson possessed none whatsoever, while Boswell, whom Thrale did not admire, got a top score. The women were notably more good humored than the men: 19 out of the 46 had scores of 15 or above (41 percent), versus 7 of 38 (18 percent) for men.

What place did wit hold among the women's "conversation powers"? A clue, perhaps, appears in the anecdote that immediately follows the table rating the women. The story features a witticism by the prominent bluestocking Elizabeth Montagu, who topped the women's ratings with a 20 out of 20 for conversation, along with high marks in all the other categories. For the women but not the men, Thrale added up the scores to reach an overall total. (Montagu ranked far ahead of the pack with 101, dwarfing the next highest score of 76 among the acquaintances; Thrale's ratings of herself, coming as an addendum, also total 76.) The anecdote runs as follows:

> I have heard Mr Johnson remark that nobody could ever relate any Thing that Pope *said*; we were settling it that he made no figure in Conversation, when Mrs Montagu recollecting herself observed that She had never heard him speak indeed, but She once had heard him cough: you heard then Madam says Johnson as much from him as anybody ever did.[21]

The witty Johnson (15 out of 20) started the theme, but it was the peerless Mrs. Montagu who added the comic spark; arguably, Johnson was merely a supporting player. In the following paragraphs Thrale goes on to relate other witty sayings of Mrs. Montagu and herself, as well as comic moments in other conversations among women and men—confirming that the laughable was very much in her mind as she surveyed and assessed the scenes of social performance.

Defining Wit and Humor

Thrale's final triple column for men—Wit, Humor, and Good Humor—groups together three potentially laughter-related terms. What exactly did they mean? The meanings of wit and humor were very much in flux during Thrale's own lifetime, as witnessed by her need add a note explaining what she meant by good humor: "N:B: by Good humor is meant only the Good humour necessary to Conversation."[22] A modern equivalent might be pleasantness or cheerfulness. Good humor was used in that sense, for example, by Dudley Ryder in his early eighteenth-century diary, to describe people who were friendly and nice to him. There was also a suggestion of smiling and readiness to laugh, as in his description of a convivial time with other men at a tavern: "We were exceeding merry, full of good humour."[23] One finds a similar implication in Lord Shaftesbury's description of "Improvement to the good Humour of the Company" in the course of a "diverting" conversation full of raillery.[24]

But there were non-laughing senses of the words wit and humor that were older. The ambiguity and shifts in meaning are evident in the groundbreaking English dictionary published by Samuel Johnson in 1755. Johnson generally began with what he viewed as the older, more established meanings of words. In a method that is now the time-honored practice of the revered *Oxford English Dictionary*, he quoted passages from literature to demonstrate their various meanings. "Humour" referred first to moisture, and in particular to the fluids of the body, linked in the ancient humoral theory of medicine to different qualities or moods of the individual. Traditionally, for instance, a sanguine humor, with blood prominent in the balance of fluids, was cheerful, while melancholy would result from an excess of black bile. In Johnson's definitions of humor, after moving through temperament and mood, we reach jocularity and merriment only in definition 5, as variants on the concept of grotesque imagery. Unlike the other definitions of humor, this one has no literary quotation to support it; yet it appears before definitions 6 through 9, which sport citations from such authors as Shakespeare and Francis Bacon. The lack of quotation for merriment suggests that it was a prominent meaning for humor in everyday language—more central than those below, such as petulance or caprice—yet not found in the authoritative literary sources: a newer meaning, in other words. The change over time is even more evident in the definitions of associated terms like humorous, humorously, and humorist. "Humorist" had no link to laughter at all for Johnson: a humorist is one who follows his own humor, his whim or passion. "Humorous" mainly means grotesque, odd, or capricious; its last meaning, almost as an afterthought and with no literary quotation, is "Pleasant; jocular." "Humorously," however, already had strong associations with laughter: "merrily; jocosely" edged out caprice to become the first definition, and even had the literary backing of a quotation from Jonathan Swift.

Johnson's definitions of wit at first seem even less infused with laughter. He began with the word's "original signification" of the intellect, and went on to meanings of quick imagination, genius, and judgment. One might begin to think there was nothing funny about it at all—until one comes to "witcracker": "a joker, one who breaks a jest" and "witsnapper": "one who affects repartee"—both from Shakespeare and so dating back some one hundred and fifty years before Johnson's time. Looking more closely at the supporting literary passages, Johnson's "quickness of imagination" in fact aroused laughter, as in the associated citation from Shakespeare:

> The brain of this foolish compounded clay, man, is not able to invent any thing that tends more to laughter, than what I invent, and is invented on me. I am not only witty in myself, but the cause that wit is in other men.[25]

Shakespeare's usages show that "wit" was already a laughing matter in the years around 1600. At least until the mid-eighteenth century, however, there were attempts by critics to keep wit and laughter segregated. The theorists were sure that precision of language required a firm separation, but they were fighting a strong tide of social practice and everyday language. The intellectual elitism of theoretical purists meshed with class-based snobbery like that of Lord Chesterfield, attempting to place wit on a higher plane than humor and laughter. One is reminded of the seventeenth-century French lexicographers who sought to purge the noise from laughter (Chapter 5).

Johnson's contemporary Corbyn Morris, writing in 1743, attempted a definitive disentanglement of wit from humor, along with such associated terms as raillery, ridicule, and satire. He was a major influence on Thrale's friend Arthur Murphy, who adopted Morris's categories in his enormous commonplace book on comedy—more on that later. But it seems his precise distinctions were lost on people in everyday conversation, even sophisticated ones like Hester Thrale. Morris was swimming upstream against that powerful arbiter of eighteenth-century taste, *The Spectator*—a periodical that was saved, bound, and re-read by gentlefolk for generations. Morris quoted disapprovingly a *Spectator* column by Joseph Addison that shows how wit, humor, and laughter were already blending when he wrote in 1711. Rather than define humor, Addison imagined a genealogy:

> *supposing* HUMOUR *to be a Person* . . . TRUTH *was the Founder of the Family, and the Father of* GOOD SENSE; GOOD SENSE *was the Father of* WIT, *who married a Lady of collateral Line called* MIRTH, *by whom he had Issue* HUMOUR.[26]

Humor, here, is the child of wit and mirth, that is, essentially, of cleverness and laughter. Morris saw this description as confused and imprecise, and he sought to instruct people in the correct, scientific distinctions—but it was a losing battle.

One gets the sense in Morris of nostalgia for the original meaning of wit, denoting intelligence, and an elitist wish to prevent people from calling things witty when they really were not. In Morris's scheme, wit was defined as "the *quick Elucidation* of one subject, by the sudden *Arrangement*, and *Comparison* of it, with another Subject."[27] Wit was clever, but it was not necessarily funny. In fact, he found it less likely to elicit laughter than humor, partly because it would take some wit to appreciate it. But humor too was very different from what a modern reader might expect. Again harking back to earlier meanings of the bodily fluids and their connection with an individual's character, Morris declared that it was the "*Foibles* and *whimsical Oddities* of Persons, which alone constitute HUMOUR."[28] People laughed at these, or at the representation of them—but unlike wit, they were not the result of intellectual invention. One might be amused by humor (feeling, in fact, something like Hobbes's rejoicing in superiority to it), but it was not something to cultivate or admire.

Laughter for Sale and Study

Arthur Murphy was an intimate acquaintance of Hester Thrale, a man she admired for his wit but not for his morality. It was Murphy, in fact, who introduced Samuel

Johnson to the Thrales, sparking that famous literary friendship. Although largely forgotten today, he was an astoundingly prolific author of plays and other works. Many of his plays, especially his comedies, went through multiple editions during his lifetime, including translations into French and German. Some critics have faulted him for lack of originality, as he sometimes adapted foreign plays for the English stage. But then, Shakespeare borrowed plots too. Murphy's plays delighted audiences not only in his own day but for many decades thereafter. He was an adept classical scholar, author of a translation of the Roman historian Tacitus that was standard for more than a century. He published editions of the works of Henry Fielding and Samuel Johnson, along with their biographies and that of the actor and producer David Garrick. All this was in addition to his work as an essayist and editor for the periodical press. Today, he is fairly obscure even among scholars; a few intrepid literary critics have examined his plays—but not many. Yet he cut quite a figure in his time, not only through his writings but also as an ornament to social gatherings, where he could be counted on for entertainment and laughter.

In his professional life, Murphy was a seller of laughter. He also cultivated it in social encounters. His natural comic abilities, as Thrale testified, were formidable and adaptable to audiences of every class:

> so willing to amuse you, to divert your Company, to inform, to sooth: yet no Buffoonery, no Coarseness, no meanness, but a Behaviour perfectly decorous. . . . Is your Table filled with People of high Rank & Accomplishments? nobody outshines Murphy, yet nobody is eclipsed by him; every one goes away in the same Mind concerning him. Have you a set of low Fellows, Burgesses of a Boro' or Freeholders of a County? Murphy sets them on a continual Roar.[29]

But he did not rest on these laurels. In his large compilation of laughter lore, now preserved at the Folger Library, Murphy pursued the essence of the laughable through all its guises. Comedy was his profession and also his intensive study.

Murphy's collection falls into the early modern genre of the commonplace book. In vogue throughout the seventeenth and eighteenth centuries, the commonplace book was typically a collection of extracts, drawn from an individual's reading but also sometimes including material from everyday experience. Women's commonplace books sometimes included recipes and herbal remedies. Songs and poems were also common matter for these personal aids to memory. In Murphy's case, the compiler's advanced education, voracious curiosity, and organizational zeal led to a collection that went far beyond the norm.[30] The oversize volume of 500-odd pages is carefully organized into sections corresponding to every aspect of wit, humor, and comedy. He allotted more than 100 pages to Wit, with a range of subheadings including True Wit, False Wit, and Mixt Wit. Other sections include Humour (about 40 pages), Ridicule (90 pages), Causes of Laughter (38 pages), and the hugest section, headed Comedy (most of the last 200 pages). Every page bears a label in its upper corner giving the subject heading and page number, marked off in a rectangular box. A smaller heading at the top center gives the source of that page's material, usually carried over from the previous page. He even constructed an index for reference back to authors and ideas within the sections. The extracts range from Latin citations of authors like Ovid to contemporaries such as Voltaire and Lord Chesterfield. Murphy quoted extensive passages from successful comic playwrights such as Dryden, Jonson, and Shakespeare, as well as theorists like Hobbes and Hutcheson. He was especially impressed by Corbyn Morris—not only quoting him in many of the subsections, but adding an entire section after the index to record Morris's views on various authors.

While Murphy devoted his longest section to his professional interest in comedy on the stage, he was also intent on uncovering ultimate truths about why people laugh. Under "Causes of Laughter," he looked at a number of authorities, only to deem several of them wanting. He found Hobbes, in particular, an unreliable guide. In fact, Hobbes appears in this section mainly as the target of criticism from other writers on laughter, particularly Hutcheson and Addison. Murphy was not satisfied with Addison either, complaining that in all his discussion of the subject, "it is certain that he gives no account of the cause of laughter, nor of its final causes."[31] It was the elusive "final causes" that Murphy hoped to trace. In his systematic combing of writings on laughter, he subjected them to a rigorous analysis. His dissection of the arguments pared them down into enumerated points, laid out on the page with white space for clarity, along with careful page citations. He even cross-referenced his own organization, as in his notes on Hutcheson's critique of Hobbes. After dividing the arguments into propositions one and two, and spending a couple of pages on Hutcheson's points of evidence for the first proposition, he moved on with a reference to his own earlier page: "as to the Second proposition in this Book fol. 282." This was an exhaustive and painstaking study.

While compiling many carefully referenced extracts and outlines of others' arguments, Murphy also interjected his own observations and judgments. His favorite formulas, "it is certain that" or "certainly," regularly signaled a shift into his own thoughts. He joined Hutcheson in disapproval of Hobbes's seemingly misanthropic view of laughter as a "sudden glory" in one's own superiority. So impressed was he by Hutcheson's arguments on this score that he actually laid them out in enumerated propositions twice—once in introducing them and again in summing up. He was sure, like Hutcheson, that self-loving pride could not be the mainspring of laughter. There were too many prideful moments when laughter did not occur, and too many kinds of laughter where there is no question of superiority. Pride might contribute to certain kinds of laughter, but it was no final cause. Murphy endorsed Hutcheson's idea of incongruity as the key:

> It is certain that in the use of ridicule Hobbes's <u>sudden glory</u>[double underline] may <u>mix</u> with the emotion of <u>Laughter</u>; But that <u>sudden Glory</u> can not be <u>the Cause of Laughter</u>: It is the <u>opposition</u>, the <u>Clash</u>, the <u>Contrast</u> of <u>Ideas</u> that Excites the Laugh, and the Little triumph of the <u>Mind</u> may blend itself with the Laugh.[32]

Murphy may be the first person in history to subject laughter to such intensive and extensive study, at least from the perspective of a laughter professional. The sixteenth-century physician Laurent Joubert came first but was more interested in physiology than in practice. Murphy's own favorite laughter authors, Corbyn Morris and Francis Hutcheson, each wrote only brief treatments of the subject. Morris's "Essay towards fixing the true standards of wit, humour, raillery, satire, and ridicule" comes to some 50 pages, counting his long discussion of Falstaff and other literary characters. Without this addendum, the laughter analysis is about 25 pages. Hutcheson was similarly brief, a series of three letters about laughter, another 50 pages. For Morris and Hutcheson, laughter was a sideline—important enough for some serious thought, but hardly their main preoccupation. Morris was far more noted for his writings on economics and demography than for his essay on wit. It was those more serious subjects, particularly his collection of statistics on the city of London, that got him elected a fellow of the Royal Society in 1757. Hutcheson became a professor of philosophy, noted for his essays and later magnum opus on morals and aesthetics. His ideas about laughter were a small piece of that larger and more sober whole. But for Murphy laughter was a central concern. In fact, adding up all the pages where they appear, Murphy may have expended more ink on Hutcheson and Morris's laughter ideas than they did in their original works.

Laughter as Commodity

The approaches to laughter of Thrale and her circle offer a point of entry for examining the larger picture of laughter as a commodity: an item with exchange value. Thrale's quantification of gentlemen's laughter qualities and Murphy's painstaking compilation of laughter lore—both are signs of a demand for laughter, in sociable circles and in the audience for Murphy's comedies. Thrale's ratings mesh with the experience of Dudley Ryder, earlier in the century, who worried about competing with other men in laughter-inducing social performance, especially in mixed company (see Chapter 6). On the one hand, as literati, Thrale and her friends were hardly typical eighteenth-century Britons, if there were such a thing. On the other hand, their literary activities put them in an ideal position for observing and reflecting the impact of the laughter market. Our evidence catches them in the act, so to speak, on both sides of these laughter relations—in everyday social interaction and in their engagement with commercialized laughter products, the jestbook and the stage comedy.

By the late eighteenth century the sale of laughter commodities had been developing for some two hundred and fifty years. Jestbooks and comedy had begun to flourish already during the Renaissance. But laughter products gained ever greater prominence with the growth of a market-based consumer culture. John Brewer has pointed to how this development of a public market for cultural products was especially strong in England, where, in contrast to Continental Europe, the royal court had lost much of its cultural cachet.[33] It was public taste and the market that increasingly ruled, although the public was by no means a unified body.

Murphy's search for a "final cause" of laughter was based on an assumption of inherent funniness. By implication, if one knew the cause, one could make it happen (and Murphy, as we know, was good at this). The idea is one of transactional exchange—you give me the funniness, I laugh. Conceptually, the cause of laughter has nothing to do with the relationship between you and me. This is the commodified view of a seller of laughter. Murphy was impressed by Hutcheson, but even though he quoted some of the philosopher's ideas about the relational value of laughter and the social bonds it works to form, his main interest was elsewhere. Similarly, of course, the "jestbook" idea that inspired Thrale is a commodity view. Yet Thrale had reservations about Murphy's laughter-inducing skills. He could set any company laughing, whether gentry or lowborn, and even one-on-one, he would mobilize his talents to amuse. But: "All this without the least Spark of Regard for you or the least desire of ever seeing you more."[34] Thrale may have been unfair to Murphy; he continued to be helpful to her after many closer friends had cut ties over that scandalous remarriage. But what bothered her was a perceived lack of real relationship, a mere exchange of talent for amusement. She knew that the laughable had exchange value but was troubled when it seemed to be only that.

Thrale's description of her journal as a "jestbook" shows a hint of the jocular in itself—not because of the amusing content, but because the jestbook genre had traveled downmarket since its Renaissance heyday. Learned humanists were early promoters of jest collections, ushering them into print as well as keeping manuscript jokes and anecdotes for their own enjoyment. But even in the early days, the erudite wit of humanists jostled with less elevated productions. In the eighteenth century there was a range of audiences at different price levels, but even if bought by the prosperous, the jestbook had low intellectual standing. In reality, the style of laughter in Thrale's memories was in one sense conditioned by the laughter market—finding exchangeable value in laughable moments and assessing the social value of laughter performance. At the same time, with its Latin-derived "-ana" title, the work marked itself off along lines of class and education from the laughter of the streets.

Jestbooks and other products hawking popular humor in the mid-eighteenth century have formed the basis of a revealing study by Simon Dickie. In the same period as Thrale's early life, he found repetition of conventional types of humor that had little place in the laughter Thrale found memorable. There was a lot of unsavory laughter in comic publications: laughter at deformities, at crude sexual and scatological humor, at sexual violence, and at devalued social groups such as country yokels and the Welsh, Irish, and Scots.[35] Dickie points out that the politeness and sentimentality cultivated in some elite circles had scant effect on the broader picture of popular entertainment, where themes that already would have been condemned as buffoonery by the sixteenth-century *Courtier* still held sway.

The persistence of "low" laughter—particularly body-based humor of sex and lower bodily functions—emerges also from Vic Gatrell's work on late eighteenth-century satirical prints. These products were created by artisans but consumed by a largely elite audience interested in the doings and misdoings of the political class. Their sexual and scatological humor was masculine in tone and appeal, with sometimes misogynist tones in the treatment of female bodies. But Gatrell, harking back to the ideas of Bakhtin that we examined in Chapter 1, sees these productions as liberating in their disrespectful treatment of the powerful. Puncturing the pretenses of dress, decorum, and class, the ribald humor could equalize bodies by highlighting their common, messy physicality. Although Gatrell found women more likely to have "prissy" objections to such departures from decorum, he also found evidence of women who enjoyed "low" body humor. The governess Ellen Weeton, an educated woman, wrote amusedly of farts and of an occasion when a man's shorts gave way during a race. Even in church she could be diverted by the double meaning of "doing business," reimagining the announcement of a town business meeting into an occasion for concerted defecation by all the townsfolk.[36]

Gatrell's book is full of fascinating information about the prevalence of bawdy humor through the eighteenth century, as well as its eclipse in the early decades of the nineteenth, as ideas of respectability increasingly came to rule over public culture. At the same time, he presents powerful evidence of how the materials of the laughter market could imprint themselves on everyday laughter experience. In the case of Ellen Weeton, Gatrell shows how her comic vision was modeled on the kinds of satirical images that were hawked in public prints. She described her image as a "caricature," presenting it in visual terms that evoked the territory of the prints. The townspeople were arranged on a circular platform, rears facing inward; they expressed themselves in phrases appropriate to the speech bubbles that were already a common feature of cartoons: "I am ready" or "I can stop no longer." Then on the signal from the clerk, "behold! an effusion of matter flowed forth till it formed a hill as high as the platform." As she described the scene in a letter to her brother, the shared amusement enabled by their intimate relationship was strongly inflected by the public culture of satire.

There is some room for doubt about whether body-based humor is really liberating, despite the attractions of the work of Bakhtin and Gatrell. As we have seen, medieval elites were delighted to participate in carnival mayhem and may have been some of its main promoters. They turned the scene to comedy when the king shat in a peasant woman's basket and roused her anger (Chapter 1). The consumers of salacious satirical prints, likewise, were mainly from the upper crust. It was particular elite individuals whose comeuppance they enjoyed, not the overturning of hierarchy itself. Conversely, the "priggish" crowd that Gatrell placed on the anti-laughter side included genuine political radicals like Mary Wollstonecraft and Francis Place. Would their cries against oppression have been better if they too had relished bathroom jokes? And opponents of ribaldry did love to laugh, just at different things. Fanny Burney, whom Gatrell describes as "convention-ruled to the core," frequently bubbled over with laughter. Although strait-laced in sexual matters, she made fun of conventions she thought ridiculous—such as the idea that genteel people should not laugh![37] She even enjoyed the slightly risqué amusement of a masquerade.[38]

There was laughter at a lot of things, both in public culture and in private. Here as in every other time and place, laughter is too varied to pin down to a single type. The laughter of Thrale's journal was not the belly laugh of carnival. Here, even in the occasional joke that touched on the failings of indecorous bodies, it was the verbal wit that took precedence. Thrale remembered a bon mot from Mrs. Montagu that touched obliquely on the territory of illicit sex. Aware of recent scandals among the aristocracy and playing on the vogue for books titled "Every Man his own Broker/ Brewer/etc., she asked, why isn't there a book called Every Man his own Cuckold?"[39] This sally was rather tame in comparison with the explicit satirical prints, but hardly showing the prudery sometimes ascribed to the intellectual women of Montagu's bluestocking circles. Even Murphy, who sold laughter for a living, devoted zero space in his compendium to the idea that the body could be inherently funny. It was contrast and clash of ideas that excited laughter—and in fact, even in the bawdy satirical prints one can find this clash at work, in the contrast between pretentions of greatness and the crude effusions of the body.

Obviously, the witticisms of Thrale and her friends were very different from the laughter products hawked in the streets. Yet, they were part of the same commodity culture, even though they were not actually bought and sold, and even though their elite sensibility was not for everyone. They were exchangeable goods, and their authors reaped rewards of increased appreciation and respect. Contemporaries could recognize the parallel between displays of ability and commodity exchange, as in this comment from Hannah More: for a woman,

> talents are only a means to a still higher attainment . . . merely to exercise them as an instrument for the acquisition of fame and the promoting of pleasure, is subversive of her delicacy as a woman, and contrary to the spirit of a christian.[40]

Here talents that were exchanged for fame and pleasure were still partaking of a crude public bargain and seeking a selfish reward. For a woman, involvement in this market might be seen as degrading—a clue, perhaps, to Thrale's differential scale of ratings according to gender. For men of talent, the display of ability was the business of life, and, in everyday sociability, they might come to be rated for it in the lady's private assessment.

Laughter Makes (or Breaks) the (Gentle)man

The risk of being judged for laughter qualities and found wanting brings us to another of Thrale's less valued acquaintances, James Boswell. He evidently did not cut an impressive figure in her society, and he in turn was not pleased at her intimacy with his hero Johnson. The son and heir of a Scottish laird, Boswell was an elite figure yet an outsider in English society, where the Scots were a regular butt of ridicule, in daily conversation as well as popular print. His intimacy with Johnson led to his most famous work, his biography of the great man. He also produced voluminous documentation of his own life, an extreme exemplar of the growing trend toward self-writing.

Boswell's relationship to laughter was in some ways similar to that of Samuel Pepys a century earlier. He too loved to laugh—but he had many more worries about his own laughter. His *London Journal*, kept during a sojourn in the capital in 1762–63, is the self-conscious record of a young man of 22 enjoying a new life of independence and seeking a career. He was regularly merry and laughing with company, although he recounts a period in his life, at the age of 17, when he suffered from what we would call severe depression. In his recovery, "many a struggle was in my mind between melancholy and mirth."[41] By 1762, he was trying to construct an identity of gentlemanly dignity, suitable to both his birth and his assimilation into English society. As the eldest son of an old landowning family, Boswell was proud of his status, yet as a Scot making his way in England, he could not be assured of the respect that he felt was his due.

His goal of more dignified comportment made him wish to curb his own comic tendencies, although he did not always succeed. His youthful journal is full of resolutions against excessive jocularity, usually occasioned by feelings of regret at his frequent lapses in dignity. He saw in himself the "shocking fault" of "sacrificing almost anything to a laugh." This love of hilarity appears clearly in the numerous occasions of merry company that mark his pages, as they did those of Pepys. Most of these instances he viewed positively, as benign enjoyment of sociability. Yet repeatedly, he felt that he went too far. Curbing this tendency was especially difficult because he had already set a pattern of behavior, in an earlier visit to London, as "a heedless, dissipated, rattling fellow who might say or do every ridiculous thing" and was accustomed "to laugh at everything."[42]

It was especially hard to keep himself in line when socializing with Scottish friends he had known at home. Soon after he reached London in 1762, the Kellie/Macfarlane family arrived to claim his old acquaintance. Since they knew him so well and so recently, he could not enact his new dignified role "without the appearance of strong affectation."[43] So, to his later regret, he "let myself out in humorous rhodomontade rather too much."[44] On another occasion, at tea, more "jocularity and loud mirth went round," and though he "seemed easy," he was hurt by "the not ill-meant though coarse gibes of this *hamely* company."[45] He was more troubled by his own behavior at a later dinner with his Scottish friends: "I was very hearty at dinner, but was too ridiculous. This is what I ought most to guard against. People in company applaud a man for it very much, but behind his back hold him very cheap."[46]

Similarly, Boswell chided himself for too much joking and laughing with Robert Temple, the younger brother of his good friend William Temple. William passed his London lodgings on to Boswell when he left, but for a while they were shared with young Bob, who was soon heading for Cambridge. Mostly they got along, but Boswell could not keep him in line:

> as he is very young and has not read much, he can be a companion to me in no other way than in laughing and talking harmless lively nonsense. . . . I have unluckily let myself too much down by my extreme jocularity before him, so that when I want to assume any superiority over him, the little dog immediately rebels and cries, "Come, come, James, you are wanting to be the Great Man. But it won't do." . . . I wish I had kept him all along at a due distance, for too much familiarity, especially with those much younger than ourselves, is always attended with disagreeable circumstances. I really find this is what I am most apt to fall into; and as it often makes me look little and so gives me pain, I must guard against it.[47]

On occasion he did succeed in hitting the style he aspired to. He congratulated himself for his success in intellectual conversation with his friend William Temple and a new acquaintance from Cambridge, talking of authors like Voltaire, Rousseau, and Hume:

> I talked really very well. I have not passed so much rational time I don't know when. The degree of distance due to a stranger restrained me from my effusions of ludicrous nonsense and intemperate mirth. I was rational and composed, yet lively and entertaining.[48]

His resolution to cultivate seriousness was strengthened by his acquaintance with Samuel Johnson. Boswell was captivated by Johnson's brilliance and warmly sympathetic to his conservative views on upholding the traditions of religion and social hierarchy. Once he met Johnson, he began filling his journal with snatches of the master's conversation. Johnson's pronouncements on various subjects were often witty, and Boswell found him entertaining as well as instructive. But their meetings were not "merry" like jaunts with his boon companions Erskine and Dempster. When back with his Scottish friend Dempster, dining with him and his sister, he marked the difference: they were "lively" company, "But conversation without a subject and constantly mixed up with ludicrous witticisms appears very trifling after being with Mr. Johnson."[49] Johnson's views on laughter reinforced Boswell's earlier resolve to rein in his own love of it. Johnson declared "low jocularity" to be

> a very bad thing. "You ought no more to think it enough if you laugh than you think it enough if you speak. You may laugh in as many ways as you speak; and surely every way of speaking that is practised cannot be admired." This was a very good lesson for me, who am addicted to low jocularity. I am determined to get rid of it.[50]

The laughter of wit and intellect had value, but not mere sociable silliness.

Boswell appears to have had limited success in shedding his addiction to low jocularity. He wanted to be seen as witty—"rational and composed, yet lively and entertaining." As we know, however, Hester Thrale was not impressed with his wit, and she was not the only one. She gave him high marks for "good humor," a score that may have been pumped up by his readiness to laugh at the sallies of others, particularly those of his idol, Johnson. But good humor was not one of the qualities that gained her highest respect; besides Johnson's zero and her husband's low score here, she claimed only 10 out of 20 for herself.

Boswell's desire to change his laughter habits was an attempt to adjust his natural inclinations to the values of the society he hoped to impress. It was also an attempt to move away from the habits and associates of his youth toward a more elevated intellectual plane. He retained some fondness for the enjoyments of his boyhood and even made a collection of the chapbooks that had been his favorite entertainment. The Dicey publishing house was a prolific purveyor of these cheap, flimsy publications; Simon Dickie has described their productions as appealing to the "barely literate." But while their audience could reach into the lower classes, it clearly was not limited to them, as the privileged young Boswell was a fan. In 1763, he visited the Dicey establishment and bought up dozens of the pamphlets, which he had bound up into a volume labeled "Curious Productions."

Not all of the "Curious Productions" were laughter material; Boswell mentions "Jack and the Giants" as a favorite, and a pamphlet on Jack takes pride of place as the first item in the volume. But he had certainly been consuming products from the low end of the laughter market. Dicey's stock in trade was largely reprints from the popular past. The "Wise Men of Gotham," whom Boswell remembered fondly, were subjects of a venerable jestbook dating back to the sixteenth century (attributed, doubtfully, to the Montpellier medical graduate Andrew Boorde, whom we met in Chapter 3). Boswell was surely pleased to find the foolish Gothamites in a two-part Dicey edition for his collection. Also in the collection was old Mother Bunch, who made her first appearance in the 1604 Pasquil's Jests, before spinning off into her own chapbooks full of slightly bawdy advice on love. The pranks of the "Frolicksome Courtier," another jestbook hero, included buttering the buttocks of a woman who tried to cheat him of the butter she was selling, then having his dogs lick them off. There was also *Wanton Tom, or the Merry History of Tom Stich, the Taylor*—in two parts. Boswell planned one day to write a story for children in the chapbook style, a task that "will require much nature and simplicity, and a great acquaintance with the humours and traditions of the english common people."[51] The qualities of nature and simplicity in the "Curious Productions" might be open to debate, but they certainly were exemplars of the lowbrow laughter market.

There is food for thought in the combination of Boswell's fondness for this boyhood reading and his concerns about excesses of "low jocularity." When Boswell felt himself lowered by inappropriate hilarity, what was it that marked the boundary of respectable laughter? Were the "hamely" Scots of his early acquaintance joking about bums, farts, sex, and the other topics of Rabelaisian earthiness that marked the satirical prints studied by Gatrell? Were they engaging in crude, jestbook-style humor of the sort studied by Dickie and embodied in the "Curious Productions?" We know that Boswell retained a taste for risqué humor long past his youth. After the death of Henry Thrale in 1781, he amused his friends with scurrilous verses imagining a sexual relationship between Hester Thrale and Dr. Johnson.[52] Perhaps he would not have been discomfited by some of the jestbook targets Dickie identified—deformity, sexual violence, and lower-class stupidity—which he could have joined in deriding. On the other hand, as a Scot, he was one of the common figures of jestbook fun, along with the Irish and Welsh. It was his own personal dignity that Boswell found threatened by being "too ridiculous"—from the loosening of barriers to familiarity more than the subject matter of jest. Of course, Boswell knew nothing about Thrale's private rating system. But he was very aware that he might be judged for his laughter behavior.

★★★

The world of Hester Thrale was an exclusive one, populated by many active participants in the literary market. Obviously, they were not representative of English society, let alone the rest of Europe. Yet the development of cultural products as public commodities was broadly shared, including the selling of laughter materials. We can find hints of the intersection between the laughter market and social practice in different times and places: Madame de Sévigné finding echoes of Molière's plays in her own life; Dorothy Osborne, Maria Thynne, and even Martin Luther turning the comic stereotype of the shrew into matter for private fun. Thrale's system of ratings, however playful, highlights an intensified demand for social performance in the realm of laughter.

The historian Daniel Wickberg has even argued that there was more laughter in English conversations by the eighteenth century, based on the coining and increased usage of such terms as ridicule, banter, and raillery.[53] Does the linguistic evidence mean that people actually laughed more? I'm not sure of that—but I do think the changes in language suggest an increased valuation of laughter and an increased sense that there are special skills involved in eliciting it. Both of these changes were fed by the laughter market. The view of laughter as a valuable commodity and as a response to performance emerged from a long historical development of buying and selling laughter.

Notes

1 Hester Lynch Thrale, *Thraliana: The Diary of Mrs. Hester Lynch Thrale (Later Mrs. Piozzi) 1776–1809*, ed. Katharine C. Balderston, 2 vols. (Oxford: Clarendon Press, 1951), 1:329.
2 For a recent biography, see Ian McIntyre, *Hester: The Remarkable Life of Dr Johnson's 'Dear Mistress'* (London: Constable, 2008).
3 See Katharine C. Balderston, "Introduction," in Thrale, *Thraliana*, 1:xi.
4 Thrale, *Thraliana*, 1:57.

5 Thrale, *Thraliana*, 1:50.

6 Thrale, *Thraliana*, 2:1000.

7 Thrale, *Thraliana*, 1:6.

8 Quoted in Leo Damrosch, *The Club: Johnson, Boswell, and the Friends Who Shaped an Age* (New Haven and London: Yale University Press, 2019), 215.

9 Quoted in Damrosch, *The Club*, 215.

10 Thrale, *Thraliana*, 2:1008.

11 Anthony Ashley Cooper, Earl of Shaftesbury, *Sensus Communis: An Essay on the Freedom of Wit and Humour* (London, 1709), 93.

12 Shaftesbury, *Sensus Communis*, 54.

13 Francis Hutcheson, *Thoughts on Laughter and Observations on the Fable of the Bees* (Glasgow, 1758), 2, *Eighteenth Century Collections Online*.

14 Hutcheson, *Thoughts on Laughter*, 37.

15 Hutcheson, *Thoughts on Laughter*, 41.

16 Thrale, *Thraliana*, 2:1087n.

17 Thrale, *Thraliana*, 1:545–46.

18 Thrale, *Thraliana*, 2:768, 770.

19 Thrale, *Thraliana*, 1:329; Joseph Spence, *Crito, or, A Dialogue on Beauty* (London, 1752), 44, https://archive.org/details/critoordialogueo00spen/mode/2up.

20 Thrale, *Thraliana*, 1:329–30.

21 Thrale, *Thraliana*, 1:331–32.

22 Thrale, *Thraliana*, 1:330.

23 Dudley Rider, *The Diary of Dudley Ryder 1715–1716*, ed. William Matthews (London: Methuen & Co., 1939), 71.

24 Shaftesbury, *Sensus Communis*, 14.

25 Samuel Johnson, *A Dictionary of the English Language: In Which the Words Are Deduced From Their Originals, And Illustrated In Their Different Significations by Examples From the Best Writers, to Which Are Prefixed, a History of the Language, And an English Grammar* (London: W. Strahan, 1755), s.v. Wit, https://catalog.hathitrust.org/Record/009310086.

26 Corbyn Morris, *An Essay Towards Fixing the True Standards of Wit, Humour, Raillery, Satire, and Ridicule* (London, 1744), xx (Italics in original).

27 Morris, *Essay*, xii (Italics in original).

28 Morris, *Essay*, xxv (Italics in original).

29 Thrale, *Thraliana*, 1:151.

30 Arthur Murphy, Commonplace Book of Arthur Murphy on Humor and Comedy, ms. at Folger Shakespeare Library. The Folger volume is not Murphy's only compilation in the genre. On his smaller commonplace book on the drama, see J. Homer Caskey, "Arthur Murphy's Commonplace-Book," *Studies in Philology* 37, no. 4 (October 1940): 598–609.

31 Murphy, Commonplace Book, 281.

32 Murphy, Commonplace Book, 286.

33 See John Brewer, "'The Most Polite Age and the Most Vicious': Attitudes towards Culture as a Commodity, 1660–1800," in *The Consumption of Culture 1600–1800: Image, Object, Text*, ed. Ann Bermingham and John Brewer (London and New York: Routledge, 1995), 341–61.

34 Thrale, *Thraliana*, 1:151.

35 Simon Dickie, *Cruelty and Laughter: Forgotten Comic Literature and the Unsentimental Eighteenth Century* (Chicago and London: University of Chicago Press, 2011).

36 Vic Gatrell, *City of Laughter: Sex and Satire in Eighteenth-Century London* (London: Atlantic Books, 2006), 361.

37 Gatrell, *City of Laughter*, 348; Anca Parvulescu, *Laughter: Notes on a Passion* (Cambridge and London: MIT Press, 2010), 44.

38 Fanny Burney, *The Early Journals and Letters of Fanny Burney, vol. 1 1768–1773*, ed. Lars E. Troide (Kingston and Montreal: McGill-Queen's University Press, 1988), 97–100.

39 Thrale, *Thraliana*, 1:332.
40 Hannah More, *Strictures on the Modern System of Female Education* (1799), 2:12; cited in Brewer, "The Most Polite Age," 354.
41 James Boswell, *Boswell's London Journal 1762–1763*, ed. Frederick A. Pottle (New York: McGraw-Hill, 1950), 77–78.
42 Boswell, *London Journal*, 62.
43 Boswell, *London Journal*, 63.
44 Boswell, *London Journal*, 68.
45 Boswell, *London Journal*, 116.
46 Boswell, *London Journal*, 121.
47 Boswell, *London Journal*, 298.
48 Boswell, *London Journal*, 257–58.
49 Boswell, *London Journal*, 304.
50 Boswell, *London Journal*, 321.
51 Boswell, "Curious Productions," flyleaf inscription, Widener Library, Harvard University.
52 Damrosch, *The Club*, 356–57.
53 Daniel Wickberg, *The Senses of Humor: Self and Laughter in Modern America* (Ithaca: Cornell University Press, 1998), 54–6.

CODA

The Lessons of Laughter

This book opened with the contrast between the anti-laughter advice of Lord Chesterfield and the celebration of laughter in Jane Austen's novel *Pride and Prejudice*. To Chesterfield, audible laughter was beneath the dignity of the highborn gentleman. To Austen, as to her contemporary Fanny Burney, such pompous restraint was, in a word, laughable. This striking clash of eighteenth-century views underlines the fact that there is no single story of laughter at any time. The divide also highlights important points in laughter's history. Strikingly, people laughed in spite of what pundits were telling them—even among the educated classes who were most exposed to the naysaying. At the same time, these opposing views come from parallel trends in the valuation of laughter—one aiming to suppress hostile or disturbing laughter, the other highlighting laughter's positive side. Both belong to the early modern era, and they mark a shift into the world of modern laughter.

There was a long tradition of focus on negative aspects of laughter in Western Christian thinking, and the weaponizing of laughter in Renaissance competitiveness only underlined its aggressive edge. But purposeful reactions against malicious laughter date to the same era, with courtly attempts to curb excess and turn wit and laughter to civilized use. New standards of bodily comportment sought to restrain physical humor and unbridled laughter, while proponents of gentler laughter emphasized laughter's uses in easing and enhancing social relationships. Chesterfield's contempt for the contortions and noise of laughter was paired with a famous wit; purveyors of laughter published collections of his bon mots, some of which found their way into Arthur Murphy's commonplace book. One can see Austen and Chesterfield as advancing different versions of the movement toward "civilizing" laughter. For Chesterfield, amusement was refined with elite dignity to the point of the noiseless smile. For Austen, it was a positive means of drawing people together—without the boisterous physicality of the laughter of carnival celebrants or even Felix Platter, but retaining its power to forge social bonds.

DOI: 10.4324/9781003247517-9

One finds both of these parallel lines of development in Baldassare Castiglione's sixteenth-century *Courtier*. The ideal sophisticate would be tamed in both directions, neither cavorting like a buffoon nor engaging in malicious mockery. The first type of taming focused especially on the physical aspects of laughter, as elites cultivated a sense of disgust at physical excess and emphasis on bodily control. The other civilizing trend, favoring genial and benevolent laughter, was more concerned with intangibles—the emotions aroused by hostile versus pleasant laughter and its social effects of conflict versus bonding. If Castiglione and other early proponents of courtliness can be seen as embracing both trends, Benvenuto Cellini gives us an untamed version of hostile and ebullient laughter. No one would claim that aggressive laughter is gone in the modern era or that Cellini was a typical laugher, but laughing in the face of one's enemies went out of fashion among aspirants to gentility. The elaborate rules of the duel, developed in these early modern centuries, prescribed very different modes of dealing with elite male honor and insult, channeling and expressing aggression.

Madame de Sévigné was a descendant in the same spirit as Castiglione, able to maintain friendly relations with the objects of her jests, while being an adept at courtly decorum and etiquette. Yet the larger picture of laughter at court was much less innocuous, controlled in body while potentially cruel in spirit. It was rare for the courtly gathering to break into open laughter at clumsy dancing—Saint-Simon even thought it a first—but shaming ridicule was a staple. Sévigné's friend La Rochefoucauld declared that ridicule was "more dishonoring than dishonor itself"—because taking it seriously as insult only made one look even more ridiculous.[1] Chesterfield, who thought an audible chuckle beneath him, was ready to bite with his wit. One of his sallies, quoted in Murphy's commonplace book, might have landed a lesser man in court for defamation in the previous century:

> Ld Chesterfield told by Miss Chidley, that it was a slanderous World, and that Fame reported she had been brought to bed of Twins:—It is a rule with me, Ma'am, not to believe above half of what I hear.[2]

So, there were two early modern modes of taming unruly laughter, both of them cultivated by privileged social classes. But the Chesterfield mode of aristocratic superiority was in decline during the eighteenth century, as Enlightenment ideas, political revolutions, and the growing industrial age undermined its prestige. Proponents of Enlightenment thinking in France prided themselves on their wit and gaiety. At the close of the century, Jane Austen and Fanny Burney could simply laugh at excessive elitist (and male) gravity. Certainly, one can find continuing strains of blasé contempt for common amusement among elites, but laughter has risen steadily in social approval since the eighteenth century. People have always enjoyed laughter in everyday life, but in the modern age disdain for laughter has waned even among grouchy intellectuals.[3] A "sense of humor" is widely seen as a valuable trait. It was in the early modern period that laughter overcame the dual strains of negativity it faced in Western society, from both religious authorities and elite purists.

How much did this enhanced reputation of laughter come at the cost of suppression of some of its infinite varieties? Along with developing conventions of behavior to manage laughter, there were certainly official moves to police the laughter of the lower classes, especially when they were laughing at social superiors. The curbing of popular festivities like carnivals and maypole dances aimed partly to prevent illicit sexuality or violence, but the hilarity also worried reforming moralists, especially in Protestant regions. Excesses of frivolity might pave the path toward vice. Ribald humor also became a target, as people resorted to courts to defend themselves against insults involving cuckoldry, whoredom, or bastardy. At the same time, laughter at sexual foibles and innuendo was a staple of public, commercial comedy, from theater to jestbooks and other popular print. While the public culture of the nineteenth century became less tolerant of bawdry, most famously in Victorian England, the realm of private laughter remains less clear.

The trends toward taming laughter were largely at the level of social convention and prescription, as well as being bounded by class and by the nearly infinite range of "laughter communities" across Europe. Looking at laughter in practice, we find people turning laughter to their own uses in ways that often do not match the conceptions of authorities. In fact, laughter and humor were always resistant to predictable control—one reason why elite-dominated courts like the Star Chamber wanted to quash obstreperous laughter among social subordinates. In all the many forms in which we encounter it in social relations, laughter plays by its own rules. This quality of laughter is a given in modern society, but its possibilities are often forgotten when we look at the past and find grim-sounding pronouncements from the famous, powerful, or well-published. Among Calvinists, despite complaints about humorlessness and the policing of morality, people actually did laugh, just as some women laughed at early modern misogyny, finding spaces of play to manage the strictures that surrounded them.

★★★

I've said that laughter has not a history, but histories. In one sense that statement refers to the laughter stories of individuals, both those recounted here and those that have gone unrecorded. It also refers to multiple strands of historical change. Alongside the "civilizing process" came the growth of the laughter market, in which exchangeable laughter material became detached from its social context. The commercialization of laughter was a very long development, stretching from the early printed jestbooks into the present day. In the nineteenth century, the market for laughter products grew exponentially from its early modern beginnings. As Louise Lee recently remarked about the market for humor in Victorian England: "the distinct difference in the Victorian age is its excessive mercantile transmissibility: the new and myriad pathways for dissemination through exponentially expanding local, national and international print cultures, theatrical performances, circuses and revues." Jokes were "produced on an ever-expanding scale—industrialised even—with the voracious appetite for new material often outstripping supply."[4]

What difference did the commercialization of laughter make? Its effects are challenging to tease out, especially since in the twenty-first century we are still, and even more thoroughly, immersed in a culture full of laughter commodities. The canned laughter of situation comedy is emblematic of this immersion in commercial laughter; it can become such a normalized part of our experience that we expect to hear it. Similarly, the laughter of comic performance strongly colors our perception of the laughable, even though the bulk of our actual laughter occurs in social interactions that may not even be humorous. In the early modern period, one can observe many points of intersection and influence between daily occasions of laughter and the marketed laughter products of the surrounding culture. When Martin Luther teased his wife with misogynistic tropes, and still more when Johann Dietz re-enacted the violent shrew-taming of comic literature in his own marriage, we can see the impact of their consumption of canned comedy. Comic stereotypes enabled them to frame their male superiority as play—good-naturedly in the one case, less so in the other. Madame de Sévigné drew on the plays of Molière to label her foolish neighbor, as well as to endorse the witty barbs she traded with her son. Defendants in libel cases drew their comic insults from the conventional butts of public humor.

Other implications of the changes in laughter over time are more speculative but intriguing. I've said that the commercialization of laughter was a separate line of development from the taming of laughter and its rising prestige. But were these really separate? Did the selling of laughter boost its perceived social value? We know that things that are not monetized in modern society—"housework," for example—tend to be downgraded in social importance. Laughter may be a case of the contrary. In addition, the spread of impersonal laughter may have lessened laughter's reputation as hostile and threatening. Commercial comedy is sold for pure pleasure, and the audience's laughter has little impact on their everyday social relationships. Even essentially malicious laughter against stereotypical targets may seem harmless when the targets are not actually present. Canned laughter may create the impression that laughter is less important than it actually is, even as the demand for salable laughs could reinforce the reliance on stereotypes. Thus, Dickie found predictable targets in the mass-market jokebooks of eighteenth-century England, from the Irish and Scots to the poor or disabled.[5]

On the other hand, if commercialization extracts laughter from its normal habitat of social relations, it also creates virtual communities of response to the laughable, giving laughter a modern form of social power. Perhaps even more than interpersonal laughter, this power can promote both harmony and hostility. The spread of laughter through media can unite a disparate audience into shared feeling and implicit agreement. I have pointed elsewhere to the way in which crime sensationalism fostered common emotional reactions that helped build the non-rational aspects of the early modern "public sphere."[6] The commercialization of laughter surely played a part in forging common sensibilities as well. Its operations in this regard are not necessarily benign, of course, as shared laughter at a common target can harden lines of social division, both in the early modern period and in modern times. One need only look at the repellent antisemitic "humor" of Nazi propaganda to see those possibilities.

★★★

One effect of commercialization has had a strong impact on ideas about gender and laughter: the rise of the joke. The modern joke, complete with punch line, is a distinctive form of laughter product: detachable from its social context and capable (if successful) of reproducing laughter in multiple retellings to different audiences. Older ideas of jest included a much broader repertoire of amusement. (Note that Felix Platter and Dorothy Osborne did not need punch lines in their laughing relationships with future mates.) Jokes are told in sociable contexts as well as in professional/commercial performances; one might think of sociable jokes as mini-performances. We have observed this aspect of social performance in Hester Thrale's ratings of her acquaintances in the late eighteenth century. As the performance of exchangeable jokes came increasingly to be perceived as the core element of humor and laughter, the always-gendered associations of laughter shifted. As Bob Nicholson has observed, in the nineteenth century female modesty came to seem incompatible with joking. By the end of the century, a Dundee newspaper was referring to "the old theory that women have no sense of humor" while attempting to assure its readers that a woman who wrote jokes could still retain her feminine charm.[7]

But how old in reality was the idea that women lack a sense of humor? The idea of "sense of humor" is largely a nineteenth-century development, but if we take the concept more broadly to mean the ability to either evoke laughter or respond to jest, we do not find the exclusion of women going back very far. Early modern moralists were more worried, in fact, that women might laugh too much or too loudly or too suggestively. In the sixteenth century, Castiglione assumed that ladies would jest; Juan Luis Vives wanted good wives to tell funny stories to their husbands, not assuming that it took a special skill to do so. Felix Platter's mother and the Abbess of Olsberg both loved to play practical jokes. When Sir Nicholas Le Strange compiled funny sayings from his family and friends in the early seventeenth century, his mother and other women were among the jesters. Sévigné championed laughter, while Samuel Pepys appreciated the company of a "fine, witty lady," even when she did not appear to be sexually available. Of course, women were long adjured not to talk too much, and to avoid exposure in the public space that was increasingly marked off from the privatized household. In Hester Thrale's journal we see signs of how the association of laughter with performance and the market could downplay women's humor, even in Thrale's own setting among brilliant female wits. In her differential table of qualities for men and women, men were rated on their wit and humor, while women were valued for vaguer "conversation powers." It appears that the growing association of humor and laughter with marketable performance clashed with ideas of female nature and decorum; certainly that was the view put forward by Hannah More, even though she too was admired by contemporaries for her ready wit.

Naturally, women have continued to laugh on through the nineteenth century and into the present. But the idea that women lack a sense of humor became commonplace in the nineteenth century, persisted into the twentieth, and is not yet dead. As recently as 2007, an article headed "Why Women Aren't Funny" appeared in *Vanity Fair* magazine.[8] After its nineteenth-century spread in public commentary, the idea of women's humorlessness became enshrined in scholarly studies in the twentieth century, especially among psychologists of the Freudian school.[9] Modern studies of mixed-gender interaction often find more use of aggressive humor by men, although not necessarily more laughter or more humor overall.[10] Both sexes report high valuation of a sense of humor in their partners. Women appear to value performance of humor, such as joke-telling, in prospective mates, while men look more for receptivity. Women's uses of humor have often taken forms that differ from punch line performances. But the settings in which humor and laughter have been studied are quite limited. In the United States, for example, many studies use the readily available populations of college students or frequenters of local bars, and material for cross-cultural comparison is largely lacking. Female comic performers have countered the "old" stereotype of humorless women, with notable successes. But we know less about the gender dynamics of the everyday encounters where most laughter lives.[11]

Laughter has featured in love affairs and other intimate relationships across time and cultures. In his comparative study of romantic love, for example, William Reddy quotes a medieval lyric from India about the love of Krishna, in which "he laughed with an abundance of passion for the pleasure-of-love."[12] The laughter of lovers appears to be one aspect of laughter that the naysayers of Western culture were never able to stifle. In the early modern period, we find much laughter among lovers, including the courtship laughter of Felix Platter and Magdalena Jeckelmann, the laughter of women like Dorothy Osborne who could use the freedom of intimate relationships to mock gender stereotyping, and the laughter that brought other women under suspicion of sexual looseness. What one does not find in the early modern era is the modern demand for a sense of humor as a priority in choosing a mate. The shift toward sense of humor as a staple virtue of the ideal partner came gradually across the nineteenth and twentieth centuries. Clearly, this change was connected with changes in courtship and marriage toward a more emotional rather than economic focus. Over the early modern period, economic activity moved increasingly out of its former center within the household. Practical considerations remained important in courtship, but already in the seventeenth century there was increasing freedom for youth to choose their own partners. They could give more priority to their feelings, rather than bow to familial control—a trend we find even among young women of the English gentry like Osborne and Thynne. The greater freedom of youth was a change that occurred first at lower social levels, where kin groups had less interest and power for consolidating property holdings and political influence. Aristocrats, and especially royals, have been the last to gain freedom in marital choices.

★★★

People love to laugh now and don't feel bad about it, but in Western culture this has not always been so. While laughter has always been a powerful social agent, its nature and uses have been contested and evolving. Early modern laughers show us both the power of laughter and its changing fortunes in different contexts. We can trace to the early modern period the modern high valuation of laughter and sense of humor, now a staple of social approval from casual acquaintance to life partner. We can also trace to the early modern period the dominance of commercialized laughter in concepts of what (and who) is funny. This development has privileged the extractable joke and humor performance in judgments of the laughable, fueling such modern stereotypes as the idea that women lack humor. It's a complicated and not always laughable story! But these histories of laughter reach deep into daily experience, in the early modern era and in our own.

Notes

1 François, duc de La Rochefoucauld, *Maximes*, ed. Jean Lafond (Paris: Imprimerie Nationale, 1998), 116, no. 326.
2 Murphy, Commonplace Book, 53; the lady, Elizabeth Chudleigh, really had given birth in secret, however.
3 For example, see the discussions in Peter L. Berger, *Redeeming Laughter: The Comic Dimension of Human Experience*, 2nd ed. (De Gruyter, 2014), Proquest Ebook Central; Willibald Ruch, "Foreword and Overview. Sense of Humor: A New Look at an Old Concept," in *The Sense of Humor: Explorations of a Personality Characteristic*, ed. Willibald Ruch (Berlin: De Gruyter, 1998), 3–14, Proquest Ebook Central. For different views, however, see Dietmar Kamper and Christoph Wulf, eds., *Lachen—Gelächter—Lächeln: Reflexionen in drei Spiegeln* (Frankfurt am Main: Syndikat, 1986); Michael Billig, *Laughter and Ridicule: Towards a Social Critique of Humour* (Sage Publications, 2005), DOI: 10.4135/9781446211779; F. H. Buckley, *The Morality of Laughter* (Ann Arbor, MI: University of Michigan Press, 2003), https://doi.org/10.3998/mpub.12004.
4 Louise Lee, ed., *Victorian Comedy and Laughter: Conviviality, Jokes and Dissent* (London: Palgrave Macmillan, 2020), 13, ProQuest Ebook Central.
5 Simon Dickie, *Cruelty and Laughter: Forgotten Comic Literature and the Unsentimental Eighteenth Century* (Chicago and London: University of Chicago Press, 2011).
6 Joy Wiltenburg, *Crime and Culture in Early Modern Germany* (Charlottesville: University of Virginia Press, 2012).
7 Bob Nicholson, "'Capital Company': Writing and Telling Jokes in Victorian Britain," in *Victorian Comedy and Laughter*, 109–39, 125.
8 Christopher Hitchens, "Why Women Aren't Funny: What Makes the Female so much Deadlier than the Male," *Vanity Fair* 49, no. 1 (January 2007): 54, Gale OneFile: Contemporary Women's Issues.
9 See Nancy A. Walker, *A Very Serious Thing: Women's Humor and American Culture* (Minneapolis: University of Minnesota Press, 1988), 74–83.

10 For a recent review, see J. Hoffmann et al., "Gender Differences in Humor-related Traits, Humor Appreciation, Production, Comprehension, (Neural) Responses, Use, and Correlates: A Systematic Review," *Current Psychology* (2020), https://doi-org.proxy.library.upenn.edu/10.1007/s12144-020-00724-1.

11 There are ongoing efforts to promote further study; for example, see the special issue on gender in *Humor: International Journal of Humor Research* 33, no. 2 (May 2020).

12 William M. Reddy, *The Making of Romantic Love: Longing and Sexuality in Europe, South Asia, and Japan, 900–1200 CE* (Chicago: University of Chicago Press, 2012), 260.

BIBLIOGRAPHY

Primary Sources

Adams, Thomas. *The Blacke Devil or the Apostate Together with the Wolfe Worrying the Lambes*. London, 1615. Early English Books Online.

Aquinas, St. Thomas. *Summa Theologica*. Translated by Fathers of the English Dominican Province, 1947. https://www.ccel.org/ccel/aquinas/summa.SS_Q168_A4.html.

Aughterson, Kate, ed. *Renaissance Woman: A Sourcebook: Constructions of Femininity in England*. London and New York: Routledge, 1995.

Bangs, Benjamin. *Memoirs of the Life and Convincement of that Worthy Friend, Benjamin Bangs, Late of Stockport in Cheshire, Deceased; Mostly Taken from His Own Mouth, by Joseph Hobson*. London, 1757. Eighteenth Century Collections Online.

Booy, David, ed. *Personal Disclosures: An Anthology of Self-writings from the Seventeenth Century*. Aldershot: Ashgate, 2002.

Boswell, James. *Boswell's London Journal 1762–1763*. Edited by Frederick A. Pottle. New York: McGraw-Hill, 1950.

———. comp. "Curious Productions." Collection of chapbooks, 1763. Houghton Library, Harvard University.

Burney, Fanny. *The Early Journals and Letters of Fanny Burney*. Edited by Lars E. Troide. Vol. 1, 1768–1773. Kingston and Montreal: McGill-Queen's University Press, 1988.

Burton, Robert. *The Anatomy of Melancholy*. Edited by Holbrook Jackson. New York: Vintage Books, 1977.

Castiglione, Baldassarre. *The Book of the Courtier*. Translated by Leonard Epstein Opdycke. New York: Charles Scribner's Sons, 1903. https://archive.org/stream/bookofcourtier-00castuoft/bookofcourtier00castuoft_djvu.txt.

———. *The Book of the Courtier*. Edited by Daniel Javitch. Translated by Charles S. Singleton. New York: Norton, 2002.

———. *Il Libro del Cortegiano*. Edited by Giulio Preti. Torino: Einaudi, 1965. http://www.letteraturaitaliana.net/pdf/Volume_4/t84.pdf.

Cellini, Benvenuto. *The Autobiography of Benvenuto Cellini*. Translated by George Bull. Rev. ed. New York: Penguin, 1998.

————. *The Life of Benvenuto Cellini.* Translated by John Addington Symonds. 2 vols. London, 1863. https://en.wikisource.org/wiki/The_Life_of_Benvenuto_Cellini.

————. *My Life.* Translated by Julia Conaway Bondanella and Peter Bondanella. Oxford and New York: Oxford University Press, 2002.

————. *La Vita.* Edited by Lorenzo Bellotto. Parma: Fondazione Pietro Bembo, 1996.

Cochrane, Eric, and Julius Kirshner, eds. *University of Chicago Readings in Western Civilization 5: The Renaissance.* Chicago and London: University of Chicago Press, 1986.

Contat, Nicolas. *Anecdotes typographiques: où l'on voit la description des coutumes, moeurs et usages singuliers des Compagnons imprimeurs.* Edited by Giles Barber. Oxford: Oxford Bibliographical Society, 1980.

Crawford, Patricia, and Laura Gowing, eds. *Women's Worlds in the 17th-century England: A Sourcebook.* London and New York: Routledge, 2000.

Cust, Richard, and Andrew Hopper, eds. *The Court of Chivalry 1634–1640. British History Online.* http://www.british-history.ac.uk/no-series/court-of-chivalry.

d'Aubigné, Theodore-Agrippa. *His Life, to His Children; Sa Vie à ses enfants.* Translated by John Nothnagle. Lincoln and London: University of Nebraska Press, 1989.

Davis, Norman, ed. *Paston Letters and Papers of the Fifteenth Century.* Oxford: Clarendon Press, 1971.

de Croÿ, Marguerite. Lettres. Archives Départementales du Nord, Lille, France.

Dietz, Johann. *Master Johann Dietz, Surgeon in the Army of the Great Elector and Barber to the Royal Court.* Translated by Bernard Miall. London: George Allen & Unwin, 1923.

Equiano, Olaudah. *The Interesting Narrative and Other Writings.* Edited by Vincent Carretta. New York: Penguin, 2003.

Glueckel of Hameln. *Glikl: Memoirs 1691–1719.* Edited by Chava Turniansky. Translated by Sara Friedman. Waltham, MA: Brandeis University Press, 2019. https://doi-org.proxy.library.upenn.edu/10.2307/j.ctv102bd6s.

Goldberg, P. J. P., ed. and trans. *Women in England c. 1275–1525: Documentary Sources.* Manchester and New York: Manchester University Press, 1995.

Hair, Paul, ed. *Before the Bawdy Court: Selections From Church Court and Other Records Relating to the Correction of Moral Offences in England, Scotland and New England, 1300–1800.* New York: Harper & Row, 1972.

Halkett, Anne. *The Autobiography of Lady Anne Halkett.* Westminster: Camden Society, 1875. https://archive.org/stream/autobiographyofa00halkrich#page/n5/mode/2up.

Harsdörffer, Georg Philip. *Frauenzimmer Gescprächspiele.* Edited by Irmgard Böttcher. Deutsche Neudrucke, Reihe Barock. 8 vols., 13–20. Tübingen: Max Niemeyer, 1968.

Helmholz, R. H. *Select Cases on Defamation to 1600.* London: Selden Society, 1985.

Hobbes, Thomas. *Humane Nature, or, the Fundamental Elements of Policy.* 1650. Early English Books Online. https://www.proquest.com/books/humane-nature-fundamental-elements-policy-being/docview/2240906975/se-2?accountid=14707.

————. *Leviathan.* Edited by J. C. A. Gaskin. Oxford: Oxford University Press, 1996.

Hutcheson, Francis. *Thoughts on Laughter and Observations on the Fable of the Bees. In Six Letters.* Glasgow, 1758. Eighteenth Century Collections Online. Gale.

Johnson, Samuel. *A Dictionary of the English Language: In Which the Words Are Deduced from Their Originals, And Illustrated In Their Different Significations by Examples From the Best Writers, to Which Are Prefixed, a History of the Language, And an English Grammar.* London: W. Strahan, 1755. https://catalog.hathitrust.org/Record/009310086.

Joubert, Laurent. *Traité du Ris, Contenant ses causes, et mervelheus effais, curieusemant recerchés, raisonnés et observés.* Paris, 1579.

————. *Treatise on Laughter.* Translated by Gregory David de Rocher. Alabama: University of Alabama Press, 1980.

La Rochefoucauld, François, Duc de. *Collected Maxims and Other Reflections*. Translated and edited by E. H. and A. M. Blackmore and Francine Giguère. Oxford and New York: Oxford University Press, 2007.

———. *Maximes*. Edited by Jean Lafond. Paris: Imprimerie Nationale, 1998.

Le Strange, Sir Nicholas. *"Merry Passages and Jeasts": A Manuscript Jestbook*. Edited by H. F. Lippincott. Salzburg: Institut für Englische Sprache und Literatur, 1974.

Lowe, Roger. *The Diary of Roger Lowe, of Ashton-in-Makerfield, Lancashire, 1663–74*. Edited by William L. Sachse. New Haven: Yale University Press, 1938.

Luther, Martin. *D. Martin Luthers Werke. Kritische Gesamtausgabe. Tischreden*. 6 vols. Weimar: H. Böhlau, 1912–1921.

———. *Works*. 55 vols. Vol. 54, *Table Talk*. Edited and translated by Theodore G. Tappert. Philadelphia: Fortress Press, 1967.

Martin, Randall, ed. *Women Writers in Renaissance England: An Annotated Anthology*. Harlow: Pearson, 2010.

Ménétra, Jacques-Louis. *Journal of My Life*. Edited by Daniel Roche, translated by Arthur Goldhammer. New York: Columbia University Press, 1986.

Morris, Corbyn. *An Essay Towards Fixing the True Standards of Wit, Humour, Raillery, Satire, and Ridicule*. London, 1744. Eighteenth Century Collections Online. Gale.

Ms Arch Papers Oxon, Oxfordshire History Centre, Oxford, UK.

Murphy, Arthur, comp. *Commonplace Book of Arthur Murphy on Humor and Comedy* [manuscript], ca. 1760–1780. Folger Shakespeare Library.

Newcastle, William Cavendish, Duke of. *The Phanseys of William Cavendish Marquis of Newcastle Addressed to Margaret Lucas and her Letters in Reply*. Edited by Douglas Grant. London: Nonesuch Press, 1956.

Ordinary of Newgate's Account, The. Old Bailey Online. https://www.oldbaileyonline.org/index.jsp.

Osborne, Dorothy. *Dorothy Osborne: Letters to Sir William Temple*. Edited by Kenneth Parker. Aldershot, UK: Ashgate, 2002.

———. *Letters from Dorothy Osborne to Sir William Temple (1653–1654)*. Edited by Edward Abbott Parry. London: J. M. Dent, and New York: E. P. Dutton, 1914. http://digital.library.upenn.edu/women/osborne/letters/letters.html.

Ostovich, Helen and Elizabeth Sauer, eds. *Reading Early Modern Women: An Anthology of Texts in Manuscript and Print, 1550–1700*. New York and London: Routledge, 2004.

Otten, Charlotte F., ed. *English Women's Voices 1540–1700*. Miami: Florida International University Press, 1992.

Paré, Ambroise. *The Apologie and Treatise of Ambroise Paré*. Edited by Geoffrey Keynes. New York: Dover, 1968.

———. *Oeuvres complètes*. Edited by J.-F. Malgaigne. 3 vols. Paris, 1840–1841.

Pepys, Samuel. *The Diary of Samuel Pepys*. Edited by Robert Latham and William Matthews. 11 vols. Berkeley and Los Angeles: University of California Press, 1970–1983.

———. "The Diary of Samuel Pepys." https://www.pepysdiary.com.

Petrarca, Francesco. "Letters on Familiar Matters." In *University of Chicago Readings in Western Civilization 5: The Renaissance,* edited by Eric Cochrane and Julius Kirshner, 37–41. Chicago and London: University of Chicago Press, 1986.

Platter, Felix. *Tagebuch (Lebensbeschreibung) 1536–1567*. Edited by Valentin Lötscher. Basel and Stuttgart: Schwabe, 1976.

Platter, Thomas (1499–1582). *The Autobiography of Thomas Platter, a Schoolmaster of the Sixteenth Century*. Translated by Mrs. Finn. London, 1839. Hathi Trust Digital Library. http://hdl.handle.net/2027/hvd.32044011383924.

———. *Thomas Platter: Ein Lebensbild aus dem Jahrhundert der Reformation*. Edited by Horst Kohl. Voigtländers Quellenbücher Band 21. Leipzig: R. Voigtländers Verlag, 1912.

Platter, Thomas (1574–1628). *Journal of a Younger Brother: The Life of Thomas Platter as a Medical Student in Montpellier at the Close of the Sixteenth Century.* Translated by Seán Jennett. London: Frederick Muller Limited, 1963.

Rütiner, Johannes. *Diarium 1529–1539.* 5 vols. Edited by Ernst Gerhard Rüsch. St. Gallen: Vadiana, 1996.

Ryder, Dudley. *The Diary of Dudley Ryder 1715–1716.* Edited by William Matthews. London: Methuen & Co., 1939.

Saint-Simon, Louis de Rouvroy, duc de. *Historical Memoirs of the Duc de Saint-Simon.* Edited and translated by Lucy Norton. 3 vols. London: Prion Books, 2000.

———. *Mémoires de Saint-Simon.* 41 vols. Edited by Arthur de Boislisle. Paris, 1879–1919.

———. *The Memoirs of Louis XIV, His Court and the Regency.* Translated by Bayle St. John. https://www.gutenberg.org/files/3875/3875-h/3875-h.htm#link2H_INTR.

Sévigné, Marie de Rabutin-Chantal, Marquise de. *Correspondance.* Edited by Roger Duchêne. 3 vols. Paris: Gallimard, 1972.

———. *The Letters of Madame de Sévigné.* Edited by A. Edward Newton. 7 vols. Philadelphia: J. P. Horn, 1927.

Shaftesbury, Anthony Ashley Cooper, Earl of. *Sensus Communis: An Essay on the Freedom of Wit and Humour.* London, 1709.

Shakespeare, William. "The Merry Wives of Windsor." In *The Arden Shakespeare Complete Works*, edited by Richard Proudfoot, Ann Thompson, and David Scott Kastan. Walton-on-Thames, Surrey: Thomas Nelson, 1998.

Spence, Joseph. *Crito, or, A Dialogue on Beauty.* London, 1752. https://archive.org/details/critoordialogueo00spen/mode/2up.

St. Clair, William, and Irmgard Maassen, eds. *Conduct Literature for Women 1500–1640.* 6 vols. London: Pickering & Chatto, 2000.

Thrale, Hester Lynch. *Thraliana: The Diary of Mrs. Hester Lynch Thrale (Later Mrs. Piozzi) 1776–1809.* Edited by Katharine C. Balderston. 2 vols. Oxford: Clarendon Press, 1951.

Vasari, Giorgio. *Lives of the Most Eminent Painters, Sculptors and Architects.* Translated by Gaston du C. De Vere. London: Medici Society, 1915. https://archive.org/stream/livesofmostemine10vasauoft/livesofmostemine10vasauoft_djvu.txt.

Vaughan, William. *The Spirit of Detraction, Coniured and Conuicted in Seuen Circles. . . .* London, 1611. Early English Books Online. https://www-proquest-com.proxy.library.upenn.edu/eebo/docview/2240852009?&imgSeq=1.

Vives, Juan Luis. "Instruction of a Christian Woman (1541)." In *Conduct Literature for Women*, edited by William St. Clair and Irmgard Maassen. 6 vols., 1:17–318. London: Pickering & Chatto, 2000.

Wall, Alison D., ed. *Two Elizabethan Women: Correspondence of Joan and Maria Thynne 1575–1611.* Devizes: Wiltshire Record Society, 1983.

Watt, Isabella M., M. Wallace McDonald, and Jeffrey R. Watt, eds. *Registres du Consistoire de Genève au temps de Calvin, 1554.* Vol. 9. Geneva: Droz, 2015.

Reference Works and Archives

Archives Départementales du Nord, Lille, France.

Borthwick Institute for Archives, University of York. http://www.hrionline.ac.uk/causepapers/.

Calendar of State Papers Relating To English Affairs in the Archives of Venice, Volume 6, 1555–1558. Edited by Rawdon Brown. London, 1877. British History Online. http://www.british-history.ac.uk/cal-state-papers/venice/vol6.

Calendar of State Papers, Spain (Simancas), Volume 1, 1558–1567. Edited by Martin A. S. Hume. London, 1892. British History Online. http://www.british-history.ac.uk/cal-state-papers/simancas/vol1.

Calendar of State Papers, Spain (Simancas), Volume 2, 1568–1579. Edited by Martin A. S. Hume. London, 1894. British History Online. http://www.british-history.ac.uk/cal-state-papers/simancas/vol2.

Cheshire Record Office, Chester, UK.

Dictionnaire de l'Académie français, Le. 1694. https://artflsrv03.uchicago.edu/philologic4/publicdicos/.

Dictionnaire du Moyen Français (1330–1500). http://www.atilf.fr/dmf.

Goetze, Alfred. *Frühneuhochdeutsches Glossar.* Berlin: Walter de Gruyter, 1967.

Grande Dizionario della Lingua Italiana. 21 vols. Edited by Salvatore Battaglia. Turin: Unione Tipografico-editrice Torinese, 1961–2009.

Grimm, Jacob, and Wilhelm Grimm. *Deutsches Wörterbuch* (1889), repr. ed. Munich: Deutscher Taschenbuch Verlag, 1999.

Howard-Drake, Jack. *Oxford Church Courts: Depositions 1589–1593.* Oxford: Oxfordshire County Council, 1997.

———. *Oxford Church Courts: Depositions 1609–1616.* Oxford: Oxfordshire County Council, 2003.

———. *Oxford Church Courts: Depositions 1616–1622.* Oxford: Oxfordshire County Council, 2005.

———. *Oxford Church Courts: Depositions 1629–1634.* Oxford: Oxfordshire County Council, 2007.

Letters and Papers, Foreign and Domestic, Henry VIII, Volume 2, 1515–1518. Edited by J. S. Brewer. London, 1864. British History Online. http://www.british-history.ac.uk/letters-papers-hen8/vol2.

Letters and Papers, Foreign and Domestic, Henry VIII, Volume 3, 1519–1523. Edited by J. S. Brewer. London, 1867. British History Online. http://www.british-history.ac.uk/letters-papers-hen8/vol3.

Letters and Papers, Foreign and Domestic, Henry VIII, Volume 4, 1524–1530. Edited by J. S. Brewer. London, 1875. British History Online. http://www.british-history.ac.uk/letters-papers-hen8/vol4.

Letters and Papers, Foreign and Domestic, Henry VIII, Volume 5, 1531–1532. Edited by James Gairdner. London, 1880. British History Online. http://www.british-history.ac.uk/letters-papers-hen8/vol5.

Matthews, William, *British Diaries: An Annotated Bibliography of British Diaries Written between 1442 and 1942.* Berkeley and Los Angeles: University of California Press, 1950.

OED Oxford English Dictionary. Oxford, UK: Oxford University Press, 2002.

Oxfordshire History Centre, Oxford, UK.

Ponsonby, Arthur. *English Diaries: A Review of English Diaries from the Sixteenth to the Twentieth Century with an Introduction on Diary Writing.* London: Methuen & Co., 1923.

Tesoro della Lingua Italiana delle Origini. Edited by Pietro G. Beltrami and Lino Leonardi. http://tlio.ovi.cnr.it/TLIO/.

Secondary Sources

Althoff, Gerd. *Family, Friends and Followers: Political and Social Bonds in Early Medieval Europe.* Cambridge and New York: Cambridge University Press, 2004.

————. "Vom Lächeln Zum Verlachen." In *Lachgemeinschaften: Kulturelle Inszenierungen und Soziale Wirkungen von Gelächter im Mittelalter und in der Frühen Neuzeit*, edited by Werner Röcke and Hans Rudolf Velten, 3–16. Berlin and New York: de Gruyter, 2005.

Amussen, Susan D. "The Gendering of Popular Culture." In *Popular Culture in England, c. 1500–1850*, edited by Tim Harris, 48–68. New York: St. Martin's Press, 1995.

Amussen, Susan D., and David E. Underdown. *Gender, Culture and Politics in England, 1560–1640: Turning the World Upside Down*. London and New York: Bloomsbury Academic, 2017.

Apte, Madahev L. *Humor and Laughter: An Anthropological Approach*. Ithaca, NY: Cornell University Press, 1985.

Baecque, Antoine de. *Les éclats du rire: la culture des rieurs au XVIIIe siècle*. Paris: Calmann-Lévy, 2000.

Bakhtin, Mikhail. *Rabelais and His World*. Translated by Hélène Iswolsky. Cambridge, MA: MIT Press, 1968.

Bayless, Martha. "Medieval Jokes in Serious Contexts: Speaking Humour to Power." In *The Palgrave Handbook of Humour, History, and Methodology*, edited by Daniel Derrin and Hannah Burrows, 257–73. Cham, Switzerland: Palgrave Macmillan, 2021. https://doi.org/10.1007/978-3-030-56646-3_13.

Beam, Sara. *Laughing Matters: Farce and the Making of Absolutism in France*. Ithaca: Cornell University Press, 2007.

Beard, Mary. *Laughter in Ancient Rome: On Joking, Tickling, and Cracking Up*. Berkeley: University of California Press, 2014.

Beasley, Faith E. *Salons, History, and the Creation of Seventeenth-Century France: Mastering Memory*. Aldershot, UK, and Burlington, VT: Ashgate, 2006.

Beik, William, ed. *Louis XIV and Absolutism: A Brief Study with Documents*. Boston and New York: Bedford/St. Martin's, 2000.

Ben-Amos, Ilana Krausman. *Adolescence and Youth in Early Modern England*. New Haven: Yale University Press, 1994.

Berger, Peter L. *Redeeming Laughter: The Comic Dimension of Human Experience*. 2nd ed. De Gruyter, 2014. Proquest Ebook Central.

Bideaux, Michel, ed. *Européens en Voyage (1500–1800): Une Anthologie*. Paris: Presses de l'université Paris-Sorbonne (PUPS), 2012.

Bilger, Audrey. *Laughing Feminism: Subversive Comedy in Frances Burney, Maria Edgeworth, and Jane Austen*. Detroit: Wayne State University Press, 1998.

Billig, Michael. *Laughter and Ridicule: Towards a Social Critique of Humour*. London: Sage Publications, 2005.

Bok, Sissela. *Exploring Happiness: From Aristotle to Brain Science*. New Haven: Yale University Press, 2010.

Boose, Lynda. "Scolding Brides and Bridling Scolds: Taming the Woman's Unruly Member." *Shakespeare Quarterly* 42 (1991): 179–213.

Bowen, Barbara C. "A Neglected Renaissance Art of Joking." *Rhetorica* 21, no. 3 (Summer 2003): 137–48.

————, ed. *One Hundred Renaissance Jokes: An Anthology*. Birmingham, AL: Summa Publications, 1988.

Boyle, Marjorie O'Rourke. "Gracious Laughter: Marsilio Ficino's Anthropology." *Renaissance Quarterly* 52, no. 3 (Autumn 1999): 712–41. http://www.jstor.org/stable/2901916.

Braet, Herman, Guido Latré, and Werner Verbeke, eds. *Risus Mediaevalis: Laughter in Medieval Literature and Art*. Leuven, Belgium: Leuven University Press, 2003.

Bremmer, Jan, and Herman Roodenburg, eds. *A Cultural History of Humour: From Antiquity to the Present Day*. Cambridge, UK: Polity Press, 1997.

Brewer, Derek. "Prose Jest-Books Mainly in the Sixteenth to Eighteenth Centuries in England." In *A Cultural History of Humour: From Antiquity to the Present Day*, edited by Jan Bremmer and Herman Roodenburg, 90–111. Cambridge, UK: Polity Press, 1997.

Brewer, John. "'The Most Polite Age and the Most Vicious': Attitudes towards Culture as a Commodity, 1660–1800." In *The Consumption of Culture 1600–1800: Image, Object, Text*, edited by Ann Bermingham and John Brewer, 341–61. London and New York: Routledge, 1995.

Briggs, Asa. *A Social History of England*. New York: Viking Press, 1983.

Brockliss, Laurence, and Colin Jones. *The Medical World of Early Modern France*. Oxford: Clarendon Press, 1997.

Brown, Pamela Allen. *Better a Shrew Than a Sheep: Women, Drama, and the Culture of Jest in Early Modern England*. Ithaca: Cornell University Press, 2003.

———. "Jesting Rights: Women Players in the Manuscript Jestbook of Sir Nicholas Le Strange." In *Women Players in England, 1500–1600: Beyond the All-Male Stage*, edited by Pamela Allen Brown and Peter Parolin, 305–14. Aldershot, England, and Burlington, VT: Ashgate, 2005.

Brown, Pamela Allen, and Peter Parolin, eds. *Women Players in England, 1500–1600: Beyond the All-Male Stage*. Aldershot, England, and Burlington, VT: Ashgate, 2005.

Bryson, Anna. *From Courtesy to Civility: Changing Codes of Conduct in Early Modern England*. Oxford: Clarendon Press, 1998.

Buckley, F. H. *The Morality of Laughter*. Ann Arbor, MI: University of Michigan Press, 2003. https://doi.org/10.3998/mpub.12004.

Burckhardt, Jacob. *The Civilization of the Renaissance in Italy*. Translated by S. G. C. Middlemore. 2 vols. New York: Harper & Row, 1958.

Burke, Peter. *The Fortunes of the Courtier: The European Reception of Castiglione's Cortegiano*. University Park, PA: Pennsylvania State University Press, 1995.

———. *The Historical Anthropology of Early Modern Italy: Essays on Perception and Communication*. Cambridge: Cambridge University Press, 1987.

———. "Languages and Anti-languages in Early Modern Italy." *History Workshop Journal* 11 (1981): 24–32.

———. *Popular Culture in Early Modern Europe*. 3rd ed. Farnham, UK, and Burlington, VT: Ashgate, 2009.

———. "Representations of the Self from Petrarch to Descartes." In *Rewriting the Self: Histories from the Renaissance to the Present*, edited by Roy Porter, 17–28. London and New York: Routledge, 1997.

———. *Varieties of Cultural History*. Ithaca, NY: Cornell University Press, 1997.

Burke, Peter, William Grange, Martina Kessel, and Jonathan Waterlow. "Forum: Humour." *German History* 33, no. 4 (December 2015): 609–23.

Capp, Bernard. *England's Culture Wars: Puritan Reformation and its Enemies in the Interregnum, 1649–1660*. Oxford: Oxford University Press, 2012.

———. "Separate Domains? Women and Authority in Early Modern England." In *The Experience of Authority in Early Modern England*, edited by Paul Griffiths, Adam Fox, and Steve Hindle, 117–45. New York: St. Martin's Press, 1996.

———. *When Gossips Meet: Women, Family, and Neighborhood in Early Modern England*. Oxford: Oxford University Press, 2003.

Carrell, Amy. "Historical Views of Humor." In *The Primer of Humor Research*, edited by Victor Raskin. Berlin and New York: de Gruyter, 2008.

Caskey, J. Homer. "Arthur Murphy's Commonplace-Book." *Studies in Philology* 37, no. 4 (October 1940): 598–609.

Cavallo, JoAnn. "Joking Matters: Politics and Dissimulation in Castiglione's Book of the Courtier." *Renaissance Quarterly* 53, no. 2 (Summer 2000): 402–24. http://www.jstor.org/stable/2901873.

Chafe, Wallace L. *The Importance of Not Being Earnest: The Feeling Behind Laughter and Humor.* Amsterdam: John Benjamins Publishing, 2007.

Chey, Jocelyn, and Jessica Milner Davis, eds. *Humour in Chinese Life and Letters: Classical and Traditional Approaches.* Hong Kong: Hong Kong University Press, 2011.

Cohen, Thomas V. "The Lay Liturgy of Affront in Sixteenth-Century Italy." *Journal of Social History* 25, no. 4 (1992): 857–77.

Cohen, Thomas V., and Elizabeth S. Cohen. *Words and Deeds in Renaissance Rome: Trials before the Papal Magistrates.* Toronto: University of Toronto Press, 1993.

Cohen, Thomas V., and Lesley K. Twomey, eds. *Spoken Word and Social Practice: Orality in Europe (1400–1700).* Leiden and Boston: Brill, 2015.

Cohn, Samuel Jr., Marcello Fantoni, Franco Franceschi, and Fabrizio Ricciardelli, eds. *Late Medieval and Early Modern Ritual: Studies in Italian Urban Culture.* Europa Sacra vol. 7. Turnhout, Belgium: Brepols, 2013.

Coxon, Sebastian. "Friendship, Wit and Laughter in Heinrich Bebel's Facetiae." *Oxford German Studies* 36, no. 2 (2007): 306–20. DOI: 10.1179/174592107x254986.

Cressy, David. *Dangerous Talk: Scandalous, Seditious, and Treasonable Speech in Pre-Modern England.* Oxford: Oxford University Press, 2010.

———. "Purification, Thanksgiving and the Churching of Women in Post-Reformation England." *Past & Present* 141 (November 1993): 106–46. http://www.jstor.org/stable/651031.

———. *Travesties and Transgressions in Tudor and Stuart England: Tales of Discord and Dissension.* Oxford: Oxford University Press, 2000.

Crum, Roger J., ed. *Renaissance Florence: A Social History.* New York: Cambridge University Press, 2006.

Damrosch, Leo. *The Club: Johnson, Boswell, and the Friends Who Shaped an Age.* New Haven and London: Yale University Press, 2019.

Darnton, Robert. *The Great Cat Massacre and Other Episodes in French Cultural History.* New York: Basic Books, 1984.

Dauber, Jeremy. *Jewish Comedy: A Serious History.* London and New York: W. W. Norton & Company, 2017.

Davis, Natalie Z. *Society and Culture in Early Modern France.* Stanford: Stanford University Press, 1975.

Davison, Kate. "Occasional Politeness and Gentlemen's Laughter in 18th Century England." *The Historical Journal* 57, no. 4 (2014): 921–45.

Daybell, James, and Andrew Gordon, eds. *Cultures of Correspondence in Early Modern Britain.* Philadelphia: University of Pennsylvania Press, 2016.

———. *Women and Epistolary Agency in Early Modern Culture, 1450–1690.* London and New York: Routledge, 2016.

Dean, Trevor. "Gender and Insult in an Italian City: Bologna in the Later Middle Ages." *Social History* 29, no. 2 (2004): 217–31.

Dean, Trevor, and K. J. P. Lowe, eds. *Crime, Society and the Law in Renaissance Italy.* Cambridge and New York: Cambridge University Press, 1994.

Dekker, Rudolf M. *Family, Culture and Society in the Diary of Constantijn Huygens Jr, Secretary to Stadholder-King William of Orange*. Leiden and Boston: Brill, 2013.

———. *Humour in Dutch Culture of the Golden Age*. Basingstoke, UK and New York: Palgrave, 2001.

Derrin, Daniel, and Hannah Burrows, eds. *The Palgrave Handbook of Humour, History, and Methodology*. Cham, Switzerland: Palgrave Macmillan, 2020. https://doi.org/10.1007/978-3-030-56646-3_4.

De Waal, Jeremy. "The Reinvention of Tradition: Form, Meaning, and Local Identity in Modern Cologne Carnival." *Central European History* 46, no. 3 (September 2013): 495–532.

Dickie, Simon. *Cruelty and Laughter: Forgotten Comic Literature and the Unsentimental Eighteenth Century*. Chicago and London: University of Chicago Press, 2011.

Douglas, Mary. "Social Control of Cognition: Some Factors in Joke Perception." *Man: The Journal of the Royal Anthropological Institute* 3 (1968): 361–76.

Duchêne, Roger. *Madame de Sévigné ou la chance d'être femme*. Paris: Fayard, 1982.

Dulieu, Louis. *La médecine à Montpellier. Tome II: La Renaissance*. 7 vols. Avignon: Presses Universelles, 1975.

Dunbar, Howard Hunter. *The Dramatic Career of Arthur Murphy*. New York: Modern Language Association, 1946.

Elias, Norbert. *The Civilizing Process: The History of Manners*. Translated by Edmund Jephcott. New York: Urizen Books, 1978.

———. *The Court Society*. Trans. Edmund Jephcott. New York: Pantheon, 1983.

———. "Essay on Laughter." Ed. Anca Parvulescu. *Critical Inquiry* 43, no. 2 (2017): 281–304.

Epstein, Pamela. "Advertising for Love: Matrimonial Advertisements and Public Courtship." In *Doing Emotions History*, edited by Susan J. Matt and Peter N. Stearns, 120–40. Champaign, IL: University of Illinois Press, 2014.

Eva Illouz, ed. *Emotions as Commodities: Capitalism, Consumption and Authenticity*. London and New York: Routledge, 2017.

Ewin, R. E. "Hobbes on Laughter." *The Philosophical Quarterly* 51, no. 202 (January 2001): 29–40. https://www.jstor.org/stable/2660519.

Fairchilds, Cissie. *Women in Early Modern Europe 1500–1700*. Harlow, England: Pearson Longman, 2007.

Favre, Robert. *Le rire dans tous ses éclats*. Lyon: Presses Universitaires de Lyon, 1995.

Fietz, Lothar, Joerg O. Fichte, and Hans-Werner Ludwig, eds. *Semiotik, Rhetorik und Soziologie des Lachens: Vergleichende Studien zum Funktionswandel des Lachens vom Mittelalter zur Gegenwart*. Tübingen: Max Niemeyer Verlag, 1996.

Fletcher, Anthony. *Gender, Sex and Subordination in England 1500–1800*. New Haven and London: Yale University Press, 1995.

Foka, Anna, and Jonas Liliequist, eds. *Laughter, Humor, and the (Un)Making of Gender: Historical and Cultural Perspectives*. New York: Palgrave Macmillan, 2015.

Fox, Adam. "Ballads, Libels and Popular Ridicule in Jacobean England." *Past & Present* 145 (1994): 47–83.

———. *Oral and Literate Culture in England 1500–1700*. Oxford: Clarendon Press, 2000.

Fox, Adam, and Daniel Woolf, eds. *The Spoken Word: Oral Culture in Britain 1500–1850*. Manchester and New York: Manchester University Press, 2002.

Fox, Cora, Bradley J. Irish, Cassie M. Miura, and Michael C. Schoenfeldt, eds. *Positive Emotions in Early Modern Literature and Culture*. Manchester, UK: Manchester University Press, 2021.

Gallucci, Margaret A. *Benvenuto Cellini: Sexuality, Masculinity, and Artistic Identity in Renaissance Italy*. New York: Palgrave Macmillan, 2003.

Gatrell, Vic. *City of Laughter: Sex and Satire in Eighteenth-Century London*. London: Atlantic Books, 2006.

Ghislain, André Joseph. "Notice sur Marguerite d'Autriche, Gouvernante des Pays-Bas." In *Correspondance de l'empereur Maximilien Ier et de Marguerite d'Autriche*. 2 vols. 2:422–65. Paris: J. Renouard, 1839.

Ghose, Indira. *Shakespeare and Laughter: A Cultural History*. Manchester and New York: Manchester University Press, 2008.

Goddard, Cliff, and Kerry Mullan. "Explicating Verbs for 'Laughing with Other People' in French and English (and Why it Matters for Humour Studies)." *Humor: International Journal of Humor Research* 33, no. 1 (2020): 55–77. https://doi.org/10.1515/humor-2017-0114.

Goffman, Erving. *The Presentation of Self in Everyday Life*. Garden City, NY: Doubleday, 1959.

Gowing, Laura. *Domestic Dangers: Women, Words and Sex in Early Modern London*. Oxford Studies in Social History. Oxford: Clarendon Press, 1996.

———. "Women, Status, and the Popular Culture of Dishonour." *Transactions of the Royal Historical Society* Sixth series 6 (1996): 225–34.

Greenblatt, Stephen. "Mutilation and Meaning." In *The Body in Parts: Fantasies of Corporeality in Early Modern Europe*, edited by David Hillman and Carla Mazzio, 221–42. New York and London: Routledge, 1997.

Griffiths, Paul. *Youth and Authority: Formative Experiences in England, 1560–1640*. Oxford: Clarendon Press, 1996.

Guarino, Gabriel. "Taming Transgression and Violence in the Carnivals of Early Modern Naples." *The Historical Journal* 60, no. 1 (2017): 1–20.

Gundle, Stephen. "Laughter Under Fascism: Humour and Ridicule in Italy, 1922–43." *History Workshop Journal* 79, no. 1 (2015): 215–32.

Gurevich, Aaron. "Bakhtin and his Theory of Carnival." In *A Cultural History of Humour*, edited by Jan Bremmer and Herman Roodenburg, 54–60. Cambridge, UK: Polity Press, 1997.

Hammond, Nicholas. *Gossip, Sexuality and Scandal in France (1610–1715)*. Oxford and New York: Peter Lang, 2011.

Hampton, Timothy. "The Theology of Cheer, Erasmus to Shakespeare." In *Positive Emotions in Early Modern Literature and Culture*, edited by Cora Fox, Bradley J. Irish, Cassie M. Miura, and Michael C. Schoenfeldt, 91–106. Manchester, UK: Manchester University Press, 2021.

Hay, Jennifer. "Functions of Humor in the Conversations of Men and Women." *Journal of Pragmatics* 32 (2000): 709–42.

Heal, Felicity. *Hospitality in Early Modern England*. Oxford: Clarendon Press, 1990.

Heltzel, Virgil B. "Chesterfield and the Anti-Laughter Tradition." *Modern Philology* 26, no. 1 (August 1928): 73–90.

Hendrix, Scott H., and Susan C. Karant-Nunn, eds. *Masculinity in the Reformation Era*. Kirksville, MO: Truman State University Press, 2008.

Herborn, Wolfgang. "Das Lachen im 16. Jahrhundert: Die Chronik des Hermann von Weinsberg als Quelle für eine Gemütsäußerung." *Rheinisch-westfälische Zeitschrift für Volkskunde* 40 (1995): 9–30.

Heyd, David. "The Place of Laughter in Hobbes's Theory of Emotions." *Journal of the History of Ideas* 43, no. 2 (April–June 1982): 285–95. http://www.jstor.org/stable/2709204.

Hillard, Derek, Heikki Lempa, and Russell A. Spinney, eds. *Feelings Materialized: Emotions, Bodies, and Things in Germany, 1500–1950*. New York: Berghahn Books, 2020.

Hillman, David, and Carla Mazzio, eds. *The Body in Parts: Fantasies of Corporeality in Early Modern Europe*. New York and London: Routledge, 1997.

Hintz, Carrie. *An Audience of One: Dorothy Osborne's Letters to Sir William Temple, 1653–1654*. Toronto: University of Toronto Press, 2005.

Hitchings, Henry. *Defining the World: The Extraordinary Story of Dr. Johnson's Dictionary*. New York: Farrar, Straus and Giroux, 2005.

Hofmann, J., T. Platt, C. Lau et al. "Gender Differences in Humor-Related Traits, Humor Appreciation, Production, Comprehension, (Neural) Responses, Use, and Correlates: A Systematic Review." *Current Psychology* (2020). https://doi-org.proxy.library.upenn.edu/10.1007/s12144-020-00724-1.

Holcomb, Chris. *Mirth Making: The Rhetorical Discourse on Jesting in Early Modern England*. Columbia, SC: University of South Carolina Press, 2001.

Holmes, Janet. "Politeness, Power and Provocation: How Humour Functions in the Workplace." *Discourse Studies* 2, no. 2 (2000): 159–85.

Horlacher, Stefan. "A Short Introduction to Theories of Humour, the Comic, and Laughter." In *Gender and Laughter: Comic Affirmation and Subversion in Traditional and Modern Media*, edited by Gaby Pailer, Andreas Böhn, Stefan Horlacher, and Uli Scheck, 17–47. New York and Amsterdam: Rodopi, 2009.

Hunt, Margaret R. *Women in Eighteenth-Century Europe*. Harlow, UK: Longman, 2010.

Hutton, Ronald. *The Rise and Fall of Merry England: The Ritual Year 1400–1700*. Oxford: Oxford University Press, 1994.

Ingram, Martin. "Charivari and Shame Punishments: Folk Justice and State Justice in Early Modern England." In *Social Control in Europe 1500–1800*, edited by Herman Roodenburg and Pieter Spierenburg, 288–308. Columbus, OH: Ohio State University Press, 2004.

———. *Church Courts, Sex & Marriage in England, 1570–1640*. Cambridge: Cambridge University Press, 1987.

———. "Ridings, Rough Music and the Reform of Popular Culture in Early Modern England." *Past & Present* 105 (November 1984): 79–113.

Jaeger, Stephen. *The Origins of Courtliness: Civilizing Trends and the Formation of Courtly Ideals, 939–1210*. Philadelphia: University of Pennsylvania Press, 1985.

Jancke, Gabriele. *Gastfreundschaft in der frühneuzeitlichen Gesellschaft: Praktiken, Normen und Perspektiven von Gelehrten*. Vol. 15. Berliner Mittelalter- und Frühneuzeitforschung. Göttingen: V&R Unipress, 2013.

Jansen, Sharon L. *The Monstrous Regiment of Women: Female Rulers in Early Modern Europe*. New York: Palgrave Macmillan, 2002.

Jones, Colin. *The Smile Revolution: In Eighteenth Century Paris*. Oxford: Oxford University Press, 2014.

Jones, Peter J. A. *Laughter and Power in the Twelfth Century*. Oxford: Oxford University Press, 2019.

Kamper, Dietmar, and Christoph Wulf, eds. *Lachen—Gelächter—Lächeln: Reflexionen in drei Spiegeln*. Frankfurt am Main: Syndikat, 1986.

Karant-Nunn, Susan C. "The Masculinity of Martin Luther: Theory, Practicality, and Humor." In *Masculinity in the Reformation Era*, edited by Scott H. Hendrix and Susan C. Karant-Nunn, 167–89. Kirksville, MO: Truman State University Press, 2008.

Karant-Nunn, Susan C., and Merry Wiesner-Hanks, eds. *Luther on Women: A Sourcebook*. Cambridge: Cambridge University Press, 2003.

Kelso, Ruth. *Doctrine for the Lady of the Renaissance*. Urbana, IL: University of Illinois Press, 1956.

Kessel, Martina, and Patrick Merziger, eds. *The Politics of Humour: Laughter, Inclusion, and Exclusion in the Twentieth Century*. Toronto: University of Toronto Press, 2012.

King, Barbara Mackey. "Delicately Corrected and Constantly Befriended: Arthur Murphy's Female Characters." *Studies in Eighteenth-Century Culture* 43 (2014): 197–217. https://doi.org/10.1353/sec.2014.0007.

Knights, Mark, and Adam Morton, eds. *The Power of Laughter and Satire in Early Modern Britain: Political and Religious Culture, 1500–1820*. Woodbridge, Suffolk: Boydell & Brewer, 2017.

Kolfin, Elmer. *The Young Gentry at Play; Northern Netherlandish Scenes of Merry Companies 1610–1645*. Translated by Michael Hoyle. Leiden: Primavera, 2005.

Kotthoff, Helga. *Spaß Verstehen: Zur Pragmatik von konversationellem Humor*. Tübingen: Max Niemeyer Verlag, 1998.

Kuhn, Christian. "Urban Laughter as a 'Counter-Public' Sphere in Augsburg: The Case of the City Mayor, Jakob Herbrot (1490/95–1564)." *International Review of Social History* 52 (2007): 77–93.

Kuhn, Christian, and Stefan Bießenecker, eds. *Valenzen des Lachens in der Vormoderne (1250–1750)*. Bamberger Historische Studien 8. Bamberg: University of Bamberg Press, 2012.

Kuipers, Giselinde. *Good Humor, Bad Taste: A Sociology of the Joke*. Berlin and Boston: De Gruyter, 2015.

Kuper, Michael. *Zur Semiotik der Inversion: Verkehrte Welt und Lachkultur im 16. Jahrhundert*. Berlin: VWB: Verlag für Wissenschaft und Bildung, 1993.

Ladurie, Emmanuel Le Roy. *The Beggar and the Professor: A Sixteenth-Century Family Saga*. Translated by Arthur Goldhammer. Chicago and London: University of Chicago Press, 1997.

———. *Carnival in Romans*. Translated by Mary Feeney. New York: George Braziller, 1980.

Ladurie, Emmanuel Le Roy, and Jean-François Fitou. *Saint-Simon ou le système de la cour*. Paris: Fayard, 1997.

Lee, Louise, ed. *Victorian Comedy and Laughter: Conviviality, Jokes and Dissent*. London: Palgrave Macmillan, 2020. ProQuest Ebook Central.

Le Goff, Jacques. "Laughter in the Middle Ages." In *A Cultural History of Humour*, edited by Jan Bremmer and Herman Roodenburg, 40–53. Cambridge, UK: Polity Press, 1997.

Levin, Carole. *The Heart and Stomach of a King: Elizabeth I and the Politics of Sex and Power*. 2nd ed. Philadelphia: University of Pennsylvania Press, 2013.

Lombardo, Davide. "De Certeau, the Everyday and the Place of Humour." *Revue d'Histoire des Sciences Humaines* 23 (2010): 75–98.

Lötscher, Valentin. "Introduction." In Felix Platter, *Tagebuch (Lebensbeschreibung) 1536–1567*. Basel and Stuttgart: Schwabe, 1976.

Loveman, Kate. "Pepys's Jests." *Notes and Queries* 50, no. 2 (2003): 188–89.

Maral, Alexandre. *Le roi, la cour et Versailles: Le coup d'éclat permanent 1682–1789*. Paris: Perrin, 2013.

Martin, Rod A. *The Psychology of Humor: An Integrative Approach*. Amsterdam: Elsevier, 2007.

Martin, Rod A., and Nicholas A. Kuiper. "Daily Occurrence of Laughter: Relationships with Age, Gender, and Type A Personality." *Humor: International Journal of Humor Research* 12, no. 4 (1999): 355–84.

Martin, R. B. *The Triumph of Wit: A Study of Victorian Comic Theory*. Oxford: Clarendon Press, 1974.

Mascuch, Michael. *Origins of the Individualist Self: Autobiography and Self-identity in England, 1591–1791*. Stanford, CA: Stanford University Press, 1996.

Matt, Susan J., and Peter N. Stearns, eds. *Doing Emotions History*. Champaign, IL: University of Illinois Press, 2014.

McIlvenna, Una. *Scandal and Reputation at the Court of Catherine de Medici*. London and New York: Routledge, 2014.

McIntyre, Ian. *Hester: The Remarkable Life of Dr Johnson's 'Dear Mistress.'* London: Constable, 2008.

Mclean, Paul Douglas. *The Art of the Network: Strategic Interaction and Patronage in Renaissance Florence*. Durham, NC: Duke University Press, 2007.

McShane, Angela, and Garthine Walker, eds. *The Extraordinary and the Everyday in Early Modern England: Essays in Celebration of the Work of Bernard Capp*. Basingstoke: Palgrave Macmillan, 2010.

Ménager, Daniel. *La renaissance et le rire*. Paris: Presses universitaires de France, 1995.

Mendelson, Sara Heller. "Child Rearing in Theory and Practice: The Letters of John Locke and Mary Clarke." *Women's History Review* 19, no. 2 (April 2010): 231–43.

———. *The Mental World of Stuart Women*. Amherst: University of Massachusetts Press, 1987.

Midelfort, H. C. Erik. *Exorcism and Enlightenment: Johann Joseph Gassner and the Demons of Eighteenth-Century Germany*. New Haven: Yale University Press, 2005.

Minois, Georges. *Histoire du rire et de la dérision*. Paris: Fayard, 2000.

Miura, Cassie M. "Therapeutic laughter in Robert Burton's *The Anatomy of Melancholy*." In *Positive Emotions in Early Modern Literature and Culture*, edited by Cora Fox, Bradley J. Irish, Cassie M. Miura, and Michael C. Schoenfeldt, 44–59. Manchester, UK: Manchester University Press, 2021.

Morreall, John. *Comic Relief: A Comprehensive Philosophy of Humor*. Malden, MA: Wiley-Blackwell, 2009.

———. "Philosophy of Humor." In *The Stanford Encyclopedia of Philosophy* (Winter 2016 Edition), edited by Edward N. Zalta. https://plato.stanford.edu/archives/win2016/entries/humor/.

Muir, Edward. *Mad Blood Stirring: Vendetta in Renaissance Italy*. Baltimore: Johns Hopkins University Press, 1998.

Nicholson, Bob. "'Capital Company': Writing and Telling Jokes in Victorian Britain." In *Victorian Comedy and Laughter: Conviviality, Jokes and Dissent*, edited by Louise Lee, 109–39. Palgrave Macmillan, 2020. ProQuest Ebook Central.

Ollard, Richard. *Pepys: A Biography*. New York: Atheneum, 1984.

Otto, Beatrice K. *Fools Are Everywhere: The Court Jester Around the World*. Chicago and London: University of Chicago Press, 2001.

Outram, Dorinda. *Four Fools in the Age of Reason: Laughter, Cruelty, and Power in Early Modern Germany*. Charlottesville and London: University of Virginia Press, 2019.

Owren, M. J., and J-A. Bachorowski. "Reconsidering the Evolution of Nonlinguistic Communication: The Case of Laughter." *Journal of Nonverbal Behavior* 27 (2003): 183–200.

Ozment, Steven. *Three Behaim Boys: Growing Up in Early Modern Germany*. New Haven and London: Yale University Press, 1990.

Pailer, Gaby, Andreas Böhn, Stefan Horlacher, and Uli Scheck, eds. *Gender and Laughter: Comic Affirmation and Subversion in Traditional and Modern Media*. New York and Amsterdam: Rodopi, 2009.

Paranque, Estelle. *Elizabeth I of England through Valois Eyes: Power, Representation, and Diplomacy in the Reign of the Queen, 1558–1588*. Cham, Switzerland: Palgrave Macmillan, 2019.

Parkin, Robert. "The Joking Relationship and Kinship: Charting a Theoretical Dependency." *Journal of the Anthropological Society of Oxford (JASO)* 24, no. 3 (1993): 251–63. https://www.anthro.ox.ac.uk/fileadmin/ISCA/JASO/Archive_1993/24_3_Parkin.pdf.

Parvulescu, Anca. *Laughter: Notes on a Passion.* Cambridge and London: MIT Press, 2010.

Paster, Gail Kern. *The Body Embarrassed: Drama and the Discipline of Shame in Early Modern England.* Ithaca, NY: Cornell University Press, 1993.

Peristiany, John G., ed. *Honour and Shame: The Values of Mediterranean Society.* Chicago: University of Chicago Press, 1966.

Pettegree, Andrew, ed. *The Reformation World.* London and New York: Routledge, 2000.

Pfister, Manfred. *A History of English Laughter: Laughter from Beowulf to Beckett and Beyond.* Amsterdam and New York: Rodopi, 2002.

Pioffet, Marie-Christine. "Le rire de Paul Le Jeune: Du rire jaune à l'humour noir." *Nouvelles Études Francophones* 22 (2007): 122–34. https://www.jstor.org/stable/25702074.

Pitt-Rivers, Julian. "Honour and Shame." In *Honour and Shame: The Values of Mediterranean Society,* edited by John G. Peristiany, 21–77. Chicago: University of Chicago Press, 1966.

Plamper, Jan. *The History of Emotions: An Introduction.* Oxford: Oxford University Press, 2015.

Plessner, Helmuth. *Laughing and Crying: A Study of the Limits of Human Behavior.* Translated by James Spencer Churchill and Marjorie Grene. Evanston, IL: Northwestern University Press, 1970.

Pollock, Linda. *With Faith and Physic: The Life of a Tudor Gentlewoman, Lady Grace Mildmay, 1552–1620.* London: Collins & Brown, 1993.

Poos, Lawrence. "Sex, Lies and the Church Courts of Pre-Reformation England." *The Journal of Interdisciplinary History* 25, no. 4 (1995): 585–607.

Provine, Robert R. *Laughter: A Scientific Investigation.* New York: Viking, 2000.

Proyer, René T., et al. "Breaking Ground in Cross-Cultural Research on the Fear of Being Laughed at (Gelotophobia): A Multi-National Study Involving 73 Countries." *Humor* 22, no. 1/2 (2009): 253–79.

Puff, Helmut. *Sodomy in Reformation Germany and Switzerland, 1400–1600.* Chicago and London: University of Chicago Press, 2003.

Purdie, Susan. *Comedy: The Mastery of Discourse.* Toronto: University of Toronto Press, 1993.

Rayfield, Lucy. "Rewriting Laughter in Early Modern Europe." In *The Palgrave Handbook of Humour, History, and Methodology,* edited by Daniel Derrin and Hannah Burrows, 71–91. Cham, Switzerland: Palgrave Macmillan, 2020. https://doi.org/10.1007/978-3-030-56646-3_4.

Reddick, Allen. *The Making of Johnson's Dictionary 1746–1773.* Cambridge: Cambridge University Press, 1996.

Reddy, William M. *The Making of Romantic Love: Longing and Sexuality in Europe, South Asia, and Japan, 900–1200 CE.* Chicago and London: University of Chicago Press, 2012.

Reinke-Williams, Tim. *Women, Work and Sociability in Early Modern London.* Houndmills, Basingstoke: Palgrave Macmillan, 2014.

Richardot, Anne. *Le rire des lumières.* Paris: Champion, 2002.

Roberts, Benjamin. "Humor." In *Encyclopedia of European Social History from 1350 to 2000,* edited by Peter N. Stearns, 5:131–39. New York: Scribner, 2001.

Robinson, Dawn T., and Lynn Smith-Lovin. "Getting a Laugh: Gender, Status, and Humor in Task Discussions. *Social Forces* 80, no. 1 (September 2001): 123–58. https://www.jstor.org/stable/2675534.

Rocke, Michael. *Forbidden Friendships: Homosexuality and Male Culture in Renaissance Florence.* New York and Oxford: Oxford University Press, 1996.

Röcke, Werner, and Hans Rudolf Velten, eds. *Lachgemeinschaften: Kulturelle Inszenierungen und Soziale Wirkungen von Gelächter im Mittelalter und in der Frühen Neuzeit*. Berlin and New York: de Gruyter, 2005.

Roodenburg, Herman. "To Converse Agreeably: Civility and the Telling of Jokes in Seventeenth-Century Holland." In *A Cultural History of Humour*, edited by Jan Bremmer and Herman Roodenburg, 112–33. Cambridge, UK: Polity Press, 1997.

Roodenburg, Herman, and Pieter Spierenburg, eds. *Social Control in Europe 1500–1800*. Columbus, OH: Ohio State University Press, 2004.

Roper, Lyndal. *Martin Luther: Renegade and Prophet*. New York: Random House, 2017.

Rosenwein, Barbara H. *Generations of Feeling: A History of Emotions, 600–1700*. Cambridge, UK: Cambridge University Press, 2016.

———. "Problems and Methods in the History of Emotions." *Passions in Context: Journal of the History and Philosophy of the Emotions* 1 (2010): 1–32.

Ross, Elaina M., and Jeffrey A. Hall. "The Traditional Sexual Script and Humor in Courtship." *Humor: International Journal of Humor Research* 33, no. 2 (May 2020): 197–218.

Rossi, Paolo L. "The Writer and the Man. Real Crimes and Mitigating Circumstances." In *Crime, Society and the Law in Renaissance Italy*, edited by Trevor Dean and K. J. P. Lowe, 157–83. Cambridge and New York: Cambridge University Press, 1994.

Roth, Carla. "Obscene Humour, Gender and Sociability in Sixteenth-Century St. Gallen." *Past & Present* 234 (2017): 39–70.

Ruch, Willibald. "Foreword and Overview. Sense of Humor: A New Look at an Old Concept." In *The Sense of Humor: Explorations of a Personality Characteristic*, edited by Willibald Ruch, 3–14. Berlin: De Gruyter, 1998. Proquest Ebook Central.

———. "Psychology of Humor." In *The Primer of Humor Research*, edited by Victor Raskin, 17–100. Berlin and New York: De Gruyter, 2008. Proquest Ebook Central.

Sanders, Barry. *Sudden Glory: Laughter as Subversive History*. Boston: Beacon Press, 1995.

Sanson, Helena L. "Donne Che (non) Ridono: Parola E Riso Nella Precettistica Femminile Del XVI Secolo in Italia." *Italian Studies* 60, no. 1 (2005): 6–21.

Saslow, James M. *Ganymede in the Renaissance: Homosexuality in Art and Society*. New Haven: Yale University Press, 1986.

Scheer, Monique. "Are Emotions a Kind of Practice (and is That What Makes Them Have a History? A Bourdieuian Approach to Understanding Emotion." *History and Theory* 51, no. 2 (May 2012): 193–220.

Schindler, Norbert. "Ein bäuerlicher Münchhausen? Die Memoiren des Zillertaler 'Hoftirolers' Peter Prosch (1789)." *Österreichische Zeitschrift für Volkskunde* 72, no. 1 (2018): 85–110.

Schindler, Norbert. "Karneval, Kirche, und verkehrte Welt. Zur Funktion der Lachkultur im 16. Jahrhundert." *Jahrbuch für Volkskunde* 7 (1984): 9–57.

Schörle, Eckart. "Die Erfindung des 'guten' Lachens: Lachdebatten zwischen 1650 und 1750." In *Valenzen des Lachens in der Vormoderne (1250–1750)*, edited by Christian Kuhn and Stefan Bießenecker, 329–50. Bamberger Historische Studien 8. Bamberg: University of Bamberg Press, 2012.

———. *Die Verhöflichung des Lachens: Lachgeschichte im 18. Jahrhundert*. Bielefeld: Aisthesis Verlag, 2007.

Schulze, Winfried, ed. *Ego-Dokumente: Annäherung an den Menschen in der Geschichte*. Berlin: Akademie Verlag, 1996.

Screech, M. A. *Laughter At the Foot of the Cross*. London: Allen Lane, Penguin, 1997.

Seaver, Paul S. *Wallington's World: A Puritan Artisan in Seventeenth-Century London*. Stanford, CA: Stanford University Press, 1985.

Shepard, Alexandra. *Meanings of Manhood in Early Modern England*. Oxford: Oxford University Press, 2003.

Shrank, Cathy. "Mocking or Mirthful: Laughter in Early Modern Dialogue." In *The Power of Laughter and Satire in Early Modern Britain: Political and Religious Culture, 1500–1820*, edited by Mark Knights and Adam Morton, 48–66. Woodbridge, Suffolk: Boydell & Brewer, 2017.

Skinner, Quentin. "Hobbes and the Classical Theory of Laughter." In *Visions of Politics: Volume 3, Hobbes and Civil Science*, 142–76. Cambridge: Cambridge University Press, 2002. ProQuest Ebook Central.

———. "Why Laughing Mattered in the Renaissance: The Second Henry Tudor Memorial Lecture." *History of Political Thought* 22, no. 3 (2001): 418–47.

Smith, Moira. "Laughter: Nature or Culture." Paper delivered at the 2008 meeting of the International Society for Humor Research, Alcala de Henares, Spain. https:// scholarworks.iu.edu/dspace/bitstream/handle/2022/3162/Laughter%20nature%20 culture1.pdf.

Smith, Preserved. *Luther's Table Talk: A Critical Study*. New York: Columbia University Press, 1907.

Spector, Robert Donald. *Arthur Murphy*. Boston: Twayne, 1979.

Spierenburg, Pieter. *A History of Murder*. Cambridge: Polity Press, 2008.

Stearns Peter N., ed. *Encyclopedia of European Social History from 1350 to 2000*. 5 vols. New York: Scribner, 2001.

Steggle, Matthew. *Laughing and Weeping in Early Modern Theatres*. Aldershot: Ashgate, 2007.

Swart, Sandra. "'The Terrible Laughter of the Afrikaner'—Towards a Social History of Humor." *Journal of Social History* 42, no. 4 (Summer 2009): 889–917.

Szabari, Antónia. *Less Rightly Said: Scandals and Readers in Sixteenth-Century France*. Stanford, CA: Stanford University Press, 2010.

Taplin, Mark. "Switzerland." In *The Reformation World*, edited by Andrew Pettegree, 169–89. London and New York: Routledge, 2001.

Tarbin, Stephanie, "Raising Girls and Boys: Fear, Awe, and Dread in the Early Modern Household." In *Authority, Gender and Emotions in Late Medieval and Early Modern England*, edited by Susan Broomhall, 106–30. Houndmills, UK: Palgrave Macmillan, 2015.

Thomas, Keith. "Bodily Control and Social Unease: The Fart in Seventeenth-Century England." In *The Extraordinary and the Everyday in Early Modern England: Essays in Celebration of the Work of Bernard Capp*, edited by Angela McShane and Garthine Walker, 9–30. Basingstoke: Palgrave Macmillan, 2010.

———. "The Place of Laughter in Tudor and Stuart England." *TLS, the Times Literary Supplement* 21 (January 1977): 77–81.

Thompson, E. P. "Rough Music: Le Charivari Anglais." *Annales. Histoire, Sciences Sociales* 27, no. 2 (April 1972): 285–312.

Tierney-Hynes. Rebecca. "The Humour of Humours: Comedy Theory and Eighteenth-Century Histories of Emotions." In *The Palgrave Handbook of Humour, History, and Methodology*, edited by Daniel Derrin and Hannah Burrows, 93–108. Cham, Switzerland: Palgrave Macmillan, 2020. https://doi.org/10.1007/978-3-030-56646-3_5.

Tlusty, B. Ann. *Bacchus and Civic Order: The Culture of Drink in Early Modern Germany*. Charlottesville: University Press of Virginia, 2001.

Tomalin, Claire. *Samuel Pepys: The Unequalled Self*. New York: Knopf, 2002.

Tremayne, Eleanor E. *The First Governess of the Netherlands: Margaret of Austria*. London: Methuen, 1908. https://catalog.hathitrust.org/Record/006068884.

Treu, Martin. *Katharina von Bora*. Wittenberg: Drei Kastanien Verlag, 1996.

Trokhimenko, Olga V. *Constructing Virtue and Vice: Femininity and Laughter in Courtly Society (ca. 1150–1300)*. Göttingen: V&R Unipress, 2014.

———. "Women's Laughter and Gender Politics in Medieval Conduct Discourse." In *Laughter in the Middle Ages and Early Modern Times: Epistemology of a Fundamental Human Behavior, Its Meaning, and Consequences*, edited by Albrecht Classen, 243–64. Berlin: Walter de Gruyter, 2010.

Ulbrich, Claudia, Kaspar von Greyerz, and Lorenz Heiligensetzer, eds. *Mapping the 'I': Research on Self-Narratives in Germany and Switzerland*. Leiden and Boston: Brill, 2015.

Underdown, David. *Fire from Heaven: Life in an English Town in the Seventeenth Century*. London: HarperCollins, 1992.

Velten, Hans Rudolf. *Scurrilitas: Das Lachen, die Komik und der Körper in Literatur und Kultur des Spätmittelalters und der Frühen Neuzeit*. Bibliotheca Germanica 63. Tübingen: Narr Francke Attempto, 2017.

Verberckmoes, Johan. "The Comic and the Counter Reformation." In *A Cultural History of Humour*, edited by Jan Bremmer and Herman Roodenburg, 76–89. Cambridge, UK: Polity Press, 1997.

———. *Laughter, Jestbooks and Society in the Spanish Netherlands*. Houndmills, UK, and New York: St. Martin's Press, 1999.

Verdon, Jean. *Rire au Moyen Age*. Paris: Perrin, 2001.

Völker-Rasor, Anette. "'Arbeitsam, Obgleich Etwas Verschlafen.'—die Autobiographie des 16. Jahrhunderts als Ego-Dokument." In *Ego-Dokumente: Annäherung an den Menschen in der Geschichte*, edited by Winfried Schulze, 107–20. Berlin: Akademie Verlag, 1996.

Walker, Nancy A. *A Very Serious Thing: Women's Humor and American Culture*. Minneapolis: University of Minnesota Press, 1988.

Warnicke, Retha M. "Lady Mildmay's Journal: A Study in Autobiography and Meditation in Reformation England." *Sixteenth Century Journal* 20, no. 1 (1989): 55–68.

Webb, Jennifer D. "All is Not Fun and Games: Conversation, Play, and Surveillance at the Montefeltro Court in Urbino." *Renaissance Studies* 26, no. 3 (June 2012): 417–40.

Welsford, Enid. *The Fool: His Social and Literary History*. Garden City, New York: Anchor Books, 1961.

Westhauser, Karl E. "Friendship and Family in Early Modern England: The Sociability of Adam Eyre and Samuel Pepys." *Journal of Social History* 27, no. 3 (1994): 517–36.

Whitaker, Katie. *Mad Madge: The Extraordinary Life of Margaret Cavendish, Duchess of Newcastle, the First Woman to Live by Her Pen*. New York: Basic Books, 2002.

Wickberg, Daniel. *The Senses of Humor: Self and Laughter in Modern America*. Ithaca: Cornell University Press, 1998.

Williams, Alison. "Sick Humour, Healthy Laughter: The Use of Medicine in Rabelais's Jokes." *Modern Language Review* 101, no. 3 (2006): 671–81.

Wiltenburg, Joy. *Crime and Culture in Early Modern Germany*. Charlottesville and London: University of Virginia Press, 2012.

———. *Disorderly Women and Female Power in the Street Literature of Early Modern England and Germany*. Charlottesville and London: University Press of Virginia, 1992.

———. "Early Modern Embodiments of Laughter: The Journal of Felix Platter." In *Feelings Materialized: Emotions, Bodies, and Things in Germany, 1500–1950*, edited by Derek Hillard, Heikki Lempa, and Russell A. Spinney, 115–26. New York: Berghahn Books, 2020.

———. "Soundings of Laughter in Early Modern England: Women, Men, and Everyday Uses of Humor." *Early Modern Women: An Interdisciplinary Journal* 10, no. 2 (2016): 22–41.

Withington, Phil. "Company and Sociability in Early Modern England." *Social History* 32, no. 3 (2007): 291–307.

———. "Intoxicants and Society in Early Modern England." *Historical Journal* 54, no. 3 (September 2011): 631–57.

———. "'Tumbled into the Dirt': Wit and Incivility in Early Modern England." *Journal of Historical Pragmatics* 12, no. 1–2 (2011): 156–77.

Wood, Andy. *Riot, Rebellion and Popular Politics in Early Modern England.* Houndmills, UK, and New York: Palgrave, 2002.

Woolf, Virginia. *The Common Reader: Second Series.* London: Hogarth Press, 1965. https://archive.org/details/woolf_commonA/mode/2up.

Wunder, Heide. *He Is the Sun, She Is the Moon: Women in Early Modern Germany.* Translated by Thomas Dunlap. Cambridge, MA, and London, England: Harvard University Press, 1998.

Wunderli, Richard M. *London Church Courts and Society on the Eve of the Reformation.* Cambridge, MA: Medieval Academy of America, 1981.

Young, Dannagal G. *Irony and Outrage: The Polarized Landscape of Rage, Fear, and Laughter in the United States.* New York: Oxford University Press, 2020.

Zijderveld, Anton C. "Humor, Laughter, and Sociological Theory." *Sociological Forum* 10, no. 2 (1995): 341–45. https://www.jstor.org/stable/684995.

———. "A Sociological Theory of Humor and Laughter." In *Semiotik, Rhetorik und Soziologie des Lachens: Vergleichende Studien zum Funktionswandel des Lachens vom Mittelalter zur Gegenwart*, edited by Lothar Fietz, Joerg O. Fichte, and Hans-Werner Ludwig, 37–45. Tübingen: Max Niemeyer Verlag, 1996.

INDEX